THE HERMIT AND US

Our Adirondack Adventures with Noah John Rondeau

William J. O'Hern

THE HERMIT AND US

Our Adirondack Adventures with Noah John Rondeau

The book and cover design and typesetting were created by Nancy Did It! (www.NancyDidIt.com)

Cover: Noah John Rondeau, courtesy Richard J. Smith, and At the Beauty Parlor Wigwam, courtesy Dr. Adolph G. Dittmar, Jr.

Back Cover: Noah John Rondeau at Indian Falls, September 1951, courtesy Dr. Roger D. Freeman

Pen-and-Ink Drawings and Maps by Sheri Amsel, Adirondack Artist and Illustrator

Grateful acknowledgment is made for permission to use the photo of Noah John Rondeau on the Cold River City map to the New York State Department of Conservation Archives.

The story, "Noah John Rondeau, Hermit of Cold River," was written by Adolph G. "Ditt" Dittmar and taken with permission from the Forty-Sixers book, *The Adirondack High Peaks and The Forty-Sixers* (The Adirondack Forty-Sixers, 1970).

Grateful acknowledgment is made to North Country Books, Inc. for permission to use portions found in "In Search of a Bow-Hunting Hermit" that originally appeared in *Life with Noah.*

Grateful acknowledgement is made to the Adirondack Museum Library for permission to use quotations from its collection of Noah John Rondeau dairies.

Grateful acknowledgement is made to Dan Lucca for permission to use his photograph of Noah and friends on the Dedication page.

The "Noah's Code" typeface used in the production of this book was created by and is copyright © David Greene, 2009. "Noah Code" is based on Rondeau's late 1940s code.

Silhouette icon of Noah John Rondeau cut by Lillian G. Clarke, gifted to Noah by Mrs. John P. Bunker, Dedham, MA.

Grateful acknowledgment is made to *Adirondack Life* magazine for permission to use Philip G. Wolff's "Knowing Noah John, A Young Man's Tale of a Hermit's Hospitality." Original material that appeared in *Adirondack Life*, May/June 2010.

In the Adirondacks

Camden, NY 13042 • www.adkwilds.com

Printed in the United States of America by Versa Press, Inc.
ISBN 978-0-9890328-2-7

EPIGRAM

Noah John Rondeau

*Friends fondly remembered
the hermit's kindness and his interest
in the forest creatures that
populated his world. "They in turn
accepted him for exactly
what he was, a warm, capable
citizen of this planet."*

—Leona Raymond Warner

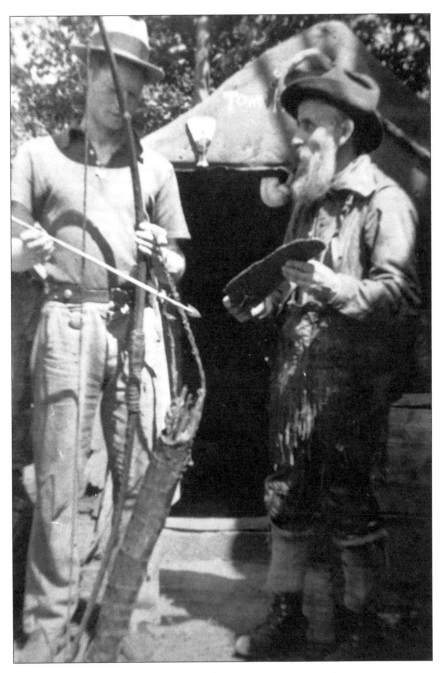

Richard Smith and Noah John Rondeau, Summer 1934.

Photographer Tony Okie. Courtesy of Richard J. Smith

DEDICATION

*To all who helped in the
creation of
The Adirondack Hermit and Us—
all caring people in
Noah's life—this book is gratefully
dedicated.*

Lt. to Rt. Noah, Frank "Scout" Pepecelli, Roy Lasher. Two members of "F-Troup."
circa late 1940s. Courtesy Dan Lucca

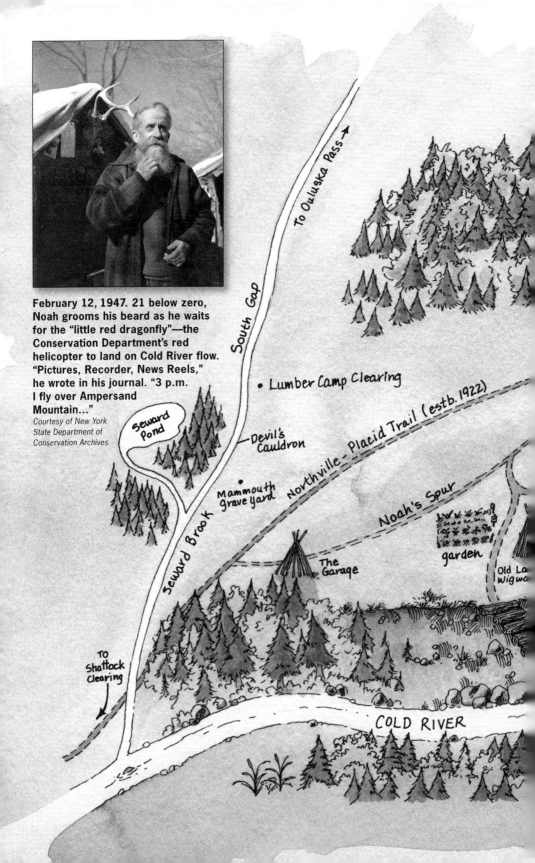

February 12, 1947. 21 below zero, Noah grooms his beard as he waits for the "little red dragonfly"—the Conservation Department's red helicopter to land on Cold River flow. "Pictures, Recorder, News Reels," he wrote in his journal. "3 p.m. I fly over Ampersand Mountain..."

Courtesy of New York State Department of Conservation Archives

To Ouluska Pass →

South Gap

• Lumber Camp Clearing

Seward Pond

Devil's Cauldron

Northville – Placid Trail (estb. 1922)

Mammouth Grave Yard

Seward Brook

Noah's Spur

garden

The Garage

Old La
Wigwa

To Shattock Clearing

COLD RIVER

CONTENTS

Section I: Rondeau's Quest for Education 16

Section II: The Hermit and Us 31

Preface

As I reflect on my wanderlust years of hiking with friends to remote lakes, frozen marshes, or distant mountains, I am reminded of the fluidity of life. People come and go, and take more than a knowledge of the vast terrain that we explored … they take a part of me. "Jay" O'Hern, as he likes to be called, is a unique individual who has filled my life with special memories.

I met Jay in 1971 through the Adirondack Mountain Club. Personable, knowledgeable, energetic, and simply fun to be with, Jay and I matched like a nut and a bolt.

I recall one memorable weekend when we climbed three High Peaks, and with full packs logged close to forty miles of hiking. Jay was wearing new boots. Both of his big toes were bloody pulps, but he did not complain. We didn't care if it was one o'clock in the morning. Rain or shine, we were both determined to become Forty-Sixers.

After our first round of High Peaks adventures, we focused our attention on the vast Moose River Plains wilds. Jay was interested in writing a book about its history, so nearly every weekend we would continue our routine of meeting at the Howard Johnson's in Old Forge, feasting on their all-you-can-eat special, and then continuing on to the entrance gate outside of Inlet, N.Y.

We'd search for old lumber camp locations, fading log roads and forgotten trails. We fueled each other's desire for exploration and adventure to the point where we exclusively bushwhacked to any location that appeared interesting on the topographic map.

Jay has a passion for interviewing old-timers, collecting memorabilia about the Adirondacks, and discovering old places—what he calls "eyewitness research." This type of research is his forte, and he has meticulously preserved taped interviews with figures who fondly remembered old-timers and former times in the Adirondacks.

Once we exhausted the Plains, we branched out to other regions of the Adirondacks—the West Canada Lakes Wilderness region, Stillwater Reservoir, Independence River, North Lake/South Lakes—any place in the Adirondacks that looked inviting. For nearly twenty-five years, during every season of the year, we explored for excitement and adventure. And we were never disappointed. We discovered hidden and illegal hunting camps, a cave I named the Bear Hunter's Den, used as far back as the Civil War according to some Indian head pennies I found inside along with crockery and metal utensils, old barrels filled with stashed camp goods that had gone unused, boats hauled in miles over the snow, hidden in errant locations.

The author's wife, Bette, is getting a lesson on how to use a GPS from Bob Bates. Bette, Jay and Bob have often explored the Cold River territory together.
Courtesy of William J. O'Hern

Family commitments and aging parents eventually slackened our times of adventure, but the miracle of our friendship has not waned. Although we do not get together as much as in the past, we remain in contact. And, when I reminisce through old photographs Jay has taken or pick up one of the books he has penned, I am reminded of a poem that which best exemplifies those many excursions with Jay. The author, whose name eludes me, wrote simply, but powerfully:

> *Our lives are filled with many*
> *Mountains to challenge*
> *Ever changing minds and*
> *Personalities.*
> *But more important than the*
> *Mountains are those*
> *Who climb beside you.*
> *You have seen the mountains*
> *With friends,*
> *Now you must always share*
> *The new life the mountains*
> *have shown you.*

Our extraordinary friendship, founded on our shared adventures, is a real treasure. But then Jay has always been good at digging up treasure where others might not bother to look—among everyday folks with whom he has quickly become friends. In this book, he shares their recollections of *their* friend Noah Rondeau, and in turn readers will feel as if they've known Noah themselves, and if they're lucky, they'll hear Jay's voice behind the lines, and here they will find yet another friend. And so the circle widens.

—Paul Sirtoli, 2014

Introduction

"I'll be satisfied if you just tell an honest account of my good friend who carved out of an unforgiving wilderness a life of happy solitude," Richard Smith said of the man he respected so well. Smith saw the historic value of Noah Rondeau's life and of the possessions he had left in Richard's care. But, Richard cautioned more than once, if I was to write "a verbal monument to a grand old man," I needed to remember to never make him "bigger than life." I realized I would also have to be careful not to glorify Richard, who was one of my own heroes. He was one of Noah's dearest friends, yet he wanted no tribute for whatever he offered me. He simply wanted to share a personal, positive image of Noah.

Smith maintained Rondeau was the finest person he had ever known, and he could choose no better partner. To rub elbows with an older, wiser man who could answer all his questions was a continual delight; it was school and holiday all in one. Smith had a supportive, understanding teacher, guide, and pal, each man tolerant of the other's various idiosyncrasies. "Anyone can have a friend, but to few is it given to have a trusting pal. The combination of both is as rare as the proverbial hen's tooth," Smith said more than once.

Many of Noah Rondeau's friends believed the hermit was an artist in his down-to-earth and organized poetry, in his well-managed flower pots and vegetable garden, in his teepee-style wood piles and hermit clothing made from animal hides, in his brilliantly colored hand-formed fish lures and tied flies, in his detailed yearly diaries, and in his meticulous, clear, and elegant Spencerian penmanship. All felt he made his very life a work of art.

The public knew the rough hermit side of Rondeau and his finger-pointing on matters of principle between himself and game protectors. Mountain climbers admired his knowledge of the back country. Sportsmen sought his time-honored woodcraft skills, his hunting and fishing insight and wisdom. Others saw a surprisingly compassionate and perceptive side of his character. This caring trait is often described in hikers' stories of their encounters with him, and most also were treated to his spirited sense of humor.

Smith had been one of the younger veterans of Noah's close-knit circle of friends. He would stick tight, eventually offering his mentor a permanent home for the final years of Noah's life. Smith took on the key role, handling building renovations and looking out for him wherever he could. "It's interesting everybody focuses on his early life at the river, and rightly so," Richard said to me. "Everybody who helped him was so important. You know, Noah brought something special to the group—I think he became the spirit and the personality. He had such a wonderful, open, playful quality about him, and yet he was so talented. Everything just fell into place, and somehow it was real pivotal about Noah."

Richard Smith and Noah J. Rondeau. Both woodsmen were sensitive to the poetry of nature behind the life of hardship—making the men interesting people.
Photo by Bill Wilkins. Courtesy of Richard. J. Smith

On Richard Smith's lengthy stays in his cabin in the Adirondack Mountains, he couldn't help but notice the one thing that all lone woodsmen learn to live with: Isolation from human companionship. I could not help but think about all the time he and Noah Rondeau spent alone in the mountains, and it was that isolation or separation that some call loneliness that inspired me to write some of these stories in the voice and style of Smith. It is an accurate accounting of how he dealt with solitude. I have based them on material gleaned from tales Richard told me.

Smith had two distinct images of Noah. One was of the Hermit of Cold River; the second was of the "grand old gentleman" who finished out his life living at Singing Pines, Richard's modest hut near Wilmington. When he felt he really got to know me well, he handed me his entire collection of Rondeau memorabilia and said, "I want you to help protect my old friend's memory. When you hear people say incorrect things about him, take up for him." I didn't fully know what that meant at the time. I understand it better now.

The Hermit and Us tells Noah's story from many first-person points of view. The personal chronicles have much in common: their Adirondack activities, Noah, his hermitage, what they experienced and what they have carried in their hearts for the hermit. The hermit, by all accounts, was a kindly man who gained the admiration of almost everyone who met him. Accounts don't get a great deal better than that.

Some of the details in their remembrances overlap, yet each memory is historically valuable now, and will prove more priceless in the future.

Wilderness Forever —Richard J. Smith
So vivid in memory are those precious moments
I have but to close my eyes to relive once again
Those wondrous days in the wilderness
Where still I pray the stately wolf and mountain lion creep.
Where once I slept on balsam beds.
Where once the flashing speckled trout caused me to leap and shout.
Where once I learned what happiness and life were all about.
Where once I gazed with rapture, watching sleepy spruces nod.
Where high upon the mountain top, I paused to thank and speak to God.

Section I

Rondeau's Quest for Education

Early in his life, even in childhood, Noah had shown an interest in the outdoors and learning. He was born in to the lower echelons of North Country society, his working-class family took jobs in the mines, the factories and lumber woods. They knew poverty among neighbors and worked with fellow French-speaking incomers who comprised part of the work force in northern New York.

Observing and knowing conditions from the inside of a rural one-room school house, Noah recognized a monstrous inequality between the French- and English-speaking children. All poor, the foreign-speaking children were overwhelmed by the language barrier. He sensed the English-speaking children had a boundless opportunity; his ilk felt only insurmountable hurdles. By as early as the third grade, the inequality in public education caused him to begin to skip school. He dropped out before entering junior high school.

Decades of woods life taught Noah valuable survival lessons.
Courtesy of Dr. Adolph G. Dittmar, Jr.

Throughout his adult life he was heard to talk about his "dozen points of failure." Lacking a high school diploma was at the head of the list.

Youth who came in contact with Noah recall his asking about their schooling. He counseled them about the benefits of a good education. He'd tell them school hadn't been easy for him. He would admit, he had little formal education but tried to make up for it by reading everything he could get his hands on.

"I got my learning back here among these lofty peaks, but the mathematics is hard to get alone," he'd say. He explained, "Some learning was harder than others but if people would just give new and difficult material a chance they'd see it won't be all that difficult." He was convinced that more students could become scholarly in the many disciplines if they would accept the struggle and at least try harder to learn their lessons.

Rondeau's hermitage, Cold River Hill. *Courtesy of Dr. Adolph G. Dittmar, Jr.*

THE HERMIT AND US

Chapter 1

A Long-Running Grumble

"Noah could be a friend to the friendly and hang on to a grudge just as long. There was something of vindictiveness in his nature; he was a hypersensitive person. A brooder."

—A. T. Shorey

A. T. Shorey, Richard Smith, Clarence Petty, Oscar Burguiere, Billy and Jean Burger, Barney Fowler, Jay L. Gregory, Doctors C.V. Latimer, Sr. and Jr. and many other friends mingled with Noah John throughout his life. All were moved, in their own ways, by the doughty woodsman, and impressed with his expert survival skills.

To Clarence Petty, Rondeau "was a man with many contradictions." Petty knew of Rondeau's defiant and often quick temper. Other residents in Coreys viewed Rondeau differently—as someone who couldn't 'make it' in society, and questioning how he would ever 'make it,' so ill equipped in the wilderness.

Rondeau had his supporters and his critics. Richard Smith had heard it all. He pointed out in his friend's defense, "Understand, Noah didn't escape from life. He escaped into it." An interesting way to put it—*escaping into life.*

Oscar Burguiere, who affectionately referred to the hermit as "Old Whiskers," hung on every word the man spoke thoroughly admiring Noah's lifestyle and vacationing at the backwoods bailiwick almost yearly over a twenty-year span.

North Country natives Billy and Jean Burger understood Rondeau's early adversarial attitude toward the game protection branch of the New York State Conservation Department. They also publicly defended Rondeau when local inhabitants' patriotic fervor during World War II prompted them to toss expletives at Rondeau for hiding out in the woods when the home front was going without many necessities because of the war demand and lack of manpower. *What was Rondeau doing for the country?*

And yet, through hard times and good times, Rondeau's fame grew. Some of his greatest support came from men and women in the 46'ers Club of Troy, N.Y. Group members' friendships with Noah grew with repeated visits to his hermitage on mountain climbing trips in the Cold River area.

Aldoph G. Dittmar was a member of the 46'ers. He remembered the hermit well: "Rondeau wore many hats: beautician, astronomer, poet, violinist, journalist, as well as hunter, guide and gardener were all roles Rondeau filled during his backwoods life." These were fitting compliments for a man who said he dropped out of life to get an education.

From all who came to know the hermit, the most commonly asked question was not how he got his food, how he kept warm, how he occupied his time, or anything to do with his physical survival in the woods through long Adirondack winters, but instead, "Why did you take to the forested mountains?"

Cold River Hermitage was once a popular hiking destination for anglers, backpackers and mountain climbers. *Courtesy of Edward J. Fox*

When Barney Fowler asked him this question, Noah's answer might have seemed ambiguous to many who read the 1961 *Albany Times Union* newspaper article, "Noah Rondeau Returns From Peaceful Wilds."

"The quest for education," he replied. From the time he was fifteen until he was thirty-three… "There about eighteen years, I sweat for education…"

Rondeau's reason was not nebulous to Fowler, who wrote the article. He penned: "Rondeau today will repeat that in the cultivation of his patch of vegetables, of the nights spent in the Cold River cabin, he learned much of people. …He will tell you, sitting in his small living room, heated by an oil burner, that he found what he was looking for."

Fowler's words celebrate the hermit and feed his saga. "Uneducated formally, he nevertheless had read of Thoreau and his *Walden*, of the battle of the ants, of the peace and quiet a philosopher might acquire when separated from civilization."

The city editor was an outdoorsman. Rondeau's life captivated Fowler's imagination and fired his zeal to pen stories that lionized the rugged life Noah had faced daily in the wilds.

He also spoke of the Adirondack back country with the passion of a man who was firmly rooted to his contemporary life, but whose heart ached to live in a world that allowed a person to escape modern complexities. But he cautioned, "The tragedy of living primitively in the midst of civilization is always the future. True primitive living in the ancient past always resulted in an early death when physical prowess ended—of abandonment by the tribe. But civilization today takes care of its own, even of those who spent… years in the wilderness as a hermit…" Fowler was referring to the monthly Social Security payments Rondeau had to rely on when he left Cold River.

The fact is, as a youngster, Noah had difficulties. Some were learning hurdles; others developed because of his individualism. He said he first became an elementary school dropout in the third grade.

Delia Rondeau provides a piece of Noah's history that focuses on his reactions to regulation. Delia Nelson Rondeau was married to William Rondeau, Noah's second-youngest brother. Delia, William, and their son Chester, who was Noah's executor, imagined how difficult Noah's day-to-day living conditions might have been, but none ever journeyed over the rough foot trails to visit his encampment. Delia's reflections were about Noah and his intra-family relationships. She characterized her brother-in-law as the black sheep of the family.

Some of what she and Chester spoke about has been documented in DeSormo's *Noah John Rondeau, Adirondack Hermit* (North Country Books, 1969).

DeSormo wrote, "Alice Corrow Rondeau, who died in 1901, only three years after Noah ran away from home, was apparently never close to her oldest son, who years afterward told one of his closest friends that he always considered his Aunt Maggie to have been more of a mother to him than his real mother."

Also shared on the taped interview was Noah's attitude toward and opinion of his father, which Delia said Noah "made quite obvious."

His boyish actions gave his father the impression Noah was more interested in enjoying action and adventure in the surrounding woodland than fulfilling chores on the family homestead and obeying commonplace rules.

As an adult, Noah frequently talked about his educational shortcomings. One excuse he laid blame to was the language gap he encountered in early grade school. The primary grades have always been an especially troubling time in many boys' academic development, but in Noah's case it is assumed he was referring to the difficulty of attending a school where only English was spoken. French was his first language, and the barrier was hard to overcome.

In Aldoph Dittmar's estimation, Noah was quite a bookish adult. During all those hours, days, and years by himself, he found himself seeking answers in books. Reading gave him a perspective he had not previously had.

Many books lined the walls of his hermitage. "Sixty at least," Smith recalled. Two well-thumbed Bibles, a dictionary, Wells's *Outline of History*, an elementary text on astronomy, books of poetry, mathematics, Darwin's book on evolution, books about philosophy and science, and Parkman's *Conspiracy of Pontiac* were among his collection.

Mary Dittmar and Noah. Rondeau was a self-taught fiddle player.
Courtesy of Dr. Adolph G. Dittmar, Jr.

Rondeau lived in the hamlet of Coreys, New York, for a while before he retreated permanently to his Cold River camp. Clarence Petty,[1] a Coreys native, knew several hermits in the area, but he said Rondeau was different from the others. He was "a rebel against all authority," but Petty "did not see him as an isolated or solitary man." He was something of a paradox. Petty explained that Rondeau "was intelligent, had an exceptional memory and read extensively." He was one of the most well-read woodsman-type persons Clarence ever knew. He was "interested in the Bible. He professed to be a Seventh Day Adventist and observed Saturday as the Sabbath. Catherine Petty, Clarence's mother, and Noah would spend a long time exchanging views each had gained from the Bible. Rondeau was also learned in the heavenly bodies. Clarence clearly recalls he was self-taught in many areas. "He was interested in astronomy and was able to tell what month it was by star positions."

> *Well, when you got to know him he was sociable, but he wouldn't talk to you unless you started talking with him. But then when you got to know him, he'd talk all day...Rondeau was a different kind of an individual. He always felt that education was denied to him. He said, 'I was denied an education.' Actually it was his own fault. His folks were highly religious. They were Catholic, Catholic people, and the reason he left at the age of eleven, he told us that his father got the priest to come in there. He said, 'You've got to come to church when your father tells you to,' he says, 'or I'm going to turn you into a little yellow dog.'* That did it right there. Noah says, 'After that,' he says, 'I want nothing to do with the Catholic religion or anything to do with it.' He turned against the whole Catholic religion. He was against it from then on. He left there at eleven. He didn't want to stay with them. His folks were highly religious. Had he stayed there and gone to school,*

he would have had an education. But it was his own doings really, and even after he got out of there and got acquainted with us and so on, he hated anybody that had any authority.

The point Clarence kept driving at was that when he was a child there was little time for anything but school and work for *all* the pupils. Families expected to take responsibility for their own welfare, and that required work and cooperation from all family members. The same thing was true of Rondeau's generation, but apparently Rondeau didn't want to play by his parents' rules.

Lt. to Rt. Archibald Petty, Paul Kelsey, Noah. March 28, 1950. Thoughout the late 1940s and 1950s Noah addressed clubs and organizations. His speaking fee was normally $25.00, a meal and travel expenses. Lecture subjects included his: Hermit Life—Cold River Style; Becoming a Hermit; Red Patches for a Hermit; Old Maids; two tales he called "Mitchell Micke Mick Swallowed the Blarney Stone" and "A Bear Eat Me Up;" Natural History of Adirondack Mountains; Cold River Valley's Flora and Fauna; Fishing, Hunting and Trapping; Wig Wams and Cabins; and Astronomy Over Cold River.

A common thread that recurrently ran through the lectures was his "lost opportunities." Topping that list was a regret of never having earned a high school diploma.
From Noah's photo album. Courtesy of Richard J. Smith.

Clarence's portrayal of Noah Rondeau is similar to the picture of him that Delia Rondeau shared. She felt some of Noah's single-mindedness had been inherited from his father, who was the "...old fashioned type. He did not believe in sparing the rod and spoiling the child." Instead he held with keeping the children (there were nine of them) in line. "I guess when he [Rondeau Sr.] told someone to do something they were expected to do it." When one of the children did not respond fast enough, he would resort to some form of physical castigation to advance his order.

Old-age never stopped Richard Smith from longing to return one last time to the Cold River country via the Upper Chubb river. *Courtesy of William J. O'Hern*

To further illustrate Noah's disinterest in any form of discipline, DeSormo shared with Delia and Chester an interview he had with a Mary Dayton, who as a young girl lived near Palmer Hill and attended the fifth grade with Noah. Mary recalled Noah had quite a bit of tomfoolery in him. DeSormo said, "Apparently they had a very strict male teacher and Noey didn't take to any form of strict discipline; he objected to it very much so. Even though he was very bright, he liked to fool around. He sat behind Mary and was in the habit of pulling her hair and sticking his tongue out at her. She would turn around and swat him every so often. 'He was that kind of guy,' Mary remembered."

In Delia Rondeau's opinion, as a lad as in adulthood, Noah had a sensitive side, but his armor plating was thick. "He was pretty headstrong; an obstinate young boy. He could charm the birds out of a tree or turn into a rage."

The story of Noah took a turn on August 8, 1898. At the age of fifteen, he left Black Brook and his home. Noah hated what he loosely termed "The Law" and "everything that was concerned with it."

The "Law" Noah spoke of was apparently a broad name that represented anything that would attempt to control his behavior or thinking. Delia said, "He wanted to think for himself; make his own decisions. And he was fed up with his father's abuse of him. He was fed up with religion; fed up with all kinds of things. Instead of just sulking, he decided to shove off. He thought that if he got himself back into the woods he wouldn't have to be bothered with that stuff."

Noah's sister-in-law's reference to him getting back into the woods had nothing to do with his move to Coreys and thereafter to the Calkins Brook-Cold River area of the Adirondacks. That move wouldn't occur until twenty years following his permanent exit from home. She was simply bringing up the fact that the Rondeau family recognized that as a youngster and teenager Noah often left home when he was displeased or sour. When he left in 1898, no one seriously considered he would never return. On the other hand, no one was surprised that he didn't!

Richard Smith took a somewhat different slant on Noah's early life. He didn't see Rondeau as a man of so many contradictions. In fact, Smith defended Rondeau.

"Oh, Noah might have lacked some self-confidence, perhaps he was a bit unruly, yes he did harbor some harsh opinions," but when his boot prints led into the mountains, he was face to face with all kinds of insecurities—yet it was there that he succeeded.

Rondeau and Smith kept in close contact from 1939 to 1967. Smith said, "He adapted easily" to the time he spent alone. In the end, he felt that time spent in the woods was the one way to salvage the kind of life he felt most comfortable living. And he came to realize that much could be learned through associations with those who accepted him—even glorified him—for just who he was.

The true-blue anglers were the first to enter Noah's isolated Cold River site. Later folks interested in climbing the nearby mountains would also discover Noah was not an unfriendly type who purposely avoided contact with his fellow man. What they would find instead was an intelligent, sometimes humorous, observant and philosophically reflective woodsman. And he would find in them a comfortable social connection.

Aside from the differences in their ages and backgrounds, I found Shorey, Smith, Petty, Burguiere, the Burgers, and Fowler all had much in common. They joined the hermit for fishing trips, tramped to the summits of surrounding mountains, hunted deer in the forest and relaxed together over long conversations on Cold River Hill.

Each agreed Noah had a wonderful mind, and they all enjoyed his choice of words. Many of his phrases were "so very quaint."

One of the homey images all held of Noah was how he would, from time to time, start his conversation with an apology to those he was addressing "on the ground that my daily talks were generally directed to chipmunks, raccoons, mice, deer, bear and tree stumps, and half my English is French anyhow, so I may stumble and break my vocabulary."

When anyone listened to his accounts of backwoods living where there was nothing but trees, mountains, animals and snow, they most often said to themselves: "But, what the devil happened to Rondeau that he got there? What does he do all day? What does he find enjoyable? What does he eat?"

That was precisely what Jean and Billy Burger wanted to know when they interviewed Noah one day in October 1941. Billy and his wife were taking notes as they talked to Noah. They were gathering material for Billy Burger's article, "Hard Times on Cold River," that would appear in the couple's home-town *The Adirondack Record-Elizabethtown Post* newspaper. In anticipation that Rondeau's replies to some of their questions would touch on sensitive subjects, the article was preceded with the following memorandum.

Editor's note: *In writing this article there is no desire to criticize or cast aspersions upon any individuals or organizations. I personally have high regard for the Conservation Commission and religious work has been my only vocation. The intent of this article is to help Rondeau's friends and the Adirondack public generally to understand some of his attitudes.*

A portion of Burger's article appears below in Noah's own words.

> *I hate Big Business because of its unfairness. A person's opinions are the result of his whole lifetime's experience. I was a Frenchman and went to school very little and was handicapped. I had to learn the English language and was pretty much as you would be if you were thrown into a Chinese school. By the time I was 15, I wanted to see with my own eyes and think with my own mind. At that age it was a stern fight and I won. They kept after me, and for ten years it was quite a transition. I became absolutely 'an overcomer.' I didn't join any church, but went to a Protestant church steadily. For a period of seven years, I went to M.E. [a Methodist] Church in Lake Placid oftener than the minister. I read the Bible more than any man of my class I ever knew.*

What I wanted above all was a first-class education. From the time I was 15 until I was 33, I sweat for an education and didn't get it. Because I wanted it, I got more than the average out of my school days. I went back to grade school after 11 years, for a term, and made a grade a day for three days, and finished 8th grade at the end of the term. I barbered at night in Upper Jay and went to school daytime. (That was in 1910 when Haley's Comet was parading in view.) I had to work for a living. The hours were long and wages small, but I learned three trades—barbering, painting and carpentry. At 33 I check up and found I wasn't getting along fast enough, so I said with the poet, 'What care I?' So I kicked it over for fair. I was a master at some of my work and honest 100 per cent, but any reward was always lacking. So I took to the woods.

Noah's Secret Code.

ᘯᒣᐟᕋ ᕪᐟᒉ ᕪᒣᕪᕪᐧ ᕪᘐ ᐧᕪᕎᕐ ᐧᕪᐟ ᕋᕐ ᐧᕐ ᕱᐧᕋᕐ ᕋᕪᕪᕪ ᕪᕐᕐᐧ ᕋᕐ
ᕋᕋᕀ ᕪᘐ ᕱᐧᕪᕋ ᕋᕪᕐᕪᕪᕩᕒᐧᕐ ᕋᕪᕐᕎ ᕐᒣ ᕽᕀ ᕋᕱᕽᕪ ᕱᕪ ᕋᕪᕪ
ᕪᕐᕐᐧᕩ ᑊᒣᕪᕓᕀ ᕪᘐ ᕪᕋᕪᕪᐧᕐᕟ ᕽᕐᕋ ᕽᕀ ᕽᕪᕐᕪᕪᕩ ᑊᕪ ᕪᘐ
ᒣᕪᕪᕁᕪᕪᕪᐧᕐ ᕪᘐ ᕪᕐᕪᕁᕐᐟ ᕪᕐᕪᕪ ᕪᕪᕽᕪ ᕱᕐ ᕋᕪᕪᕪᒣ ᕪᕀ ᕋᕪᕪ
ᕎᕐᕽᕪᕐᕐᕩᕀ ᕪᘐᒣ ᕪᘐ ᕋᕱᕁᕐᕁ ᕪᐟᕪᕪ ᕪᕩᐟ ᕪᕐᕐᕩᕐ ᕪᕪᕁᕎᕐᕐᕩᕪᕱᑊ
ᕪᕪᕪᕪ ᕪᘐ ᕪᕐᕪᐟ ᕪᐧᒣ ᕪᘐ ᕋᕱᕁᕐᕪ ᕋ ᕪᕎᕐ ᕪᕩᕪᕪ ᕪᕪᕋ ᕪᕪᕪ
ᕪᕐᕐᐧᕩᕀ ᕪᘐ ᕪᕪᕽᕽ ᕪᕪᕪᕪᕽᕪᕩᒣ ᕪᕀᕽᐧᕪᒣᕪᕪᕪᕪᕪ ᕪᕩᐟ ᕪᕪᕪᐧ
ᕪᕪᕪᕪᕪ ᕪᕽᐟᕪᕐ ᕪᕪᕪ ᐟ ᕪᐟᕪᕽᕪᕪᕪᕪᕐ ᕪᘐ ᕽᕪᕩᕋ ᕀᕐᕋᕪᕪᕐᒣ
ᕩᕪᕐ ᕪᕐᕐᕪᕩᕐ ᕽᒣ ᕋᕪᕪ ᕪᕋᕪᕩᐟᕐᕋᕪᕱᑊ ᕪᕀ ᕪᕋ ᕪᕪᕪᕪᕩᕐ ᕪᕩᐟ
ᕪᘐ ᕋᕱᕁᕐᕪ ᕽᕪᕩᕋᕐ ᕋᕐ ᕪᕐ ᕪᕪᕩᕋᕐ ᕪᕩᕐᕪᕩᕐ ᒣᕪᕪᕩᒣ ᕀᕽᕐ ᕪᘐ
ᕪᕐᕐᕪᕐ ᕪᕐ ᕪᕪᕪᕪᕋᕐ ᐟ ᕀᕪᕪᕽᕪᕩᕪᕪ

"That was when I decided to go into the woods to stay. I spent three-quarters of my time in the woods, anyway. I wanted a lot of learnin', and I figured I would have time to steddy in the backwoods. If I could have had a good education when I was a boy I wouldn't have gone into the woods. I tell people, 'Cold River is a good hiding' place for a failure.' I jest steddy now because of the satisfaction in it; figure if I could live to be five hundred years old I would be quite a scholar!"
—*NJR response to working long hours for little money with no time left for study following a fire that destroyed his few possessions.*

THE HERMIT AND US

THE HERMIT AND US
Our Adirondack Adventures with Noah John Rondeau

Section II

The Hermit and Us

Each time I arrive at Cold River Hill filled with memories, basking in the restfulness of the woodland, whether the bright afternoon light floods the site or not, in my mind the hilltop becomes the refuge that it was when Noah occupied the hermitage—when the landlord greeted company who had trekked multiple miles along a narrow path—hermit and visitors, cabins and tepees, binding then as trees and earth or fish and water. From earth to logs and logs to shelter, a seamless knit. Pilgrims never feel alone here, where a hermit they'll never meet once lived. Here something still makes this feel like his home.

Lt. to Rt. Bertha Irwin, Mary Dittmar, Noah and Madeline Dodge. 1948 "I remember Noah went fishing long before we woke up. He caught some beautiful trout and prepared a breakfast fit for royalty." —Bertha N. Irwin. *Courtesy of Dr. Adolph G. Dittmar, Jr.*

THE HERMIT AND US

Chapter 2

In Search of a
Bow-Hunting Hermit

Three quarters of the way on the Northville-Placid Trail from Averyville Road south-southwest to Duck Hole, one passes through Paint Bed Notch before reaching an unnamed mountain with a summit elevation of 3694 feet west of the footpath. Moose Creek passes by its base within a short distance. I know this rise as Bear Trap Mountain. The crag has borne its name since.

Smith always referred to the mass as Bear Trap Mountain because a friend of a friend, during one of his benders, left an illegal steel-jawed trap up there somewhere. Positive the bear trap was abandoned with its big jaws sprung open and armed to go off, everyone agreed it would be safer to stay off the mountain. In 1937, Richard's buddies Phil and Vince erected an unlawful cabin on state property from spruce logs and building materials scavenged from the scrap pile left behind after the Civilian Conservation Corps side camp was demolished.

Phil and Vince, while serving in that CCC side camp, met Noah John Rondeau, the region's most fascinating facsimile of a hermit. His encampment at Big Dam a few miles downriver was a hangout for a number of the CCC enrollees on weekends. Their visits were quite beneficial to Noah's larder, because his visitors brought him surplus food from the mess kitchen. Phil and Vince were outdoorsmen, loved life in the woods, and got along well with Noah.

Once the Corps' main project of rebuilding the dam at Duck Hole and upgrading the old government trail-lumber camp tote path into a fire control road along Ward Brook for motorized vehicles was completed, the government work camp was torn down, and Richard Smith took over the cabin in 1940 when Phil and Vince joined the Air Force.

It was an illegal structure, an outlaw camp, and eventually the game protector's path brought him to the cabin. The note the enforcer placed on the table left no doubt about his feelings. It was clear and to the point: "Your camp is illegal but I see it being a benefit. It places someone in a remote area where they could be watchful for fires (i.e. lightning, careless hunters and fishermen). It might also save a lost hunter's life. It is so well-hidden, it hurts nothing so leave it for now."

Smith held the golden age of his life was the time 1934–1949, "a time in which an extraordinary man took me into his woodland camp and became my lifelong friend," he related. He was referring to Noah John Rondeau, the Hermit of Cold River Flow, and this is the story of how they met.

A piece of Richard's past began under the "Gate to the City," the entrance to Rondeau's Wigwam City, Population 1, on Cold River Hill. It was a hand-fashioned narrow teepee archway. There Smith and his hiking partner spotted a dirt pathway that led them off the main Northville-Placid Trail toward a goal he sought in the wilds on a summer evening in 1934.

Fourteen-year-old Richard and his friend Tony Okie had been hunting since they were children. Their earliest weapon was a homemade one they had mastered years earlier—a rubber band gun. The materials were simple: a twelve-inch piece of wood, a discarded inner tube and the original-style clothes pin. The inner tube rubber did not stretch a great distance, so the clothespin bullet did not shoot far, but it was a good gun to the young frontiersmen. The cows in the pasture near their homes were their favorite practice targets.

As teens, they were well-practiced shots with .22 rifles. To trim the cost of buying ammunition, and because of the level of skill necessary to shoot accurately, they came to be "fascinated with the bow and arrow." The idea came to them, according to Richard, because of their reading about medieval battles and Robin Hood. "We fantasized about becoming crack shots with bow and arrow," he said. This interest led them once again to make their own weapons.

Several experiments in bending the stick were needed before they had just the right amount of bow to avoid a crack in the wood shaft. Cattails were initially used for arrows. A nail was carefully pushed into a cattail's fuzzy brown head and a notch was cut on the opposite end for the bowstring. It took flight fairly well but was not accurate, leading them to spend more time fashioning smooth, straight arrows with pen knife and sandpaper. Anything that moved became a target. No animal was safe, although they didn't hit much in the beginning, Richard recalled. "Any shot within a foot of the intended target was considered close." Sooner or later the bow and arrows would break and the would-be hunters were back to the drawing board.

Tony liked hanging around the local barbershop on Greenwood Street. The older men were always talking about trapping, hunting, and fishing. Tony was particularly taken with tales of the so-called "Indian," a former Lake Placid barber-turned-hermit. The following witticism was a favorite story that was often told. He said he never knew if it was really a true tale:

Richard Smith demonstrating to Noah his skill with a bow. 1934.
Photograph by Tony Okie. Courtesy of Richard J. Smith

Smith's life in the wild began after meeting Rondeau in 1934.

Photograph by Richard Wood. Courtesy of Inez Wood Buis

The so-called Indian hermit was observed coming toward his old barber shop one day. The owner of the shop said, "Watch this," to the patrons and dropped a single penny in the floor near the doorway. The "Indian" bent over in the entrance and picked up the copperhead. Of course, he dropped it quickly in his pocket as the gang in the shop stifled their laughter. The barber made an excuse to speak. "Oh that old Indian head. It's been there all day. What's the use of bending to pick up an old penny?" The man replied, "Oh no, it just so happens that ninety-nine more of them make a dollar." Now who is the fool?

For Tony, whether or not one had made a contribution to the world would become evident come Judgment Day. He believed we should help one another and try not to intentionally hurt anybody. Tony wasn't amused by the prank played on the "Indian." Rather, he admired the man's logic.

That summer of 1934, Richard and Tony hatched a plan to put together a major trek into the deep Adirondack forest. Tony declared they should seek out the Indian-hermit who years earlier had gone off to live alone in the wilds around Cold River. They imagined themselves walking through the forest with this woodsman, bows and arrows in hand. The very idea that this reclusive fellow might still be alive and that they just might be able to muster the competence to locate him appealed to their adventurous, youthful natures.

They agreed that first Tony should learn to swim in case a river crossing was necessary. Several days later, they set out in the early light of morning to find the bow-hunting recluse. They brought along the bows and arrows they had put together from blueprints and directions found in Saxon Pope's book, *Hunting with the Bow and Arrow.* "With our bows, my father's hand-me-down .30-.30 Marlin, candy bars, dried fruit and nuts, oatmeal, sandwiches, clothing, blankets," Richard recalled, they began their journey toward Four Corners—a short distance beyond Lake Placid's railroad station and their homes. From that junction they hiked alone down a dirt road until they reached the Northville Placid Trail leading to Wanika Falls and the great forest beyond. The Sawtooth Mountains loomed in the distance. Duck Hole and the Cold River were even farther away.

No one they talked to seemed to have a clear idea where along the river the hermit lived, but the lack of solid information didn't deter them. Tony had secured a rough hand-drawn map. His barber knew of the Indian-be-having hermit and was somewhat familiar with the old Cold River logging path. His suggestion was that the hermit was most likely living somewhere off that tote road in the vicinity of the old dam and lumber camp at the impoundment.

The hike to the river's edge took most of the day as they lollygagged along, shot arrows and stopped to eat their chocolate and raisins. Miles later, the pair arrived at a virgin stand of hardwoods where an aged log lean-to stood on the north bank of Cold River. At the inception of their journey, they had noble ideas of subsisting from wild foods taken off the land, so Richard found it comical that they devoured with no hesitancy a can of sardines and some dried-out "mice-nibbled doughnuts left on a shelf in the shelter." While scouting around the open-faced structure, they saw the remainder of a huge head of a trout on a crude plank table.

They found out later on that the Black Hole, a celebrated angling place, was only a short distance downriver from the lean-to. Their trek had taken them "well beyond their home's cookie jar," Richard remarked. "We realized that our original thought of subsisting on wild food was pure poppycock." Garnering what fruits, berries, and other wild edibles they might chance on was time-consuming and inefficient.

Time passed quickly. About seven o'clock in the evening, as they prepared to make camp, Tony, while off gathering limb wood, heard the ring of somebody hewing wood not far away. He reported the find to Richard. Speculation centered on whether it could be the hermit. Minding their instincts, each agreed they did not want to camp so close to the destination they sought.

Quickly, to take advantage of the remaining daylight, they repacked their supplies and followed the dull thuds southwest where they soon spotted what looked like the outline of a wigwam against the shadowing air. Furthermore "we saw a smaller wigwam," a signpost of sorts, signaling a pathway that left the main trail and headed toward the river.

Yellow and orange sparks popping in the clear evening sky led them up the slight rise as a nippy gust wafted sharp wood smoke in their direction. They came onto what turned out to be a Plains Indian-type teepee made from logs and two diminutive log buildings. What they had initially taken to be wigwams were actually crudely engineered pole buildings. They stepped straight ahead with an eye to the man wheeling an ax into a chunk of wood. Richard was in the lead and halted until the working figure straightened up, before he lifted his axe and began to swing again. Richard summoned a soft, non-threatening "Hello," so as not to alarm the man.

The short, slender body wheeled and watched the teenagers as they neared. It was then that they saw his dark mustache and the animal-skin clothing, and then and there they presumed they "were face to face with Lake Placid's barber-turned-hermit."

Richard began to address the man, but halted when he saw the hermit's eyes were fixed on the rifle he carried. "He was obviously curious," Red recalled, "for he persisted to study it as I drew closer to the fire where the brighter light afforded a better view. Then, quite unexpectedly the woods-man quizzed in a high-pitched tone, 'You must be George Smith's boy, and if you're going to deny it, then explain why you have his old chicken hawk Marlin .30-.30.' "

Smith was surprised: the man recognized the rifle he carried and knew his father! His disclosure made their journey into the mountain valley "seem like the world had just pulled in at the waist a wee bit."

"I'll venture a guess you're George Smith's youngest and that you've got fiery red hair under that cap," the woodsman continued.

With sudden recognition, Richard flashed back to his actual first en-counter with the "Indian," Noah John Rondeau:

> There was an old slashing full-grown with berry brambles, and my brothers, father and I used to chop wood on the edge of that clear-ing about a half mile beyond our homestead along the old Mili-tary Road [in Lake Placid]. July and August was when we'd pick wild blueberries, red raspberries and blackberries. I remember the pleasing sound made by the clanking lard pails as neighbors walked down the dirt road toward the sunny cutover. One man stood out. I had been told he was a barber and lived by himself in a sparse shack on Greenwood Street. Father was good friends with

him and knew he enjoyed Mother's cooking, so whenever we spotted
him we invited him in for a meal.

The after-meal observance always intrigued my brothers and
me. First there would be the offer of pipe tobacco. Following the
ritual smoke and chat, Father would move to the pegs on the
kitchen wall and remove his Marlin, and he and father's guest
would walk out to the grassy clearing for some target practice.
Both men were master shots. We boys would climb up on the rail
fence to watch and listen to the men, deep in conversation as they
fired at bottles and cans. I was amazed at Father's skill when one
time a partridge was flushed out, and he actually shot the eye out
of it. I didn't know it then, but this other man would be partly
responsible for shaping my life in the years to come. He used to say
matter-of-factly, "The best way to become known as a great
hunter, fisherman and trapper is to do a lot more of it than any-
one else, and sooner or later you are bound to be recognized as the
best in the field."

Richard declared that his father claimed the barber was an authority on survival skills and "was a storehouse of wisdom about woodcraft. It was exactly
the opposite of what I expected of a barber. Father told us the man had a bit
of a reputation about the town as being somewhat peculiar, a bit of an out-
cast. Father said Rondeau told him his working life 'would not in a million
years amount to a hill of beans.' He tired of town life and he didn't care to
have a clock direct his day. He saw himself enjoying a simple life in the wilderness. He saw trapping as a sound trade."

Smith's recollections swung back to the story about meeting up with the
bow-hunting hermit. Noah insisted that the boys bed down in one of his
wigwams that night. It was getting dark and they were tired from their
long hike.

Tony and I woke up well after sunrise. When we withdrew from
the wigwam shelter we had slept in, we surveyed Rondeau's City of
Wigwams. It looked different in the daylight. We were surprised

THE HERMIT AND US

at how comfortable we felt there. We had experienced a warm welcome. His primitive living conditions felt agreeable. Tony joked that there was no worry about us stepping on a bar of soap and slipping in the bath because there wasn't a bathtub!

Our original plans were to find the lone wolf, ask for some pointers on archery and leave; we figured our stay wouldn't take longer than a day. However, as Noah warmed to us and we to him, he invited us to stay another night—or more.

Following an unhurried breakfast of trout and oatmeal, Noah suggested we demonstrate our proficiency with our homemade bows and arrows at the edge of the vegetable garden. The target was a two-layered invention. The backstop was a large untanned piece of hide. A pine board hung in the center. Traced on the rough-cut piece of wood was a crude charcoal outline of a hat that Rondeau said stood for "the ranger man's bonnet." We were soon to learn the hermit did not care for game wardens.

Smith's Chubb River trapping cabin. *Photograph by Richard Wood. Courtesy of William J. O'Hern*

Smith and Rondeau, May 17, 1939. *Courtesy of Richard J. Smith*

Noah's bow was kept in an inky, dirtied, timeworn buckskin sheath made during the first years he built his Big Dam shanty from what building materials remained from the abandoned logging camp that once occupied the clearing. Rondeau was truly a marksman to be admired. He proved just how skillful his home-made bow and arrows were.

He explained that if he missed an animal with this gear, or game chanced to maneuver out of range, he would settle for a "flat meal," such as the old-standby flapjacks with homemade maple syrup.

The hat silhouette was a quirky mark to aim at. We never believed for a moment he ever meant that he would actually shoot at a ranger, even though he insisted his sweetest dream was to one day sail a well-placed arrow into a game protector's hat, nailing it to a tree.

His demonstration was pure theater. Noah took his sizable bow in hand, paced off 50 yards from the target, threaded an arrow that was capped with an empty rifle cartridge shell and tipped with razor-edged bits of steel taken from an old bucksaw blade, and drew the bowstring back. His appearance took on a pose of deadly seriousness. "If the shot happens to strike a bit lower than the hat, that'll be too bad. Nothing planned or deliberate, of course," he squealed in advance of releasing the arrow. "The weather affects a bow's performance, you know."

What happened next astonished both of us. When he released the arrow, it bored cleanly through the leather backing that hung on a bush by a hair's breadth beneath the military campaign-style hat's brim. We told him it was a shame he missed the crown we presumed he must have been zeroing in on, but his response told otherwise. Noah cried out gleefully, "Oh, oh! Poor shot. Too bad." Then he danced a little jig around the grassy clearing.

We exchanged glances. There was a chance that he deliberately missed the hat for our benefit, for up to that point we had seen no indication the man with the Indian-like reputation was anything but an expert marksman, even though he admitted he didn't use the bow all that much, seeing he regarded his rifle to be far superior in accuracy.

When the time neared that we planned to vamoose, Noah suggested that a fish fry "Cold River style" was called for. He called it "a farewell lunch."

Agreeing a fish fry would be pleasant, we spent a short time fishing from a log raft that was moved by poling over the waters behind the dam. Noah fished his preferred holes below the crumbling dam's log cribbing.

Richard recalled his thoughts that afternoon as he watched his host prepare the trout. "Noah looked every bit the backwoods hermit in his well-worn and patched clothing. He was so sincere. There was no doubt in my mind that he enjoyed our company."

To further prove that Smith and Okie appreciated the hermit's hospitality, gifts were exchanged at the time of departure. Prior to leaving, Richard and Tony handed Noah some store-bought arrows along with some they had fashioned.

Waving good-by, the inspired youths turned onto the footpath that led toward the arched gateway that marked the junction with the Northville-Lake Placid Trail. "Before we had walked no more than a few yards," Smith reminisced, "Noah called after us, offering the same invitation he had bid earlier. He urged us to come back whenever we were able."

Richard shared with me what he had been mulling over in his mind at the time as the young men stepped silently along the trail, each in their own thoughts. Noah had not been happy with his life on the Outside. The work he had done didn't benefit him. But Richard believed that living in the Cold River Valley, in what some would call a pauper's standard, Noah "had success written all over himself! Although his home and clothing masked the outward appearance of a successful man, Noah was successful. Ahem!"

Smith concluded, "Like Noah, it looked like I was going to choose the less-traveled path in life, even though it only lasted less than a decade. "With enthusiasm and grit, I first set up living in a makeshift shack on the banks of the upper Chubb River. Later, I relocated to the cabin at the base of Bear Trap. It was less than a half a day's tramp from Noah's place."

"We loved to hunt, fish and trap and just hang out together. It was as natural to me as slipping into a union suit. Noah taught me how to study the wildlife in my territory. He introduced me to Doc Latimer's Camp Seward and the men in the doctor's fishing and hunting parties—like Oscar Burguiere. Oscar became a close friend."

Richard Smith took naturally to life in the mountains. Noah's influence on him over his seven years of living simply would forever cling to his heart.

Noah's Secret Code.

"All year long folks look forward to spending a few days here, or a few weeks. Then they go back to the cities and talk about it all winter, and plan for the next summer when they can come back again. They must find something they need here in the mountains." —NJR *philosophy as to why people yearn to return to the mountains.*

Chapter 3

Fredric C. Reeves:
My Best Days in the Adirondacks

Fredric C. Reeves, all 5-foot-3 inches and 149 pounds of him, was a 90-year-old former Adirondack guide, tanned, trim and from the first words he wrote, brimming with enthusiasm and rolling with reflections.

"This is like going back down memory lane!" he declared. "For a minute, I had to stop and think of all the good times that I have had in and about the Cold River country. It has been years since I was in that country. So! I am going to start with the trail beginning near the gate at Ampersand Park."

It was March 20, 1991, and Fredric's nephew, Peter Reeves Sperry of Doylestown, Pennsylvania, had sent me a superb photograph of Rondeau's deserted shacks on Cold River Hill. He pointed out, "I took this when my uncle and I were on a pack trip through the Cold River region shortly after the woods were opened [in 1953]."

Peter's photo offering was the finest image I had collected of Cold River City after its heyday. Uninhabited, vacant, and desolate, the campsite still held some reminders of the former owner. "I saw evidence of bow and arrow making in one of his shacks," Peter wrote, "and a pamphlet about archery lying on a table…" He suggested I contact his uncle in Fort Pierce, Florida: He has wonderful recollections of and personal anecdotes about Rondeau…"

Peter was right on the button. His uncle had much to say. His description tugged at the back of my mind.

"I lived at Coreys for a short time and that is when I met Rondeau. He was not a very colorful person then…

"The first time that I met Rondeau was about 1922. I was staying at the Forester Hotel. The Forester was run by Mrs. Fred Wood and then her son operated it for a number of years. It's since been sold and is now called the Cold River Ranch, Inc. I recall Rondeau had some kind of connection with the hotel. He probably did some infrequent guiding for certain guests.

"Rondeau lived in a house there at Coreys. He didn't own it. A summer resident let him stay there during the off season, probably in trade for some caretaking chores. I was in his house a few times.

"I will always remember the box stove with the chair in front of the open stove door. Rondeau wasn't very careful. He used the chair to prop up sled-length logs that got fed into the firebox. It was very dangerous.

"Rondeau never believed in cutting wood—preferring instead to burn it sled length. Well, one day he went to Saranac Lake and when he returned home his house was all in ashes. He said that he lost everything—claimed that he had over a thousand dollars in furs and the same amount in cash. I remember it clearly.

"Rondeau had no place to go but the woods. He foraged the best he could. He also got hand-outs from the lumber camps. He was great friends of the Hathaway and Petty families. He used to stay with the Hathaways every Christmas. I think Bill and Clarence Petty really took a shine to him.

"[After the fire] I didn't see Rondeau for a long time. I remember one time after he had established himself at his city, I was fishing back at Cold River. I decided to stop in to Rondeau's. When I arrived, he was sitting there in his rocker looking over Cold River and admiring the view of Santanoni…Rondeau kiddingly asked, 'Do you want to buy a mountain, Fredric? Santanoni is for sale.' Later I remember asking him just how he happened to settle at the Big Dam and this is what he told me.

"It seems that the State of New York accused Ferris J. Meigs of the Santa Clara Lumber Company of cutting timber on State owned land. The State had men in this territory for two years counting stumps. At the same time the State had two surveying teams, one started at Tahawus and the other team started at Axton. It seems that the two teams did not meet and so they started over again and again. Every time they covered the territory their lines didn't meet. Rondeau said that survey left a slice of land the shape of a flat iron, the base at Cold River and the point up on Seward, making this gore no man's land. The State still went ahead and sued the

Noah and Fred Reeves enjoyed trout fishing. *From Noah's photo album. Courtesy of Richard J. Smith*

Santa Clara Lumber Co. The State lost the case. Rondeau then told me that he asked Meigs for permission to stay at the Big Dam and that Meigs granted Rondeau the right to stay there for as long as he liked.

"As Rondeau was telling me this, it made me think of what George Morgan told me about taking on the State of New York and winning the case. Morgan did not say who his client was but I wondered if this was the case. At that time Morgan owned the Raquette Falls House. Morgan, in his day, was a brilliant lawyer, but alcohol won out.

"Rondeau had a lot of trouble with the Conservation Department. I had heard they did everything they could to get him out of Cold River country. I heard Earl Vosburgh was the main source of trouble. I don't know the story but furs were planted and they got Rondeau for illegal furs. Rondeau had quite a time with that and he lost his guide license. That is why he carved on a big pine log that laid across the lumber road that went up along side of Boulder Brook this message: 'EARL VOSBURGH IS AN ALL AMERICAN SON OF A BITCH.'

"I always thought that Ross Freeman and Earl Vosburgh were in on planting a doe at Rondeau's house [at Coreys] and then Earl V. came and arrested him and got him…[locked up] in jail.

"One time, Lucien Martin and I were in the Cold River Country and stayed all night at Rondeau's place. That evening he played the violin for a while. I will never forget in the middle of the night, we were awakened by some noise. When we got up to see what was going on, there was Rondeau standing on the bank overlooking the Big Dam and preaching to the stars. We listened to him talk from the teepee we were sleeping in for a good half hour. The next morning we asked him about that and he told us that he was 'practicing my speech, otherwise I would lose it.'

"Rondeau, as I recall, made his living trapping. Maybe he also made a little money from the Conservation Department by keeping the trails open, but I don't know if that is so. I do not believe he had any other income. The times that I stopped at the so-called city, I would introduce him to the party that I was guiding. He would want to hear what news I could give him about Tupper and such. I would never stay too long. I also never asked him too much about his misfortunes.

"The last time that I saw Rondeau was at Saranac Lake in front of the Woolworth Department store. I talked with him for a few minutes—told him that I had just been to his dwellings with my nephew. He said he had not been there in several years. He was getting a little feeble at that time.

"The only chain that hung from the teepee when Peter and I were in there was the one he used for cooking. It hung from a tripod he had made out of poles which was of set over the fire pit."

In old age, Noah was often spotted walking a town's streets.
Courtesy of Richard J. Smith from Noah's photo album

THE HERMIT AND US

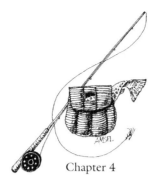

Chapter 4

Charlie and Polly Russ's "Indian Surprise"

Each summer when Charlie Russ smells the smoke from an outdoor fire and tastes the red and black raspberries his wife, Dorothy, and he pick from brambly thickets along a country roadside, he thinks of the Adirondacks and of lower and upper Ausable Lake, the family cottage at St. Hubert's, his stint in the Keene Valley church that helped prepare him for the ministry, and his past treks in the surrounding mountains.

Charlie is now a full-time Connecticut resident, but that is because his health concerns limit his movements, not because he prefers to remain away from his Adirondacks.

His written and visual memories spoke to me—old pictures with their captions told of adventure and youth and better times. They rolled back the years as I turned the pages. Photograph #1 immediately captured my attention. "Noah John Rondeau and Polly, Aug. 9, 1934."

The picture showed a younger, beardless Noah improving Polly's hold on his bow and arrow. Written out in the margin area of Charlie's journal is a conversation that he had with Noah, recorded shortly after meeting the hermit. "My first trip to Cold River was because my competitive hiker-brother John wanted to climb Santanoni. It gave me a chance to go up Seward and Donaldson.

"On my July 25–29, 1933, backpack, my brothers John and Dick and I started out together by way of Slant Rock, where we spent the first night. Then it was on to Mount Marcy, and down to the Flowed Lands, where we spent the second night. The next day we headed to the Duck Hole by way of the trail along Lake Henderson. We made our Cold River camp at the dammed-up Hole. The next day while I headed out to climb Seward, Donaldson, and Emmons, John went up Bradley Brook to climb Santanoni. Dick stayed at Duck Hole camp. John and I planned to rendezvous with Dick at Duck Hole by evening. The following day's plan was to hike north on the N-P Trail as far as Moose Pond.

Polly Russ learning a lesson or two about archery from Noah. *Courtesy of Charley Russ*

"Of the two of us that were bushwhacking, I'm the one that got confused in the woods (July 27th). I descended from the summit of Donaldson and headed in the wrong direction. The end result did not actualize in a disaster though."

> *In due time I heard the heavy flow of water. I knew I had to be*
> *near the site of the big dam and that sound was the water spilling*
> *over a still functional dam. I only recall it was a log dam. I do*
> *remember that was where the old Indian was camping out in*
> *rather an elaborate all-year-round hut. From him, I learned of*
> *my errors in direction after descending Donaldson. I had heard*
> *of this Indian sometime earlier this summer.*

Late that midsummer day the Connecticut boy pulled off the straps on his tightly woven pack basket and rested at a spot he described as the gateway to one of his "grandest trekking adventures ever to come about." In 1933 Noah John Rondeau had not yet had hundreds of images of his way of life captured in hundreds of snapshots, nor had be become the legendary "Hermit of Cold River Flow." Charlie had heard of the existence of the man who lived in the Cold River Valley during a conversation with George Marshall. Marshall had tagged the hermit "The Indian." During the early hours of the evening of July 27, Charlie came face to face with "The Indian."

Few natives in the territory had much of an idea what his purpose was, and Rondeau did not enlighten them on this matter. But Russ was immediately moved by the man as he gave him some idea of, as Russ told it, "where I might be."

"Other people that I knew referred to him as 'The Indian.' I don't think I ever took that too literally and yet the teepee and bow and arrows almost reinforced the Indian idea. I remember him as one who successfully lived like an Indian in the wilderness. I found him to be sociable right off. He was easy to talk to. He was friendly and welcomed me. I recall it was Mr. Marshall that told me about him over at Johns Brook Lodge.

I asked The Indian how far it was to Cold River Camp, an ancient lean-to in a clearing 20 or 30 feet back from the Cold River. It was located about where the trail to Axton came out. It was near the Ranger's cabin. I remember one could see smoke from the Ranger's place at the lean-to."

"The Indian replied, 'Oh, about seven miles.'

"Initially that seemed very strange. I had thought it would be about three miles until he further explained where I was located in the valley. [Rondeau] was standing over a fire when I approached, cooking his supper. ...He had a bow and arrow there and evidently had just finished making a fresh batch of arrows, for there were several sticking in a log by the fire, and numerous wood shavings and scraps of flint and feathers were lying about.

"I was immensely impressed with his camp. His living arrangements were simple and unpretentious and I don't remember any clutter or mess. I had seen many camps that were worse and I envied his lifestyle. He had a garden. He fished a lot and hunted with a bow and arrow. I took to him right away. He told me that the Ranger [who lived in the Shattuck Clearing outpost] would bring him things and that once or twice a year he would go to town for supplies. He told me that he would take a load of carefully prepared pelts to sell or barter. He showed me some skins and pelts that he was working on. He offered me some coffee and even wanted to put me up for the night, but I didn't want to wait.

"His coffee wasn't anything special except that it was hot, plentiful and black. I don't remember using any sweetener unless it was honey which he had gathered himself. Much of what we talked about on that first visit was about coming off Mt. Donaldson and getting mixed up in directions.

"I couldn't believe the campsite I planned on reaching was so far off when The Indian pointed out the way I should go. It seemed as though he was pointing due west, right into the dim afterglow of the setting sun. It was on pure faith of his knowledge that I set out in the dark for camp and my brothers. A glow from the rising moon filtering through the trees allowed me to follow the trail by looking up into the sky. When complete darkness came on and the moon rose higher, that also simplified matters.

In the short time Russ spoke with Rondeau, he "received clues to the mystery of The Indian." He was amicable but didn't mince words. He was forthright, not a bit ornery and didn't growl when he talked—all things Russ had learned through hearsay. The hermit was an experienced woodsman—"old" to young Russ—and possessed an exacting knowledge of the lay of the land as well as a store of backwoods wisdom. Living in the wilds might have been his way to get away and forget something, Russ speculated. He would have liked to stay and learn more. Rondeau "had a lifetime of experience and he treated me to tales of living back there" but Russ had to move on.

It was the wee hours of the next morning when he reached Cold River camp and shared "Indian" lore and his memorable adventure with his brothers. On the 28th of July, the trio left Cold River and headed toward the Sawtooth Range, Ward Brook, and far-off Flowed Lands. From there they would continue on to Mt. Marcy and The Range.

Later that summer Charlie wanted to return to Noah's camp. Once more he planned a circular route to climb more summits and to further acquaint himself with "The Indian." He longed to stay just for a day, just to talk and

Lt. to Rt. John Russ, Kay and Polly Russ. "We pushed her from the rear and we pulled her from in front and Kay went up The Chimney's steep slide to the summit of Mount Colden." —Charlie Russ, August 25, 1932. *Courtesy of Charlie Russ*

Noah made a game of demonstrating how accurate his aim was with a bow and arrow. June 1935 with H.S. Webber's party. *Courtesy of Richard J. Smith from Noah's photo album*

indulge in weighty religious discussion and thoughts about classics both had read, for he knew Noah John was "a philosopher of sorts." Just once more he wanted to experience Noah's camp hospitality, to maybe eat out of his pot. He knew it would also seem a fortune to the hermit to receive some staples such as flour, sweetened canned milk, coffee, dehydrated vegetables and rice, lentils and barley. On the next trip he would put some of those goods into his pack basket

Charlie was like so many other hikers that came along the trail and expressed an interest in staying at the hermit's woodland abode. He wanted to learn more about Rondeau and wanted also to share this special character with his sister.

"My second trip began August 21, 1933. I was once again headed into the Cold River area with my brother Dick and sister Polly. I wanted him and Polly to see The Indian and his camp."

Charlie had described Rondeau's encampment to his siblings. "I tried to answer all of Polly's questions." How did he manage to keep warm? Was he cold and uncomfortable in the winter? Why did he once keep a fox for a pet? What hazards did he face deep in the woods? These were some of the questions she posed. Charlie just knew he had to have another face-to-face meeting with the man.

The teenager also knew the idea of killing a bear or a deer or catching fish was like a cat stalking and pouncing on a mouse. It was an inherent talent for some people. He later heard Noah say that "even people that don't know much about it [finding wild food] or pay much attention to it, if they were crowded back to it, they could soon adjust themselves to that because it's natural."

So it was that Charlie promised his hiking enthusiast sister, Polly, that he would take her on his next Cold River trip to the little, one-man town.

That trip was aborted, and an entire year passed before Charlie and Polly had another opportunity to enter the deep woods. Charlie began:

"We started out early on August 6, 1934. Our purpose was to explore a different approach to Cold River Camp. From there we would take the trail that parallels the Cold River. On Aug. 9th, Polly and I visited with Noah at "the city."

> *Reading through my journal, I see frequent comments on the beautiful stands of virgin timber. Lumbering hadn't taken all of them by any means. Where the lumberjacks did cut there was second-growth timber coming along very nicely, even young conifers such as balsam, spruce, tamaracks, and so forth.*
>
> *I vividly remember breaking camp on the morning we reached The Indian. About half-way between from the lean-tos beyond Shattuck Clearing and Duck Hole, we struck the turn-off which led over to The Indian's cabin. Polly seemed to have been feeling fine. We made good time. We dropped our packs by his gate-of-sorts and approached The Indian's establishment. As we approached the edifices, Polly began to have some apprehensions about meeting this strange character. I had a bit of concern about her, but it all was dispelled when we saw no one was around.*

As the Russes approached the hermitage, they had a view of tall wooden tee-pees made from many poles. The pole structures appeared on the skyline with the mountains as a backdrop.

The Indian was down at the river fishing when we arrived. We looked down at him from the bluff and waved. He noticed our greeting and within minutes came back up, climbing the bank on a set of log stairs built into the cliff face. He was carrying some nice fish. He seemed tickled pink that we'd stopped in just to see him. "Sure I remember the night you came down off of the Sewards," Noah said. He remembered every detail of it from the previous year.

His welcome brought a sudden release of tension. We were impressed by him and his collection of teepees and huts, and in spite of our anxieties, we really looked forward to spending time with him. After a very brief period of general conversation with him, Polly realized she had had no reason to be concerned about anything. We found Rondeau to be warm, friendly and an interesting person.

He offered us coffee as he pointed toward some benches for us to sit down. "I must get me a bear this season," he quipped when he directed our attention to an animal skin that was mantled over the wood back. "This one is getting a mite ragged," he said, directing his comment more toward Polly as he pointed to a well-worn hide draped over a hand-made rocker. It was the only comfortable chair in sight. We mentioned the use of animal skins and learned from him that bear skin "will make any hermit a serviceable jacket." He said he kills a bear every few years but takes a deer every year. The woodsman has excellent sewing skills. He produces sturdy jackets, pants, and boots out of deer skins, too. Once seated, he asked us where we were from. We told him we lived in Hartford, Connecticut and came in the summers to St. Hubert's, where our family had a cottage and land bought by my paternal grandparents about 1875. I may have told him that I had walked all the way from Hartford to St. Hubert's the year before.

A CCC worker standing at the sluiceway of the old Moose Creek outlet dam about a mile from the CCC side camp. Polly and Charlie were surprised to see construction along the Cold River. *Courtesy of Gay Prue*

I know I asked him point blank, "Don't you get mighty lonely out here by yourself?"

Noah replied, "Yes, yes—but I get used to it. I used to get lonesome long ago when I first came here. The world is getting mightily sinful nowadays. It's pretty black; the day of judgment isn't far off. Yes, yes. This generation will see it. Why, everything is written in the text [the Bible]. All this trouble in Europe, why that's all just written. Why you take the Jews now, we know from the Bible just how long it was that the Jews were the chosen people. For example, '____ ____ ____ ____' " (He quoted as fast as he could, passage after passage from the Old and New Testaments, especially from Revelation.)

Noah continued, "So it was just 2,000 years that the Jews were in favor and then they were cast out. That's why you see the Jews all over the world oppressed. You see, it had to be equal. For the last 2,000 years the Gentiles have been in favor, ending in 1999. But their time is coming, yes, yes. Why you can read it all in the New

Civilian Conservation Corps side camp near Mountain Pond. 1935. *Courtesy of Gay Prue*

THE HERMIT AND US

Testament '_____ _____ _____ _____' [more quotes]. It tells all about the world war. Yes, the world is mighty sinful. Lots of people are going to be cast out. Not even the church can save them. Look how many churches there are in the United States. They will all be wiped out. It is written thus '_____ _____ _____ ____.'"

Noah then talked about himself. I can't recall the details excepting when he told of Mr. Van. [Henry Van Hoevenberg built and operated an impressive log lodge on Clear Lake, now called Heart Lake. On June 3, 1903, fire destroyed the hotel. The present owner of the property is the Adirondack Mountain Club.] He apparently had worked for Mr. Van. I remember he spoke highly of him. Somewhere in his story he told about coming to Cold River and how he lived. He showed us his whole camp. He pointed out how he made his bow and arrows. That led to a discussion of nature and killing nature's animals, and that led to religion. He started quoting more Bible passages, especially Revelation, which brought us into politics. He seemed to be not at all interested in theology. He had no use for ecclesiastical theology, for priests or ministers, but had a strong sense of the divine. He seemed to be well informed about the war he saw breaking out in Europe, and saw it as fulfilling Biblical prophecies, and there was more, I'm sure, that I have forgotten.

Polly inquired about getting food. As I recall, he told us about all this and that the nearest grocery store was thirty-five miles away. We dumped our pack baskets and gave him some presents of food. The conversation went on. First it was about himself, how as a boy he had tried to get work, then it turned to Mr. Van Hoevenberg again, then to Germany and the present European crisis, then to religion. I was surprised how well he knew the Bible. He, just like Grandma Russ, saw in current events a fulfillment of the Biblical prophecies. He must have memorized the whole book of Revelation. At one point, he said that the Bible is the only thing he reads.

Noah could quote Matthew 24. He accepted that the time was coming for the Lord to come again. He believed the end was nearing

Lt. to Rt. Gay Prue, Earle Conto, Harold Potter. Civilian Conservation Corps workers by tent near the Ward Brook Fire Control truck road. 1935. *Courtesy of Gay Prue*

every door. He believed the 'good old Bible' from the beginning to the end—just compare today with Matthew 24. We are living in the days He is speaking about, all these we are having every day. Let's be ready for His coming. Greet Him with a shout, for He tells us in His word to watch and pray. Many wars will come upon us, many earthquakes in those days, all of these. And just as quickly he switched to talking about hunting and fishing, and soon had his bow and arrow out to show us how it was done.

The hermit's bow and arrows he made himself. It's claimed the bow has a 75-pound pull. Noah claimed he has made forty kills with it. The most abundant meat he relies on comes from small game like chipmunks, squirrels, partridge, and so forth. He has killed deer and a bear with the bow, but he really relies on his rifle to fill his larder during the hunting season. First he demonstrated the efficiency of his homemade equipment. Next he handed the long bow over to us. He wanted us to actually try shooting with his homemade hunting equipment The target was a simple, small piece of untanned deerskin tacked to a tree. With the utmost care not to do anything to offend her, he showed Polly exactly how to do it.

I mean by "the utmost care not to offend"—Noah seemed to be a bit uneasy with teaching a pretty gal. He had to stand close. Because of that, he appeared to be extra cautious in helping Polly in his close contact with her. I saw him kick a paper or some object out of their way as if to make things neater.

He was very patient and seemed to be amused at our ineptitude at shooting accurately at the target. When I tried it, I lost the first arrow. We spent a long while looking for it. The next one went short, but on the third try I hit the mark. Polly did better than I did. It was getting late by the time our lessons were over. We suggested that our time to depart was drawing close.

"No, no, it's still early and you only have a little way to go," he blurted. Why wouldn't we stay and have some more coffee? It wouldn't take long, and "besides people didn't come around here very much."

*So we stayed. Not only did we have coffee, but fish, carrots,
bread, and butter which the Ranger had recently brought him.
All the while, the Indian kept talking about the virtues of bow
and arrow hunting. Meanwhile, the Ranger and his boy came in
to camp. He seemed highly amused at the conversation we were
having, but I didn't think he was any more amused than we were.
The Indian so much wanted to have us write him a letter some
time. He gave me his address and I gave him ours.*

*As we were leaving, he reminded us again to write and promised
he would do the same. I don't recall his exact words, but they were
happy ones. To my regret, neither Polly nor I corresponded. I don't
know why. I did send a Christmas card that first year after we'd
seen him.*

*The walk to the upper Cold River lean-to was short and passed
very quickly. We were no sooner out of hearing than we looked at
each other and burst into spontaneous laugher. Our reaction must
have been an automatic response, a venting of delight.*

**Lt. to Rt. Bill Dufreane and Gay Prue, 3-C squad leader, in Company 208. 1935.
Rest break on Chicago pneumatic compressor and Cleveland H-77 Sinker on truck
trail. Blasting rock to open a roadway to Duck Hole.** *Courtesy of Gay Prue*

I never did ask his reason for living in the wilderness. I did wonder why, but I thought that was none of my business and that he would bring the subject up if he wished me to know. He never elaborated too much.

Off to the side of the Cold River trail we saw remains of deserted lumber camps. I do indeed remember seeing a number of them. We investigated each. I thought we might find some interesting items in the lumber shanties.

We spent that night in the shelter near Duck Hole. The next day we traveled the identical route we had taken in 1933 back to Flowed Lands. All I remember about that is that we were always sloshing through swamps.

From Flowed Lands we turned toward Skylight Notch and climbed Skylight. On the 11th we reached Johns Brook Lodge via the Hopkins Trail. We took my trail (one I cut out) and came home through Rooster Comb Pass.

On trip four, on August 20th, 1934, brother Ernest and I returned to the Cold River area so that we might climb Santanoni for the view, which I wanted Ernie to see. I had not been able to view it on my earlier trip because of rain and fog. We spent our first night out at Moose Pond. Ernest and I utilized planks and hardware from a deserted lumber camp in the area to build a make-shift shelter that we then used for the night.

After climbing Santanoni, Panther and Couchsachraga we returned to our make-shift Moose Pond camp for the night. The following day, Aug. 21st, we went to shelter at Duck Hole. We found a group of boys, older than us, camping there and got to talking with them. We learned they were members of the Harvard Mountaineering Club. After they left I was in the midst of reading out loud in English a French story that I had brought along, when two men, very much absorbed in conversation, arrived.

"There, there we are, we'll stick 'em right in there. That will be a fine place," one of the men was saying as he pointed to the small open field. Then he saw us relaxed in the lean-to.

"Hello boys. Camping here tonight? We just come along down here to see about the camp and the bridges we're going to put in here."

"Bridges in here?" we exclaimed.

"Why, yes, of course. We've got to bridge that stream, thar, you know." He was pointing downstream to the Moose Creek outlet. "And we're going to put the horses right in there. Why the road itself will be in here in jig time."

"Road? What road?"

"Why, didn't you fellows know we're building a road back here?"

"You mean the one they're putting in from Axton along the Ward Brook Trail? Why, I didn't know you were bringing it in as far as this."

"Yes, sure. It will come clear up to the Duck Hole. Why, we've got trucks up there, back on the top of the hill. This is the CCC job, you know. Come on, I'll show you."

We accepted his invitation and went with him to tour the CCC road under construction. Sure enough, not 500 yards back of the lean-to was the vanguard of a troop of CCC workers, busily engaged in cutting down trees. The man now talking to the workers said, "These boys'll have something to tell their grandchildren about. Yes sir. Come here and I'll show you something you can tell your grandchildren about—what the CCC is doin'. I'll show you the CCC ain't loafin'!"

We walked on. Long lines of men were busy with hoes, picks, and shovels, digging out the banks and leveling a roadbed.

"See this here boulder?" he pointed out to us. "These will all be dragged out by horses. The larger ones will have to be blasted. See, I'll show you how it's done. We put that big chain right around 'em like that and haul them away. I suppose you boys wonder why we chop those trees down and leave such a big stump?" The stumps, all of them, were at least five feet high.

"Well, you see, we hitch a team of them horses onto the stumps and haul them right out by the roots. Do you want to see something else? Well, I've got to stay here, but you two go on up

1935. Scene along the once wide road opened by the 3-C's to Duck Hole. Today these rock cliffs are shrouded from view by foliage and the road is now a narrow footpath. *Courtesy of Gay Prue.*

the road a ways. You'll see a' plenty. We've got it almost done up the hill a ways."

So we left our guide and official—maybe the boss of the federal government operation—and proceeded along the new road on a tour of inspection. We observed long lines of men working with picks and shovels. You would never know the place as being the same old narrow foot trail that I had taken with Polly a little more than a week ago. We came to the point where the Long Lake trail branches up there near Mountain Pond. The whole area was an absolutely changed sight. The tree bearing the signboards which nine days ago was well off the side of the trail was now the only tree standing and that, plump in the middle of the roadbed. A little further back, on the Ward Brook Trail, were two men drilling 17" holes in the rock for blasting. It was all done by hand, and they told us it took all day to drill one-and-a-half holes. We watched them work a while and then we went on.

CCC squad at Cold River side camp, 1935. Front row squatting: Lt. to Rt. Bill Conness, Harold Potter, __ Bushey, Gay Prue and Elmer Jock. Center row: Gebo State foreman, Clarance Elmer, __ Lamay, Phil McCalvin, Earl Contro. Back row: Culley, __, R.E. Hayes, forester boss. *Courtesy of Gay Prue*

On the hill there were men digging drainage ditches. The road was practically completed beyond that. We walked on over the crest of the hill, marveling at the elaborate bridges that they had built, the wooden culverts, and the huge stones and trees that they had moved.

A deer came out of the woods, sniffed around uneasily, and walked along the road ahead of us. She was frightened finally by the approach of a couple of trucks. It was 5:00 PM then and a shout from the foreman, way back where we had come from, ended work for the day. We turned back again towards camp. Great groups of men passed us. They were jolly, and many of them spoke to us as we passed.

"Well, what did you see?" the officer that had been our guide said as we neared camp. "Tomorrow the boys'll have the road down by the Cold River Camp. [He was referring to the aged upriver lean-to that was set in a small clearing beside Cold River.] "You fellows unquestionably will be the last to enjoy the Cold River lean-to."

After a good supper Ernie and I settled down for the night.

Charlie and Ernest had no way of knowing then what the CCC officer meant by his parting statement. Had they returned at a later date, they would have found a temporary CCC side camp in that location. It was at this camp that CCC-er's, all young men, such as Phil McCalvin and a friend named Vince (his last name has been forgotten), both natives of Saranac Lake, worked.

Phil and Vince are representative of the numerous young men who came to meet Noah during those few years the seasonal CCC side camp stood. It provided temporary shelter while the Corps' main project following construction of the Ward Brook truck trail was to rebuild the aged logging dam at Duck Hole, following the work to open the original double track wagon route along the Ward Brook for motorized vehicles.

The tent "city" generally consisted of large, military-issue wall tents set on wooden platforms. When the camp closed, and Phil and Vince separated

1935. Noah John Rondeau. Over the weekend, Gay Prue and Phil McCalvin brought bread from the camp. "Rondeau welcomed us. He liked our company."
—Gay Prue. *Courtesy of Gay Prue*

THE HERMIT AND US

from the CCC, they built a small cabin hidden in the woods around the base of Bear Trap Mountain from the discarded material left behind when the camp was torn down. It was from this same dump that Noah also salvaged many useful items, including the galvanized trash cans he used for storing his root crops, and cans in which he stored his valuables in the woods at a location he called his Mammoth Graveyard. Soon Vince rambled away from Lake Placid, and in 1940, when McCalvin joined the Air Force, Phil turned the cabin over to his younger friend, Richard Smith.

On August 22nd, Charlie and Ernie left Cold River and Duck Hole. "I took with me a bit of the balsam bed Polly had made as a memento," he shared. By the close of August 24th he had climbed the Colden Chimney, ascended over Marcy, and camped at Sno Bird Camp near Mt. Haystack, before returning to St. Hubert's.

Seven decades plus some additional years have passed since Charlie Russ visited Noah John Rondeau, but Charlie has never forgotten the magnetic dreaminess of the hermit's camp and the voice of a person he quickly came to regard as a "dignified" man with "personal magnetism."

Noah's Secret Code.

⊹⊙ ⊘ ⊣⸍ᛁ⸍ ⟨⸍⨯⊖ ⊢ `⊖⸍₁ ⸍⊤ ⨯⊤ ⸍⊖⸍ ⸍⊢⸍⸍⸍ ⊹⊙ `⨯⊢⨯⊖ ⸍⸍
⊖⸝⸍⨯⸍⊢⸍ ⸍⸍ ⊤⸍⨯⨯⸍⊐ Ⓞ⸍⸝ ⊢⸍⸍⸍⸝⊖⸜ ⸍⸍⸍ ⊤⊖⊖ ⸍⊤ ⸍⊢⊖⨯
⸝⊖⸍⨯⊢⸝⨹⊖ ⸍⊢⸍⸍ ⸍⊢⊖⊤ ⸝⊖ ⨯⊢⸝⊢⸝⸝ ⸍⸍ ⸍ ⸝⸍⸍⸝⸝
⸝⨯⸍⊖⸍ ⸍⊢⸍⸍ ⸝⸍⸍⸝⸍⊖₁ ⊢⸍ ⸝⸝⸍ ⸍⊖ ⸜ ⸝⸝⸍⸍⸝⊖⨯₁ ⸝⸍⸝⸝
⊢`⨯⊤⊐ ⊹⊙ ⸍⊖⊖ ⸍⊢⊖ ⸝⨯⸍⊖⸍ ⸍⸝⸝⊢⸍⸍⸝ ⸝⊢⸝⊖ ⸍⊤ ⊖⨯
⸍⊢⸍⸍ ⊖⊖ ⨯⸍⸍⊖ ⸍⊤⸝ ⊤⊢⸝⸝⸍⸝ ⸝⊖⊢⸝⸝ ⨯⸍⊖ ⸝⊖⸝⊤⊖⸍⸍ ⸝⸝
⸝⸝⸍ ⊢⸍ ⨯⊢⸍⊖ ⊖⊢⸍⊢ ⸍⊢⊖ ⸝⸝⊐

"I've got some ideas of my own that I'd like to explain to folks. For instance, too few of them realize that they're living on a round planet that rotates in space and travels rapidly. I see the planet orbits, nine of 'em that we know of, first as being made perfect and put in line with the sun." —NJR's reply when asked what were some things he still would like to learn.

Chapter 5

Phil Wolff:
"Nothing Beat Cold River"

Phil Wolff at 94 is one of the few people still living who remembers the Cold River hermit. In the summer of 2010, he shared his reminiscences about camping in the Adirondacks and what he learned from his visits with Noah John Rondeau.

Backpacking gear was much simpler in the 1930s. *Courtesy of Phil Wolff*

Truck parked beside a tent platform at the CCC Cold River side camp.
Photograph by Phil Wolff. Courtesy of Phil Wolff

Phil Wolff's teenage world was filled with adventure during the latter half of the 1930s, but nothing surpassed going to the Mayor of Cold River's camp with hiking partner Frosty Bradley. He values the nature lessons learned with the hermit. It was fun sharing time and meals at the "village," a term Rondeau used when referring to the hermitage he presided over and—best of all—Phil and Frosty had Noah's undivided attention.

Today, Phil enjoys sharing stories of his backwoods treks with son David, his wife, and their sons DJ and Stephen, who in turn salute him by calling out in unison "PHIL" from the top of each of the High Peaks they summit in their quest to become Adirondack 46ers.

Noah was "one of the original proponents of energy efficiency," Phil began. His tale of the hermit's hospitality rolled from his mind easily. By the time Wolff began canoe trips and backpacking treks, Rondeau had long established his two semi-log cabins and teepee-like stacks of tree-length firewood on Cold River Hill.

"In the early 1930s I spent summers living with my Aunt Margaret and Uncle Ollie Bartz at Bartz Dairy in Saranac Lake. My camping partner, Frosty Bradley, the Boy Scout Executive of the Adirondack Council, was headquartered at Saranac Lake. As two Eagle Scouts in our early 20s, hiking, mountain-climbing and canoeing were good excuses to go camping. We prided ourselves on living and eating well in the woods with the lightest possible loads.

"At the time, a contingent from the Barnum Pond Civilian Conservation Corps Camp at Paul Smith's was rebuilding a dam at the outlet of the Duck Hole for fishing and as a nesting place for migratory birds. A camp

Phil Wolff's camp was below the Duck Hole dam spillway.
Photograph by Phil Wolff. Courtesy of Phil Wolff

THE HERMIT AND US

The Duck Hole dam's new cribbing refurbished by the CCCs.
Photograph by Phil Wolff. Courtesy of Phil Wolff

was set up six miles in, on a fire road between Axton and Coreys. On Fridays a forest ranger would drive a truck with supplies into camp and bring out men to spend the weekend at home or at Barnum Pond Camp. He would take the men back either late Sunday night or Monday morning. Ranger Ray Searles, of Lake Clear, was a good friend, and he would let us ride along. In exchange, we helped with trail work."

Wolff and Bradley found a site for their campsite near Big Dam—"by 1936 a weakening log dam on Cold River." Wolff said the site was, "ideal because of the accessibility of many High Peaks" and was within a mile of where the ranger could drive along the old Cold River lumber company road. "We were within 'Rondeau territory.' Ranger Searles suggested that one of our first projects should be a visit to the hermit. Rondeau unofficially looked after the area, which was used by many hikers and hunters. The ranger said we should avoid mealtime, and once we saw the condition of his camp, we understood why."

OUR ADIRONDACK ADVENTURES WITH NOAH JOHN RONDEAU 75

Phil's first glimpse of the hermitage. *Photograph by Phil Wolff. Courtesy of Phil Wolff*

Rondeau lived by a set of unwritten guidelines. Searles knew Noah was awfully persnickety about folks following his rules. The forewarning helped the young men avoid Noah John's pronounced contrarian streak.

Phil soon learned much about the locally-known hermit's propensity for the natural world.

"We arrived at the Town Hall one morning and were greeted by Noah, who was in his 50s, with a hearty hello and a handshake. We were surprised at his short stature. We had been told Noah's two weaknesses were smoking and reading, so we brought two packs of pipe tobacco and some magazines. Our gifts were right on target. We told him of our plans and where we were camping. Judging from his reaction, we passed muster, although later we learned from Ray that Noah had checked out our credentials with him.

"After a spell of talking, we decided it was time to go. Noah wanted to prepare a cup of coffee as a gesture of hospitality. Remembering the dishpan and dirty dishes in the pole summer kitchen, we declined and returned to set up camp.

"One afternoon we returned to camp after a hike up to Lake Henderson to find a note from Noah to check our river site. Fearing that some animal had attacked our 'Cold River refrigerator,' Frosty hurried down to check and returned with two beautiful rainbow trout. The menu for our evening meal immediately changed to trout, as you can't beat a meal of fresh trout

Cold River City. *Photograph by Phil Wolff. Courtesy of Phil Wolff*

cooked in pancake batter. After supper we made a quick trip to thank Noah. Bringing our own cups and tea bags, we arrived in time to enjoy the delicious aroma of Noah's pipe. Twice a year he had a large package of uncut tobacco leaf he called 'imported stuff' shipped to him from a mail-order house in Virginia. This had an unusual scent that Noah claimed was an excellent bug and vermin repellent. We observed one of the reasons we were warned not to accept Noah's hospitality when he brewed his re-boiled coffee grounds through an old sock.

"As we sipped our tea and Noah his coffee, we relaxed into one of our 'opinion exchanges,' as our host called them. According to Noah, discussions can end up with disagreements and destroy the best of friendships.

The hermit's huts were constructed from salvaged materials.
Photograph by Phil Wolff. Courtesy of Phil Wolff

Big Dam, built by the Santa Clara Lumber Company, once impounded a huge reservoir known as Cold River Flow. It was the backbone that allowed logs to be flushed downriver to Raquette River. Vague evidence today remains of the once substantial dam that spanned the river below Cold River Hill. *Photograph by Phil Wolff.* *Courtesy of Phil Wolff*

We soon grew to appreciate the woods philosophy Noah lived by. Animals, he believed, live by eating various things that maintain a balance in nature, which they do instinctively. Sports who killed just to prove they were smarter than the game they killed really got his dander up. He would get emotional about man's quest for superiority and the use of guns, traps and fishing gear to prove it. Noah loved living things in the wild, but felt no sorrow if he killed something in order to eat, because in nature's cycle, he said, he was allowed to do this. In exchange, he would cut down cedar trees to provide food for the deer when they had difficulty traveling in deep snow.

Rondeau was curing a pair handmade leather mittens.
Photograph by Phil Wolff. Courtesy of Phil Wolff

"Noah fished by tying a fish hook (one of man's civilized achievements that somehow fit into his philosophy) to a line and, about 18 inches above the hook, attaching the line to a piece of driftwood. For bait he used large white grubs, which he found easily by knocking over a rotting tree stump. He would locate a pool of running water and then release the driftwood, tying the line off to shore and allowing the driftwood to float so it looked, in his words, 'inviting to fish.' Noah was energy—efficient, leaving to do something else and returning later for his catch.

"Muskrats, squirrels, raccoon, rabbits, and woodchuck supplied small quantities of fresh meat. In early summer, duck nests in the ponds provided eggs, although he would never remove more than two eggs from a

THE HERMIT AND US

nest. Noah was fairly good with his homemade bow and arrows. In the fall he would occasionally hunt down a couple of male ducks, but he would never kill a wild goose. Geese are monogamous and he did not believe in separating a pair.

"Noah said he had neither a fishing nor hunting license. He also had various systems set up around camp and area trails to check if a stranger was in 'his township.'

"Noah made his words and deeds clear, but there were many subjects we weren't supposed to discuss. He was not interested in world and local news, and we had been forewarned not to ask him why he chose the life he did. There were many rumors dealing with Noah and World War I, and he would

"Robin" Noah demonstrating his accuracy with a homemade bow and arrows.
Photograph by Phil Wolff. Courtesy of Phil Wolff

A contented hermit puffing "the goose egg," his favorite meerschaum pipe, a gift from Lillian and Billy Burger. *Photograph by Phil Wolff. Courtesy of Phil Wolff*

have been the right age to be drafted. Although religion was also off-limits, he felt the Ten Commandments were 'just common sense' and 'made civilization possible.' He also believed in a form of evolution and the existence of a supreme being, which, he said 'you could call God if you wished.'

"Several interesting opinion exchanges with Noah began by talking about killing animals for food, and one of our longest was about self-defense. What would he do if he surprised a bear and her cub? Since he [at that time] did not use a gun, he said it would be time to stop and carefully retreat. Noah always carried a sharp hunting knife. If there was no good retreat, it came down to surprise—and a knife can be quite a surprise to an animal that has never encountered one before.

"One problem Noah had was money, or lack thereof. He would accept gifts but never ask for something unless he could work or pay for it. Noah trapped muskrats and mink in season, selling the skins in the fall for a few dollars, which he used to buy the limited supplies he needed. I called to his attention that this did not quite follow his philosophy that he only killed to eat, and I thought I had him. But from his facial expression I knew he had me. He first skinned the dead animal, removing the edible parts and stretching the skin to dry. Anything that remained was left for other animals and birds. Nothing went to waste.

"Noah was a wealth of information on edibles that provide a balanced diet without requiring a trip to the store. Coffee, his favorite drink next to water, was an expensive commodity, but dried and ground dandelion roots, which you could see hung from the roof of his storage shed, were an excellent substitute. For delicious greens, Noah taught us that if we kept picking the new flower buds, dandelion season could be extended. We were also introduced to a new deep-woods delicacy, cattail sprouts. As plants in marshes begin to grow, the shoots just breaking the surface can be harvested and cooked like asparagus. Another early spring vegetable Noah used was marsh marigolds. These small plants with juicy oval leaves produce yellow flowers and grow in abundance on the edges of streams. The leaf, harvested before the blooms appear, could be eaten raw in a salad or cooked like spinach. Summer offered strawberries, raspberries, blackberries and blueberries, and he competed for these with the bears. Noah had done extensive research on identifying mushrooms and lichen in the woods. Many worked well in soup made from leftover meat or sun-dried for later meals.

"Food storage, both for winter months and for summer cooking, was a problem. Jars and tins were expensive, and he believed nature did not waste things, nor should man. Noah had a good solution that he said he learned from some Native Americans. He would take a tree six to eight inches in diameter that had a center beginning to rot and saw off various lengths. He hollowed out a chunk with a chisel and hammer, creating a large hole in the center with smooth, hard side walls. He then dried the chunk. His next project would be to find a tree of approximately the same diameter as the hole he had hollowed out. He cut pieces of the green wood about an inch thick and set them out to dry as well. The green wood would split slightly and expand as it dried, providing a tight-fitting plug for the top of the hollow piece. Presto—he had a nice wooden storage container that, if put on a high shelf, larger animals would not bother and small animals, like mice, were unable to get into. Noah always said experience was a good teacher. A poorly-made container would break if a shelf broke or if a large animal knocked it over. Poor construction was 'not labor efficient' in the long run, he said.

"Hikers and hunters were a source of both food and company, offering Noah seasonings and extra unused food on their way out of the woods. Salt, sugar and flour were the most common leftovers. Occasionally in fall, hunters killed a bear. Most hunters just wanted the bearskin and a small quantity of meat, leaving Noah the remaining bounty. Since bears normally put on weight at this time of year in preparation for hibernation, it was easy for Noah to render the fat, collect the oil, and then use it in cooking through the winter. Excess fat and oil could also be made into soft soap by adding hardwood ashes. Soft soap kept well and, if properly made, could end up fairly hard.

"In the fall, the beech trees produced large quantities of nuts, which were loved by squirrels and chipmunks. Noah had a unique approach for collecting the nuts to munch on during the winter. It was a lot of work to get the meat out of the small shells, so on a sunny afternoon, Noah would find a comfortable tree to lean against and watch the chipmunks or squirrels rustle through the leaves shelling the nuts. When they had filled their cheeks with nutmeat, they would scoot off, find a hole, and deposit it. Noah would watch where the nuts were buried, collect them, and take his treasure home. Energy—efficient to the last.

"On one visit, we decided to climb the Seward peaks. The three summits were not normally approached from the riverside. A conference with Noah provided us the advice to make a good approach.

"Another time we stopped by, we told Noah about our big outing down river. Near the head of Long Lake, we took the dirt track carry that led to a farmhouse and a beautiful falls and lean-to. A most remarkable thing happened there. As we portaged our canoe and packs around Raquette Falls, a lady appeared on the porch and hollered out, 'Would you like some root beer?' What a surprise when we thought we had been roughing it in the wilds. Our 'Yesses' brought a pleasant 'Come up on the porch steps'

Raquette River House. To Phil Wolff and Frosty Bradley, the sudden appearance of the Raquette River falls farm house and a welcoming lady offering cold root beer was as a gift from Heaven. *Photograph by Phil Wolff. Courtesy of Phil Wolff*

reply. Soon a lady appeared with two drinking glasses and a quart canning jar full of soda, kept cool in the spring house. She told us it was homemade root beer. I do not think that the two of us ever had a more welcome and refreshing drink before or since. When we asked what the charges were, she said there wouldn't be any since we looked like Boy Scouts. We left with a fresh home-baked loaf of bread and four chicken eggs.

"Noah told us the farmhouse owner had been a supervisor during the logging days. He and his wife always welcomed him in for a meal and interesting talk.

"Another time, we returned to our camp to find a note tacked to the tree telling us that Ranger Searles's plans had changed. Our supply truck would be coming in on Friday and leaving early Saturday, which cut our trip short. We told Noah to be at our camp Friday afternoon so we could travel as light as possible going out, which was our way of telling him that we would like to make a present of whatever food and condiments we had left. He appeared right on time with a pack basket and a broad smile. We shared friendly handshakes all around as he prepared to leave. There were no goodbyes, just 'Keep in touch and we will return someday.' Little did we know, or Noah for that matter, what a different future was ahead for all of us."

Phil graduated from Cornell University's first class of landscape architects in 1939. In October, 1940, he married. "A growing family, a business, and World War Two changed life in many ways," Phil said. "I didn't return to hike and camp in the mountains."

The next time he talked with Noah was at the Saranac Lake Rotary Club. Noah was the guest speaker.

Following on the heels of Noah's rise to notoriety at the New York City Sportsmen's Show at Grand Central Place in New York City in February 1947, Phil recalls he was on the reviewing stand at the Saranac Lake Winter Carnival, "when I saw Noah John next. There, in the middle of the parade, was a tractor pulling a large farm sleigh. Mounted on the sleigh was the Department of Environmental Conservation replica of the Town Hall, as well as Noah John Rondeau, in a fur hat and smoking a pipe, looking like a king. As it went by I hollered, 'Cold River!' and he looked up and we waved at each other. That float got first prize."

THE HERMIT AND US

Phil developed into a well-respected Adirondack businessman working among the woods and mountains he loved. He says his being the oldest living licensed bobsled driver and becoming a 46er (climbing all 46 Adirondack peaks over 4,000 feet) are his most important lifetime accomplishments.

While his life turned out one way, he has never forgotten the hospitality of Noah John. Rondeau chose an entirely different path in life, but that doesn't mean he turned out wrong. People are like varieties of mountain flora and fauna. Some survive well in a domestic setting, being cared for and sheltered, while some need to live wild and roam free. Noah John recognized what was in his nature and accepted it.

Noah's Secret Code.

"I don't know if I could be any happier, under the circumstances. I've got the flowers and the trees; the mountains—and the stars. I have nine books on astronomy; I've read 'em over and over, and I've still got an awful lot to learn." —*NJR's take on satisfaction.*

Chapter 6

"Well, How Da Do?"
Aldoph Dittmar's Rememberances

The old-time mountain climbers are living away from the Adirondacks these days. They have left the backcountry. I read in the paper that long-time treasurer for The Adirondack Forty-Sixers, Dr. Adolph "Ditt" Dittmar, recently celebrated his 100th birthday. Ditt can no longer hike the trails in the mountains, but he still enjoys swapping stories of his long-standing twenty-nine year friendship with Noah John Rondeau.

Ditt's chronicles about his connection with the Cold River hermit are a valuable contribution to history and an inspiration to those who wistfully wonder what it would have been like to share camp at the far end of what former anglers, mountain climbers, and backpackers knew as the Cold River Flow.

"Growing up in the northern Adirondacks, I heard talk about a hermit who lived way back at Cold River Flow. Rumors claimed he hunted deer and black bear with a homemade bow and arrows and smoked enough tobacco in his secluded wooden shack that he outdid the volume of smoke that would billow from a dampened wood stove burning green wood! Reports said he scrawled warnings on logs and rocks to officers of the law, marking his territory. These were strong statements that made me question whether his bark might not be quite a bit worse than his bite. There were all sorts of theories as to what drove him to live in the woods in the first place: that he'd been jilted by a lover, in trouble with the law, or had dodged the draft."

The hearsay was just noise, but it made intriguing gossip. Ditt never believed the reports, and there were many—enough to fill a wooden nail keg. Ditt knew that anyone who lived in a remote corner of the world and survived in the wilds on his own had to be knowledgeable and industrious. Sure, he'd need to be a crack shot, but was he necessarily lonely and unhappy?

Ditt had no idea when he first heard about Rondeau that he and his future wife, Mary, would eventually become two of a small circle of friends that would help this hermit maintain his woodsman lifestyle well into old age. But the friendship wouldn't blossom until Mary and Ditt were married.

"The first I ever read of the Cold River hermit was in a brief article on January 7, 1938. in a *Troy-Record* newspaper column entitled 'Cold River Hermit Honored by 46-ers.' The 46-ers used Rondeau's hermitage as a starting, stopping and staying-over place when mountain climbing the so-called high peak region. The hermit was their first honorary member."

Rondeau was tickled with the status bestowed upon him by his newfound supporters. The article quotes Rondeau, who mailed off a thank-you letter

Lt. to Rt. "Ditt" and Mary Dittmar with son David. *Courtesy of Dr. Adolph G. Dittmar, Jr.*

"Nice Weather. At Old Lady's Wigwam. 3 PM Adolph and Mary (Newly Weds) arrive. We Spin Yarn (Talk). I get Flowers for Bride. Dr. Ditt make Birthday for the Mayor. After supper; Camp Fire- and more yarns. I lodge the newly wed in Tent- by the Beauty Parlor." —Noah John Rondeau, Saturday, September 4, 1943.
Courtesy of Dr. Adolph G. Dittmar, Jr.

to the club just before Christmas: "Two days before the 1937 holiday, I came out of the metropolis of Cold River, of which I am Mayor, and am spending three happy weeks at Bartlett Carry Club on the Saranac River. I left snow 14 inches deep at Cold River and found snow two to three feet deep in the big notch west of Seymour Mountain.

"I am feeling very happy in my own way. But the ways of the world are my enemies and I have many unpleasant and unavoidable thoughts. Such thoughts as you yourself can have if you think of China, for instance."

His "enemies"? It makes you wonder how the "ways of the world" could be seen as his enemies. We usually just think of them as the differences between human beings.

The summer of 1938, Ditt took a job as a counselor at a boys' camp in the mountains. It would also be the year he set the record straight about this "uncivilized madman," one who lived with no debt, who preferred to spend his life alone among the forest creatures.

THE HERMIT AND US

"We had planned a canoe trip that included a side trip up the Cold River as far as we could navigate. Having secured our canoes in the shallows, we felt like frontiersmen making our way along a trace footpath that would lead us to Shattuck Clearing and the intersection of the Northville-Lake Placid trail."

Rondeau's hermitage was located on a high bluff a short distance off the well-blazed Northville-Placid trail. Since Rondeau was not a true recluse, and in fact enjoyed having hikers stop by, what he did was the equivalent of standing by the expressway and flagging down passersby. With rocks, limbs and brush, he barricaded the official route of the state's Northville-Placid trail at the base of his hill where it curved away from the river and laid out a spur track that led voyagers on a climb to the top of his "Handsome Hill." The rerouting landed backpackers smack dab in front of his banner and his entrance to the "city."

"Just before we passed into Rondeau's metropolis, a piece of canvas was stretched between a wigwam and a tree, about ten feet off the ground. The banner held a hand-painted message that proclaimed we had reached the 'Gate of the City.'"

"We felt as if we were time travelers as we stepped under the banner—having just passed into another period in history. Ahead of us stood the likes of some ancient little village. A small log cabin close to the earth and half buried had a sign tacked over the door designating it as the "Town Hall." Another log, board, and batten building was labeled the "Hall of Records." Both rustic buildings were about nine feet long and seven feet wide inside and had about four-foot sidewalls and a six-foot ridge. The crudely constructed buildings were a combination of logs, boards, bits of canvas and tarpaper that were often held down with rocks, reused nails and poles. Both huts were exotically decorated with the chalky shoulder blades of beaver, antlers of bygone bucks and the skulls of bears and other animals that rattled pleasantly in a breeze.

"No one was around. We surmised that the hermit had recently left, because the coals in his outside fire pit were smoking. The coals were warm, and a frying pan with the remains of trout, which we assumed he had eaten for breakfast, was nearby. No one answered when I rapped on the cabin doors."

Did the excited and chattering group think their unannounced visit would be an intrusion? Ditt knew there were rumors. Years earlier, "Noey" had the reputation that he didn't care for trespassers. There were even some reports that he had fired on them. But that was in the past, during his teens and twenties, when he had had the most trouble with the law.

"We couldn't help but peek into his buildings. The bed and stove took up most of the space in the Town Hall. The central point was a box bed made from old boards—probably from the old lumber camps that had once been in the area. The bed was supported on top of four bullet-riddled, galvanized water pails that raised the comfortable-looking affair off the dirt floor. Natural materials comprised the mattress."

Hoping to meet Noah, Ditt and the boys waited for three hours. Those same locals he had spoken to also knew conservation officers who said they didn't care much for Rondeau living back in the woods. They held that he hunted and fished illegally. Rondeau held an equal amount of bad blood for the game protectors, especially Earl Vosburgh and Ray Burmaster. He claimed they had a vendetta against him. Over the years his trap line shelters were burned, and he was arrested three times: twice for hunting and trapping violations and once for the attempted murder of Protector Vosburgh.

Noah was found innocent each time. Having served thirty days behind bars while waiting for bail to be raised, and following his exoneration by a grand jury that found no basis for the second-degree assault charge, Noah, who was sick of "authority,"—his way of saying law enforcement—publicly announced he would execute the next game protector that messed with him. That statement prompted the Conservation Commission to deny him a guide license for the rest of his life.

"Reluctantly I made the decision to finally break from camp. We had miles of rough trail to cover before reaching the lean-to and our canoes that evening. But, as I turned from the silence of the clearing, I vowed I would return come fall and once again knock on the hermit's door."

There is no question the 1930s were difficult times. By September 1938, the year Ditt returned to Cold River and seven years since the stock market had hit bottom at 40.22 in 1931, the grip those terrible years had had on America was finally beginning to loosen. Rondeau, a heroic character?

Never, Ditt reasoned in his daydreams as he tramped along. Life could be cold and unfair; there is loss and loneliness; but he did not feel sorrow because of the man's plight. Rather, the future dentist kept his ideas grounded, knowing that like-minded people found security in nature. Living in it taught real and valuable lessons of life, with survival of utmost importance.

By an unlikely but timesaving coincidence, Noah had just entered camp, having toted a load of "civilized food" left for him when Dr. Latimer's fishing party departed the woods. He brought back butter, eggs, dry milk, and sugar from "Dr. Latimer's garbage can" and the cold spring kettle he had buried in a shaded deep pool near High Banks. Noah was more fortunate than some during the Depression's reign. He had among his patrons a few loyal sportsmen with enough wealth to go into the bush regardless of the economic conditions.

Ditt explained, "In the fall of '38 I returned to Big Dam after my tenure at the boys' camp closed. That first visit with the hermit led to many others. Rondeau became a good friend; he was the most unforgettable character

Mary Dittmar and Noah fishing Boiling Pond (aka Seward Pond) on the hermit's homemade raft. *Courtesy of Dr. Adolph G. Dittmar, Jr.*

Grace Hudowalski tries on the hermit's muskrat hat as Noah explains the fine art of sewing fur mittens. *Courtesy of Grace Hudowalski*

THE HERMIT AND US

I ever met. My files are packed with his letters, news clippings about him and notes and photos taken on the spot during my visits to Cold River 'City.'"

Ditt can still hear the voice in his head. The subject of legends crosses the dirt clearing and thrusts his arm into the air. 'How da do?" he warmly greets him.

It was Noah who told Ditt about Grace and Ed Hudowalski and about the 46-ers of Troy. [Grace was the first woman to climb all forty-six major Adirondack High Peaks.] Noah sparked Ditt's interest in mountain climbing and taught him the ways of the woods and other valuable woodcraft skills.

The Hudowalskis became lifelong friends of Adolph Dittmar. In 1939, she wrote, in *High Spots*, the Adirondack Mountain Club's Yearbook, an article straightforwardly titled "The Hermit of Cold River." I believe she summarized, in three succinct sentences, the image remembered by all who ever visited Noah:

> *"The costume and the surrounding scarcely account for the kindly face that greets one. Piercing, brown eyes sparkle from a long pointed face, and almost hidden lips twitch with a humorist's smile. He is kindly of heart, gracious of manner, merry of disposition."*

Ditt's own description, which appeared in his "Hermit of Cold River" article in the Adirondack Forty-sixers book, *The Adirondack High Peaks*, confirms Noah's unique look.

> *"He is a small man, barely five feet tall, and almost everyone has to 'talk down' to him. We usually found him clothed in a felt hat, waterproofed stiff with several coats of green paint, a deerskin leather vest, wide baggy suspender-supported trousers and, of all things, [L.L.]Bean boots. When relaxing, he sits smoking a large-bowled, curved-stem pipe. He has a tremendous beard and mustache which rival even Santa Claus at his best. His forehead is wrinkled and his skin is tanned by wood smoke, but behind it all is a man. While he claims he dislikes people and civilization, he is actually eager to have us visit him and his face always registers*

delight when the visitor arrives. When you decide it is time for you to leave, it is next to impossible to get away."

Ditt, like the majority who came in contact with Noah, was taken with the hermit. Noah was lean and fit, hardened by the demands of surviving in the wilds. He was a wry, often humorous man, slightly haggard in appearance, and with coltish tendencies among friends. He looked like a canny grandpa from pioneer times—beady piercing eyes, a dowdy-looking worn felt hat with a rounded crown, patched shirt and pants—*and when he tells a joke, he seems to swallow it, like a shot of whiskey, and feel it go down and simmer nicely.*

I had an interest in what Ditt's slant was on everything Noah did. Did he see a line of demarcation between the hermit's work and spare time? Ditt didn't make his observations from the initial September '38 daylight visit following Noah's gesture of friendship that welcomed him to step into the tobacco-whiffing Town Hall cabin. Indeed, that first meeting was a special moment in his personal history, but Ditt learned a great deal about the Cold River hermit and his part of the Adirondacks from repeated visits over more than twenty years. What he saw and what he learned was that Noah had many redeeming features: sincerity, congeniality, and honesty. The man of mystery became a friend.

Ditt was clear on Noah's dislikes. "He has no time for kings, queens, presidents, game protectors, Englishmen and Americans. He does like to read." His favorite subjects were history, biology, astronomy and evolution.

Ditt, known over the years as "the mountain-climbing dentist" to his many friends, was a fortunate man. To be sure, he began to admire Rondeau the first day he set foot in the hermitage. And yet he frankly admits there is more to the story of Rondeau than his physical survival in the woods through the long Adirondack winters.

He had an "extraordinarily complex personality." He lived the life of hunter, guide (using his camp as the jumping-off point to the surrounding

Lt. to Rt. Madeline Dodge, Noah, Mary Dittmar. 1948.

Rondeau's Beauty Parlor wigwam. "At times, Noah was a jokester. His woodsy beauty salon was an example of his kind of humor. He kept a large can of rendered bear fat and the mashed leaves of wintergreen on a shelf inside the wigwam. It was his formula for blisters and bruises. When Mary, Bertha and I arrived, we all took our turns sitting on a stump stool in front of the Beauty Parlor wigwam as Noah fussed comically to freshen our faces after the long hike in. A can was nailed on one of the log entrances. It was labeled 'Eyebrow Pencils.' The pencils were long sticks burned until charcoaled. Another can contained face conditioner. The 'beauty cream' was made of charcoal and bear's oil. A soap dish made from the skull of a bear set above the 'wet sink,' which was nothing more but an old hollow log he kept combs, brushes and whatnots in. He had them all labeled for fun." —Madeline Dodge

Following the summer trip to The Hill, Noah wrote Mary and "Ditt." A portion of the letter further illustrates his sense of funny. "By the way I think you have a nice sweet young wife, especially since she got her Eye Brows lifted at the Beauty Parlor in Cold River City. Now I don't mean that Mary was not good looking before that. But every little bit helps and I tell you it pays to employ an Artist who has the equipment..."

Courtesy of Dr. Adolph G. Dittmar, Jr.

summits,) gardener, astronomer, journalist, violinist, sage, and poet—as well as beautician.

On January 12, 1939, four months after Ditt's visit with the hermit, a snappy-sounding letter mailed from the Corey's post office arrived during a swirling North Country snowstorm.

The message included an invitation for him to return as soon as he could make a break from his new dentistry practice. There would be "something special" for supper, and a "big bed of hay" would be waiting for him in the guest wigwam.

Four years later "His Honor the Mayor" began using "Dear Old People" when he addressed the young Dittmar couple following their arrival at Cold River Hill to spend a portion of their honeymoon with the hermit.

Unique to a tee, Noah and his world had no equals. There was the man himself, a character of matchless wit and kindness. And then, there was the country: the quiet pools where trout lay in spring holes, where one can sniff a breath of truly refreshing air; forested mountains with peek holes and rocky tops to climb to in a roadless land. Adolph G. Dittmar had absorbed it all and considered the compliment of Noah's invitation one he could never refuse.

Noah's Secret Code.

$+\odot \rho_| \dashv \uparrow\uparrow^\backprime \,\, \rho^\uparrow \times \uparrow\uparrow\times \,\, \uparrow_| \,\, \rho+\theta \,\, +\theta^\prime \mathrm{o}\theta_| \,\, \rho+_|+_| \times \uparrow_\mathrm{o}-|_+|_+\square$

"It's good to look on the heavens this morning." —NJR's response after having gazed skyward through a new telescope Ditt presented to the hermit. Noah declared it as being "twice as good as Galileo's."

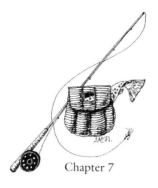

Chapter 7

Billy Burger's
Winter Trek with Rondeau

William H. "Billy" Burger of Westport, New York, was associate editor of North Country Life. *He authored "The Adirondacker" column for* The Adirondack Record-Elizabethtown Post *newspaper throughout World War II. Burger counted Noah John Rondeau among his closest life-long friends.*

Billy was familiar with the Cold River basin. He had studied the topographic map out of interest and to gain knowledge rather than with any thought of traveling extensively through the vast territory.

His first entrance into what was known then as a "trapper's paradise" was a trout-fishing trip. Crack woodsman Noah, a family friend, was his guide. Their destination was the abandoned lumber camp and dam several miles downriver from Camp One. The route followed the suggestion of the old Cold River tote road generally westward beyond Mountain Pond. The route had really been the river drivers' road. The trail was like a line drawn line though the wilderness, with no obvious need to use a compass.

Since then, Jean and Billy Burger had made numerous backpack trips to the dam and camp. The couple had slept wrapped in wool blankets, had enjoyed trout with sourdough pancakes with brown sugar topping and coffee for breakfast, and had sat atop the dam where the water flowed over the sluiceway several feet above.

Billy had heard Noah mention his snowshoe trail and trapping foxes and marten. He'd imagined the hard rigors of traveling through deep snow in the old cut-over country after freeze-up. He had gazed with curiosity and wonder at lofty peaks and crags and had an intense longing to some-day visit the land during winter in the company of his woodsman friend. The Adirondacks had a good many rugged individualists, but if an indi-viduality contest were held, he felt the hands-down winner would be Noah John Rondeau.

To answer the call of the winter trail, to see the frozen dawn, to experience the mountains in a blanket of deep snow, to observe the runs of various fur animals, to pursue the haunts of the wild during mid-winter snow was a wish he harbored. And so, on a typical February day in 1941, Billy finally took the opportunity to follow his desire. With a friend he only identifies as Bob the men met Noah, who was vacationing with Roy and Joan Hathaway at the Bartlett Carry Club. "Back With Rondeau" is Burger's report of that adventure. It appeared in "The Adirondacker" column of the August 7, 1941 issue of The Adirondack Record-Elizabethtown Post.

Noah John Rondeau, Mayor of Cold River City, was returning to his "City Hall" and "Hall of Records" to resume his winter hibernation, and we were going with him. We didn't need any alarm clock to get us up before dawn. The prospect of a thrilling trip and the smell of Mrs. Hathaway's coffee and bacon got us going in a hurry.

It had moderated to 8 below and was brilliantly clear. Roy Hathaway drove us beyond Coreys post office and about halfway from there to the bridge over Stony Creek. It was as far as the snowplow had gone. We helped Roy turn around. Noah put on his snowshoes, Bob and I our skis and we were off at 8:15 on about 18 inches of snow. We followed the snowshoe tracks of a Mr. Dreen, who was spending the winter with George Morgan at Raquette Falls. Before we reached the bridge they turned off to the right to cross the Stony Brook "delta" and from there on the road was track-less except for innumerable and often fresh tracks of deer, fox and snowshoe rabbits. The deer tracks were particularly frequent. There were few stretches of more than 100 yards in the whole 18 miles without a deer track crossing or following the road.

The sky was cloudless and the sunshine brilliant. Traveling was easy most of the way. There were from three to six inches of "powder" on fairly substantial crust. The going was distinctly better where the sun had had a chance at the snow. The only difficult place was in the green and first-growth timber on both sides of Ward's Brook lean-to. There it was pretty tough. I know, for I was breaking trail from the lean-to to Number 4.

We passed the public trail to Cold River at 10:15. This is four miles in, so we were making about two miles an hour. The lower and upper gates were soon reached, and the five-mile march beyond. The snow was deepening as we went on.

Rondeau suggested lunch of bread, butter, canned corn and cold coffee at 11:20 right in the trail. The canned corn and the cold coffee in whiskey flasks were Rondeau's ideas. Both were exceedingly good.

Lt. to Rt. Top Row: George Sausville, unidentified, Noah, Billy Burger, Katherine Kuhfahl. Bottom Row: Lt. to Rt. Hazel Gibson, Lillian Burger, unidentified. Noah at a 1930s gathering at the Burgers' Pipemakers, the name Billy Burger gave the home he built south of Westport on Lake Champlain, on the site where a man named Smith actually made clay pipes in the nineteenth century. Information about this local home industry can be found in a history of the area called "Bessboro."
Photograph by Frank Gibson. Courtesy of Jean Burger Cushman

Twenty minutes for stand-up lunch were followed by more beautiful gliding through the park. Presently we emerged in a cabin clearing, from which we got a gorgeous view of snow-capped Ampersand to the north. The telephone line branched to the left, on the road to Ampersand Pond, while we slid along the flats and up through some balsam to another gate. Then to an arched portal, where Bob and I paused for a couple of pictures.

The public trail entered on the right. While Bob pushed ahead, I hung back with Noah to locate the exact point where he usually turns off to climb the notch between Seward and Seymour, and so down to Cold River Dam.

While Bob and Noah stopped at Ward's Brook Lean-to, I started to break trail past the 10-mile point to Number 4, which is the site of an old lumber camp. As I shoved ahead, I wished I'd let the younger and faster-moving Bob do it, for the skis just about sank out of sight. However, it didn't last long, and as I got out of big timber traveling improved greatly.

Bob caught up at Number 4 and went on up the long climb over the ridge and down to the little marsh, which Rondeau says feeds into Mountain Pond. Bob waited for me in the sunshine in the marsh and we had another bite to eat. I put on my parka, which I had taken off in the early afternoon, and turned down the ear flaps. It had seemed warm during the windless, cloudless and 100 per cent sunshine of mid-day.

Abandoned lumber camp near Mountain Pond. Bette and Jay picked through several remains of Santa Clara Lumber Company's camps still visible today.
Photograph by Richard Woods. Courtesy of Inez Wood Buis

THE HERMIT AND US

We waited for Rondeau to catch up. When he didn't after 10 minutes, we pushed on slowly over the next little ridge. At the top we stopped again and Bob went back while I slid down the sharp slopes to the "corner." This was the best gliding of the day. I had been there about two minutes when I heard Bob call, "He's coming," as he shuffled into sight around a bend. We had made about 12 miles in eight hours and had 4 more to go.

A brief pause for a little food for Rondeau and we were off down the trail. He suggested we cut down to Mountain Pond to avoid a big hill to the left. We followed him and from there to Number 1, the old lumber camp on the trail.

We now kept close together, Bob breaking with skis, Rondeau following with snowshoes and I right after him on skis, although not too close to slide every chance I got! If we could have gone on that way to the dam, it would have been glorious, for me at least! For all I had to do was glide and look at the scenery. The sun was setting as we followed it west. It was one of those long sunsets you sometimes see in the mountains. From the time it dropped below the horizon somewhere near the Corner about 4:00, until it made its final disappearance nearly an hour later, I must have seen it at least a dozen times. The sunshine on the hills around Mountain Pond, the lighting up of Panther Peak in the Santanoni Range until it was all aglow with that crimson—rose —gold mass of color I defy any artist to reproduce in pigment, and the all-pervasive and very gradually fading afterglow, made the blood sing in my veins. It made me acutely sensitive to sounds that I had never been aware of before, such as the "zing" of skis on cold dry snow when gliding and leathery "creaks" of the rings of the poles as they push into the zero snow. It was one of those experiences one never forgets and is probably a foretaste of heaven!

But we were faced by the prospect of getting to camp after dark, with cabins which had been closed for five weeks of bitter cold and over a trail shrouded in complete darkness. Rondeau suggested we turn toward the Flow near its head and proceed from there to the dam in the open. He also said it would save us a half mile.

So just about dusk we followed him to the left, down through brush and trees. While he had been trailing on snowshoes all day, he was now way out in front. Bob and I had our own troubles going through that mess. We both fell three times. Twice I fell because saplings which I grabbed to break my speed came right along with me. Once it took me about five minutes to get on my feet. It wouldn't have taken much urging to have stayed right there! But after about a half hour of it we came on the frozen surface of the Flow at 6:00. I could just see the hands of the watch.

Now the last long hour, and mile, for that is what Rondeau called it, began. We cut over a couple of points, to save distance. Rondeau led, we right behind in his tracks, going very slowly. Not really fast enough to keep warm. After sundown it had got nippy again and must have been zero or below.

But what a night. The sky was perfect. Ahead and beckoning us on was that line of great planets mounting the southwestern sky—Venus, Jupiter, Saturn and Mars. Venus was so bright I thought I could see her shadow on the snow and even tried to tease her with my pole, but if it was there, it was too dim for my poor old eyes to see. To the south Sirius rode the Santanoni Range, and high above was Orion with the bright points of Betelguese and Rigel, and out in front Aldebaran. Higher up Castor and Pollux and farther north Capella, while Sirius' companion, Procyon, lingered off to the northeast. Another night I'll never forget.

But all of this didn't wholly distract attention from tired muscles, so it was welcome news when Rondeau told us the narrow hole ahead with the dim rise to the right was the dam. He suggested we take our skis off, as he was removing his snowshoes to slough through the snow to the top of the knoll. But we were tired enough to be stubborn and so fought our way to the top on skis. We were surprised when we made it and more surprised the next day when we looked at our tracks.

The doors of the two cabins were quickly opened. Snow was up to their eaves, about three feet from ground. Then fires, some talk while we rested and a supper of fried canned corn beef, bread and butter and coffee. Gosh but those sandwiches were good!

I checked the time when the fire was started. It was 7:10 p. m. We had put on skis and shoes at 8:15. I had not been off my skis for nearly eleven hours.

Presently Noah went out to one of his wigwams and brought in a "ham" from a frozen deer, which we were informed had been legally

X-C Skier near the head of Cold River Flow. *Photograph by Richard Woods.*
Courtesy of Inez Wood Buis

killed. It certainly was a buck, for the head was still on it. It was to thaw out during night. Then after a round of good hot "slings" we blew out the candles and called it a day.

Next morning it was snowing lightly and softly, in complete calm. None of us were very ambitious but we did manage to make a breakfast of cutlets from the "ham" with pancakes and coffee.

Right after breakfast, Rondeau started to prepare the big meal of the day which he calls "Slam Bang Gullion" and which he says originated in Lewis, N. Y., and which he dedicated to the Conservation Commission. This last I couldn't quite understand, or could I?

The ingredients of this potent and possibly sometimes illegal dish may interest the gourmets. The "base" was the rest of the venison from the ham, and that was a lot. To this, during the day, were added rice, potatoes (which Rondeau had raised from the river where he had them in a can to keep from freezing), tomato sauce, red pepper, salt, Crisco, butter and finally, about a half hour before serving, dumplings made with pancake flour. A huge pot of this was available with coffee at 5:00 p.m. I ate two large bowls of it a little too fast for comfort and we had more before we went to bed. Another pot was presently put on with beans and more meat. This was served for breakfast the next day with left-overs from the night before. I thought there would be a lot left for Rondeau but when we pulled out, the bottom of one pot was clearly in sight.

While we laid around most of the day, I pulled a stunt in the afternoon which should shame me to my dying day. Feeling the need of a little exercise, I skied out to a wigwam on the back trail. Then I planned to ski down as far as the bridge over Seward Brook.

I readily picked up the lower wigwam on the trail, but couldn't find the markers to show the trail from there on. I was puzzled, for I've been over it several times in summer. Peering through the trees to the left, I sighted a valley and a body of water, which I thought might be Seward Brook, although it looked larger than it should, and sure enough there seemed to

"Snow depths were often four to six deep on the level." —Noah J. Rondeau.
Courtesy of Earle Russell

be a trail heading that way, so I went down to investigate. When I got most to what looked like a dam, I thought I must be wrong, so I back-tracked to the wigwam to pick up markers. Had no better luck this time, so back I went and through this time to what looked like a dam. There were tracks, first right close by and going down to the water and then other tracks leading in a straight line right down what I thought was Cold River. I thought that was odd, while tracks close by might be Rondeau's, those others down river couldn't be.

So back to the wigwam and the final location of trail down river. A few strokes along this and it was time for supper. So back I went to report my discovery of strange tracks and other happenings.

Rondeau was baffled for a moment and then the explanation broke, to my complete chagrin. I had made an almost complete circuit of the base of the knoll on which the cabins and wigwam are pitched and what I thought was another dam, was THE dam and I thought I was looking down. Seward Brook is quite a ways down the trail, as I should have remembered. My humiliation was deepened when Bob, who I suspect wasn't sorry to get something on me, went down and found my ski tracks within five feet of the ones we had made the night before, and told me if I had only looked up to the left I'd have seen the main wigwams within stone-throwing distance.

Woe is me! I should have known better. For I should never get 100 yards off a known trail and must always carry a compass.

Stimulated by the second round of Slam-Bang Gullion the second night in camp, Noah, Bob and I launched into a profound discussion of such abstruse subjects as the probable origin of oil deposits, the size, heat and durability of the sun and the nature of energy and matter—and the relations of these phenomena, if any, to Rondeau's three big peeves: Big Business, Americanism and the Conservation Commission. It was long past Cold River bedtime when we blew out the last guttering candle. I had been looking up the river when it died.

The rest is quickly told. It was snowing lightly and was warmer the day of the trip out. I left at 8:15 to break trail, for we didn't want to battle our way up from the Flow.

It was hard going at first, over three feet of light snow. But I got to the junction with tracks to the Flow sooner than I expected and quite convinced that Rondeau was wrong in saying we had saved a half mile by taking the Flow, although it was good judgment to do this in the dark.

Bob caught up with me just beyond the Corner, although he had left an hour later. We had fine sliding down the run to Number 4 and arrived at the lean-to at 11:50 a.m. We took off our skis and had a bite to eat.

The weather was again beautifully clear and a little fresh snow on the trail made it easy running. I caught another lovely view of the peak of Ampersand at a clearing near Ampersand Pond. I found Bob waiting for me at Upper Gate. I paused for a second lunch and finished the second whiskey flask of iced coffee; I wondered what to do with the empty flask and finally slipped it down in the snow in front of the gate post, where the caretaker could not miss retrieving it in spring for deposit with other bottles in the place they belong.

Upon arrival at the bridge, I saw the plow had got that far, so I took off my skis and walked the rest of the way to Coreys post office. Saw Bob's ski tracks on the open road and found he was only about five minutes ahead, which was a reassuring discovery with which to end a memorable trip. Three cheers for Noah John Rondeau—the Hathaways and Cold River!

Noah's Secret Code.

Q?₁ᵥ|ₚ´₊| ⁄×₊×\θ₀₋| ´₀–θ →??` †?×⁄×|☺ ×?|ₚ×†□

"Mountain climbers are good folks, mostly." —*NJR in a conversation with Mary Creighton, a Christian writer who worked at Guideposts magazine. Creighton replied to Noah, "With few exceptions, they are also spiritual folk. It seems as though in the mountains one feels closer to God."*

Chapter 8

Mountain Gals of Boone's Breed: Helen Colyer Menz and Mary Colyer Dittmar

Anglers and hunters had sought Noah's outdoor advice since the 1920s, but the ever-increasing number of mountain climbers and hikers who beat a path to his door in the 1930s were a different breed. They not only showed an interest in how Noah survived in the back woods, but also in who the famous hermit really was. Understandably, this took the edge off his cynical attitude toward civilization.

Noah phrased it well when he spoke to Enoch Squires: "Well, they came along as mountain climbers and hikers and so forth, ...the people in the neck of the woods sometimes come in and steal my gun too, they've done that; but the mountain climbers, they'd buy a good pack, and they had a job somewhere and they were refined and they had education and they were interested in the mountains."

A Cold River hermit's life must have looked pretty good to the sports-people who came into the hermitage. The mountain climbers even made Noah an honorary member of both the Adirondack Mountain Club and the 46ers of Troy. He had everyone's attention, apparently for keeps, and they knew his knowledge of the animals, the plant life, and the surrounding terrain was solid.

Living back in the mountains also required a certain inclination toward quiet and stillness, a lifestyle many supporters believed Noah built from grit and determination to outwit a seemingly uninhabitable terrain.

Among Noah's most recurrent visitors were Doctor Latimer, Oscar Burguiere, Attorney Jay L. Gregory and his son Dr. William Gregory, E. R. Harmes and his son "Jack," Adolph and Mary Colyer Dittmar, Helen Colyer Menz and her husband Bill, Mary and Helen's friend Madeline Dodge of Wilmington, Peggy and Wayne Byrne, Grace and Edward Hudowalski, and of course Richard Smith of Lake Placid—but the list could go on with many other people who were a part of the hermit's life.

Listen to the words of Helen Menz at 93. She recounts her trips to the hermitage and speaks volumes without artifice and with no sensationalism about her active outdoor days.

> *I've been to Cold River four times. I never realized until I talked with you how lucky I was!*
>
> *I am not sure how much I noticed of the botany on my first trip. That was the one that Ruthie [Prince], Mary and I made in 1942. I was impressed by the hermit's neat gardens. He had two sections. One had potatoes. I wondered whether deer 'knew' that the tops were poison and so didn't eat them.*

Rt. To Lt. 1930. Helen and Mary at Camp Smokehouse, their father's hunting and fishing getaway along the Raquette River. *Courtesy Helen C. Menz*

THE HERMIT AND US

I can't remember as I write what else that he grew in the vegetable line. It seems like carrots, but deer would eat them. He did have foxgloves (digitalis), perennial sweet peas and other flowers that I don't remember.

On another trip we hiked in with 'Ditt,' Bill, and the kids. Most of them went up Couchsachraga. Bill explored to see what Noah had at camp. I had had a sore knee and stayed at a nearby lean-to. Bill said the garden plot was becoming overgrown.

In 1967, years after Noah had pulled up stakes, we returned. We bushwhacked down from Emmons after sleeping on Mount Donaldson.

On our family's Northville-Lake Placid trip in the late 1980s, we stopped at the old camp site. It was sort of sad. The one cabin still standing tilted badly and had only half a roof. The base log of the great dam was gone. There was no pond, just alder thickets. The first time that we were there, Noah rowed us across the pond that formed behind the dam in order to start up Couchy. He ended up climbing with us so the 'girls wouldn't get lost.' His garden site was still open at that time.

The ferns were thick in the garden areas. Some ferns are like black walnut trees and put compounds in the soil which inhibit growth of other plants. I saw two surviving foxglove plants and a sweet pea vine.

One time when we visited the abandoned hermitage clearing, we met a ranger who was on a 'business holiday,' as he called it. He was going to try to get the State of New York to designate the location as a special place of historic interest. I'm sure that no one would listen to him.

Noah's camp site must be entirely overgrown by now. Sure has been a long time since my first trip in.

Ruthie died a few years ago. Mary was in the nursing home fed by a tube until her death last year. Ditt would get panic spells when he couldn't breathe too well. He would have oxygen at night and a tank to use in the daytime if he felt that he needed *it. But he's gone now too. It's scary to be the only one to have survived and to still remember things. I wish that I had better penmanship and more time to write. I certainly had some great backpacks in the mountains."*

On a May morning in 1942, Helen and Mary Colyer and a friend were hiking the Northville-Lake Placid trail when they walked into the hermit's "city," located on a high bank above decaying Big Dam. The young women had been curious about Noah and the long life he had lived in the deep and silent forest. Perhaps what they found most astonishing was that anyone could be so comfortable about such a life. The friendship that resulted from this meeting endured a lifetime.

Rondeau's diary notes the arrival of the trio of women when they backpacked to Cold River.

Fri. May 29, 1942
Nice day.
Town Hall.
Bickford, Vincent (Lake Placid) come, go.
Ruth Prince, Mary Colyer, Helen Menz came.
333 years a go to day: Samuel Dee Champlain (Murderer) Killed two Indian Chiefs.

Sat. May 30
Rain and Thunder last night, cloudy today.
Mrs. Rondeau's Kitchenette.
I climb Couchsachraga with Ruth Prince, Mary Colyer, Helen Menz.
1st Kinnickinnick blossom.
6 fish for Doctors.

This is Helen's story:

Dad hunted with a pharmacist from Plattsburgh and a dentist from Saranac Lake. They hunted mostly in the Coreys-Axton area.

THE HERMIT AND US

People of all ages and backgrounds sought out Noah's digs.
Photo by Arthur Bankey. Courtesy of Bette O'Hern

That was where Dad and his partners met Noah John Rondeau. Noah John offered to do a drive for them. Years later, when Mary and I met Noah John, he immediately recalled our last name.

"He was a friend, a complex man." That is how Helen describes her association with Noah. "He did what many old-time Adirondackers would have liked to do when new regulations and laws were made in relation to hunting, camping and so forth. The old timers felt that they had lost the freedom of THEIR woods."
Her remarks about the times she spent back at the hermit's tell me Noah was not only a friend but a personal hero to her.

To paraphrase Helen: *"I've learned three things last until our end. One is our memories. The second is our family, and the third is our friends."*

Open shelters (lean-tos) were often used by Helen and Mary. *Courtesy of Helen C. Menz*

Chapter 9

Helen's First Trek to Cold River Hill

Several of Helen's letters recall the unlikely first meeting between the Colyer girls, their hiking companion and friend Ruth Prince, and Rondeau. It all began on a backpacking trip in the Adirondacks. Mary, "Ruthie" Prince, Bess Little, and Helen had climbed Seymour, Seward, Donaldson, and Emmons, the four high peaks in the Seward Mountain Range in May 1942. The cast of characters assembled at the hermitage on June 20th for an earnest assault on Couchsachraga Peak. The mustering was a mind-tingling, never-to-be-forgotten event for the women, one they often talked about through the years that followed.

I'll let Helen tell their story.

> *My first trip into Noah John's hermitage came following our successful assault of the four summits in the Seward Range. Bess hurt her ankle bushwhacking down the steep, often rocky descent off Seward Peak. She never uttered a word of pain nor mentioned the injury until we arrived back at Ward Brook lean-to, site of our temporary encampment.*
>
> *We had planned to go to Noah John's the next day. Bess persuaded us to leave her alone at the open camp. She was disappointed she had lost her footing and had injured her ankle. The swelling was pronounced. She was realistic. Rest was needed. She wouldn't be able to hike out to the trailhead in her condition, so her persuasiveness for us to continue with our plan made sense. In fact, Bess insisted*

we carry on with the original plan of climbing Couchsachraga. She had a Readers Digest to idle the hours away. Now that I think of it, we should have stayed with her. The hermitage was a good eight miles away. We shouldn't have left her alone in the woods, but we were young and didn't give any thought to any possible danger. We were comfortable in the woods.

I have no idea the exact time of day we arrived at the hermitage. Noah acted tickled pink at hearing the name Colyer. He told us he once helped our father with a deer near Calkins Brook many years earlier. [The hermit] gave us the 'grand tour' of his so-called 'city.' He showed us his wigwams, and the gardens where he grew potatoes, carrots, sweet peas, pansies and foxgloves. The 'Beauty Parlor' stood ready for customers. The 'Town Hall' cabin in which Noah lived was small. His bed was on one side. There was a bookshelf over the bed. It held Pilgrim's Progress, the Bible, a book on astronomy and another book. He had no table or chair. He told us that in winter he sat on the bed to cook. He ate from the stove so that he'd have hot food. All of his wood was pre-notched and piled teepee style so that he could get it when the snow was deep.

The teepee-type buildings, or 'wigwams' as he also called the hollow interior cone-shaped stacks of poles he prepared for future firewood, had names. The number of them varied from three to five. There were so many poles leaning together they were almost rainproof. The Trap Wigwam housed, as you might have guessed, steel traps. They hung from rings that were held by nails. He said it was used for sleeping quarters when he had an overflow crowd of guests. Mrs. Rondeau's Kitchenette was another wigwam. It had a fire pit inside. The inside back of the wigwam was piled with stones and a stone-lined hearth. He cooked in there when it rained or whenever the weather was too cold to be out of doors. His kettles were suspended over the pit by chains that were attached far above where the poles interlocked. There were buckets, empty Beechnut coffee cans, a big pan for dishwashing, a small table, and other things inside.

Foreground: Helen Colyer; Lt. to Rt.; Mary Colyer, "Ruthie" Prince and Noah. Couchsachraga Peak, 1942. Noah wrote in a letter to Mary dated April 8, 1943: "...the four in the picture are not escaped Russian Refugees as You suppose... I'll let you in on it a bit, the way they got to the Mountain Top was eating bread and Candy and drinking Lemonade..." [protected from insects with a] "diffused odor of Happy-Medium-Blend-of Kerosene, Citronella and Pine-Tar. It was captivating beyond all powers of resistance." *Courtesy Helen C. Menz*

There were two doctors in camp. They said they had been coming every year for over two decades to fish the river in June. They told us they lived in Binghamton. Their names were Dr. Gilmore Fellows and Dr. Charles Leonard Christiernin. The men were prepared to do some serious fishing and living in the backcountry during the worst of the fly season. The black flies were thick, but the veterans of the field knew how to cope during the time trout were hungriest.

The doctors were sewed into their clothing. They had sewed the slits in their shirt cuffs, the front of their shirts and socks to the pants and any other place where black flies could crawl in. The stitches were not delicate, so one could see them easily.

We had our own food. I do not remember that we ate any fish, but I would imagine that they would have offered to share their fried trout with us. That's the way of old woodsmen's etiquette. However I clearly recollect what we drank. The doctors had brought in lemon crystals for drinks. Noah John, Mary, and I were all impressed. We had never seen them before.

Noah's bailwick of wigwams was a refuge for Helen, Mary and Ruthie.
Courtesy of Edward J. Fox

"The cooking was done in an iron fry pan and an iron kettle. Both hung over the pit fireplace. The coffee pot stayed hot all day, as did the dishwater. Noah John said he continued to add more coffee grounds into the bottom half of the pot every day. When no more water would fit, the whole mess was dumped and a new pot was started. He would joke that when the dishwater got thick enough, he would make a good soup out of it. Noah John was interesting to talk with. He even got his fiddle out to give us a concert."

The girls laid aside their packs and settled themselves on a bench at Noah's plank table, set close to the open pit fire. There they ate and chatted with Noah and his fishing party guests. "Our conversation was about the woods, about climbing Couchy [Couchsachraga Peak], the hermit's stone-bordered vegetable and flower gardens, and other hikers who had come by. We were tired, so we were glad to sit and listen." All who gathered around the supper table had something in common. None were new to the woods.

Before darkness began to settle down over the forest and the birds ceased their evening songs, the women asked where they might set up their "Pioneer Featherweight" tent. It provided tight ground space for three people. "The doctors slept in the Hall of Records," one of the hermit's tiny cabins. "It was not very airy." Noah John lived in the second cabin, dubbed the Town Hall. Noah studied the girls' equipment, telling them he held they were well equipped, joking that their tent could easily fit into his pocket.

"The hermit would have nothing to do with our setting up our tent camp. He offered us the use of his yellow canvas wall tent. It was about 8 by 10 feet in size. He had it up for come-on-by hiker friends and fishermen. It was a no-frills tent—perhaps it was even a castoff from the temporary CCC tent encampment that had been located between Mountain Pond and Duck Hole, about five miles by trail upriver. The timeworn tent stood near the "stairs the former logging company had built into the bank that led down to the river." The group chatted for several hours or so and then all fell silent. It seemed a natural thing to do in the forest after a busy day's activities were done.

"We didn't worry a bit about going to Noah John's. He was like a southern gentleman when greeting us. We felt very much at ease. He smoked his pipe and visited."

The doctors were whittling on a soft pine limb with their pocket knives when from off in the distance there came a squalling bark. Noah identified it as a red fox.

Inside the tent, the air was filled with the spicy odor of freshly cut balsam boughs, and occasionally a whiff of wood smoke drifted through the open tent flaps. Outside in the dim shadows, the night noises continued, but Helen, Mary, and Ruth hardly heard them.

"As we were going to sleep, Noah John dumped two bear rugs in the tent. He thought we might be cold. I can tell you that we were not, with the bear rugs."

"In the morning we made our own breakfast. After that we were initiated in the 'Beauty Parlor' wigwam. The hermit did not have a salon back in the woods. The reference was to a pole wigwam. Noah designated the setting with a banner. The hand-painted sign read 'Beauty Parlor.' I suppose to promote good will with trail-smudged females, Noah John offered to freshen the faces of all the lady backpackers who came along. It was all good-humored antics. He had a complete backwoods cosmetic setup. In front of the opening to the Beauty Parlor wigwam was a stool. A bearskin was draped over it for comfort. Beside it hung a tin can filled with various sizes of 'eyebrow' pencils. They were really charcoal-burned sticks. Noah would present them to the user as he handed them a mirror. A washbasin and comb rested on a board-topped triangular stick-built washstand. A washcloth and towel hung from a peg on the side." Helen remembered, "We used the wash basin. It was a long way down to the dam and river just to wash up. Noah John liked being a hermit, but he also liked to have visitors—especially those who brought him reading matter."

Following their makeovers, Noah John told the women he would row them across the 'pond' so they could get started on their hike. "At that time Big Dam was still holding back quite a bit of water. It was several logs high. The 'pond' behind the dam was wide and too deep to make it possible to wade across to the bank on the far side." Not only was there a

"We relaxed with Noah as he instructed us on the best route to follow on our bushwhack to 'Couchie. In the end, he decided to tag along." —Ruth King.

Courtesy of Ruth King

Worthuer E. Colyer at Camp Smokehouse, located about two bends down the Raquette River from Axton. "Noah told Mary and me how he met our father in the 1920s. He spoke about Dad's generosity and of using our tent. *Courtesy of Helen C. Menz*

quantity of impounded water behind the dam, but also a majority of the low 'flow land' east of the dam was filled. The original bed of the river was of course flooded for miles behind the log-and-boulder dam.

"The boat was a flat-bottomed one. Sides were about twelve inches high. I'm not sure where it came from. Noah John might have made it from salvaged lumber, or perhaps it was a relic from the lumber camp that stood where Rondeau made his 'city.' I don't think it came from the former Civilian Conservation Corps camp upriver. It wouldn't have been possible to float it down through the rock-strewn Black Hole section of the river in high water. Noah John said the doctors used the boat to fish upriver."

When they reached the opposite shore, "Noah John thought he would get us started 'on the right track.' He led us to a sort of ancient woods road and pointed out which way to head off. But then, for some reason he changed his mind and decided he would accompany us all the way to Couchy. I clearly recall him puffing and groaning as we moved along. He told us that he was getting old and that we were following along one of his old trap line trails. He took us on detours to hollow trees and stumps to pinpoint jars of sugar, coffee, and tea he had stashed away in case he was forced to sleep outside.

Of course this was long ago when he trapped furbearing animals, but the jars were weather-tight and the contents were still useable. "We had known Noah John went out in winter. He stored his leftover canned goods at a bend in the river where it was deep enough not to freeze. His main problem was that he lost all the can labels to the river by spring. He never knew what food he was opening."

There was a time when Noah would build a fire, make coffee, and curl up to rest and keep warm until morning if he were far enough from Big Dam that he could not get back for the evening. "He told me," Helen recalls, "that he 'was happy if he had a log at his back,' but that now he was' too old to care about trapping' anymore. As I remember, we went most of the way through quite open woods. There were many tall trees. Some were white birch. In places, the old woods road disappeared. Every so often he would halt, remove his green enamel-painted hat and let out a groan as he repeated, 'Hard times. Hard times,' followed by 'Yes, sir, a right slump in the Depression.' Then he would point out something in the vicinity. As we made our way up the mountainside he groaned more."

"Although he complained about becoming old, he still seemed anxious to press forward. We never used a compass, so maybe he felt we should be escorted, watched, or whatever. His green-painted fedora, waterproofed 'rain hat' seemed hot. Regardless, he continued on to the peak of Couchsachraga. He let us know in no uncertain terms how glad he was he finally hit the top of Couchy. The trip didn't seem long or hard to us. He seemed to recover from it when our camera was taken out to record the event. He seemed to like having his picture taken with us."

"When we arrived back at his 'city,' thunder was beginning to roll over the mountains in the distance. A storm was approaching. We felt we had to get back to Bess at the lean-to. One night was more than enough to leave her alone, but Noah John insisted we eat before we left. I'm not sure what all food we ate. I do remember him opening a can of sausage or little hot dogs that someone had left him. We willed any food we had carried in as a token of our gratitude for his hospitality and guiding services. We had plenty more back at the lean-to. The storm had moved closer, and it was on the edge of darkness by the time we left."

"As far as our visits with Noah John when he came to Albany in 1948 and '49, his star had risen by then from poor wilderness hermit to celebrity status." The transformation came following Clayt Seagers' classic article, "The Hermit of Cold River." It appeared in the late 1947 New York State *Conservationist* magazine. Noah was airlifted in a helicopter out of the Cold River Valley to appear at the national Sportsmen's Show in New York City. Maitland DeSormo told in his biography that when he landed, "Stardom there gave Noah about four years of national recognition and numerous other engagements in big cities and small."

Helen said when they talked with him at appearances he made in the Albany shows in '48 and '49 Noah John did not like the fact that a forest ranger accompanied him. He said they 'kept a very close watch' on him. He didn't like supervision at all. He was an original hermit.

"We asked Noah John to come to our house for dinner. Clayton Seagers, who was one of the promoters of the show, made an awful fuss and told Noah he couldn't go. My husband Bill told Clayt that Noah should at least have a dinner hour. Bill promised to have him back on time, so they let him go with us to our house. Dinner conversation revolved around old times back at Cold River. He had many complaints about the close supervision at the show. He enjoyed the home-cooked meal. My husband Bill said the show's managers almost sent an escort to make sure he was returned on time. They kept such strict track of Noah John. They wanted to get their money's worth out of him. He was billed as an attraction, and so should be there to be seen."

"Mary remembers that she and Bill visited Noah John one time when he was out of his camp. He was at his sister's house in Au Sable Forks. He talked of starting a chicken farm. He had even started some building, according to her.

"I recall on our way to visit Mary and Ditt at Silver Lake, many years later, we saw some wood stacked the Noah John way near a cabin on the Wilmington Road. We stopped to see whether it was him. We had heard he had been living out of the woods. He never returned to his city following the

Noah's Town Hall's interior. *Courtesy of Peggy and Wayne Byrne*

On September 1, 1970, Helen and Mary led an expedition of their children back to Cold River Hill. A portion of the Town Hall was still standing. *Courtesy of Helen C. Menz*

Big Blow. As it turned out, it was Noah John's woodpile. He was living in a simple shack he called Singing Pines. He immediately recognized us. As Mary, Ruthie and I were given the grand tour, we could tell he was glad to see us. He told us tales of his youth. How we wished that we had a tape recorder. He told us he was working part time at Santa's Workshop. He played the role of Santa at the North Pole amusement park located along the Whiteface Mountain road. He wasn't employed there longer than one season. Noah John complained the management had 'too many rules.'

"Oh, how he grew upset as he talked about what had recently happened to him. He had owned the same old rifle for what seemed forever. He didn't really do much serious deer hunting any longer, but decided he wanted to buy a new rifle. He had sold his old one. He said he 'had never been without a gun and never wanted to live without one.' So he bought a new one. Well, the new purchase didn't set well with the Essex County welfare department. When the welfare people found out about it they docked his monthly allotment by a certain dollar figure until the cost of the gun was repaid.

Later that summer, "Ditt brought Noah out to camp at Silver Lake. Noah went down on the dock. The sun was warm. All of the kids were playing on the dock and in the water. He seemed to enjoy the activity—even getting splashed. We ate up at the camp Noah John remembered when he happened to come on to my dad in the 1920s. Both he and Dad hunted the same general territory around Axton and Calkins Brook.

"Noah John also told us tales about his boyhood and things that he did when he was growing up near Au Sable and when he lived in a lumber camp (presumably with his father) as a child.

"With all the kids, noise, and passage of years I can only remember one story. At Christmas time his father filled a flatbed sleigh with straw. All of the kids piled in. They were covered with blankets. The whole family went to a neighbor's or relative's home. They all went in to celebrate Christmas Eve. Sometimes they stayed all night. The kids slept crossways in the bed or on the floor. We should have had a tape recorder again. Noah John had a remarkable memory for people's names and factual details.

"We are bushwhacking toward Seward Pond." —Helen Menz. *Courtesy of Helen Menz*

Helen wrote on January 3, 2006, "Good luck on your new book...

> *...I have been to Noah John's hermitage several times since the 'Big Blow' of November 1950. ...when you go into Cold River this fall, look to see if there are any flowers still growing in Noah's garden for me. I will be interested to learn what you find. In 1970 I found foxgloves blooming along the trail near the site of the remaining hut. Sweet peas were climbing over the ferns. I'll bet that the ferns have all taken over by now...*

Seward Pond, September 1, 1970. "The beaver had raised the level of water so it covered what we always called 'Noah's Point,' the location of where his wigwam once stood at the edge of the water." —Helen Menz. *Courtesy of Helen Menz*

Bob Bates and Bette O'Hern standing on the remains of Noah's raft. In 2007 the level of Seward Pond a.k.a. Boiling Pond had dropped to an extremely low level.
Courtesy of William J. O'Hern

...I've found some slides of Noah John's City and his fishing pond. I took them on my 1967 trip, the year Noah died, and during the summer of 1970. The scenes show the cabin's walls were still upright but the roof had fallen in. When we went through on our Northville-Lake Placid trip in 1984, the branch with the lantern that had long hung in a tree since Noah's time (the branch eventually grew around the wire bail handle) had been sawed off. I brought home a Mason jar of Noah's sugar that I retrieved from one of his hiding places. I knew that I removed history but someone would eventually chance on to it and break it sooner or later just for fun.

The site of the Town Hall was a pile of logs and boards. In 1967 the water in Seward Pond was much higher than when Mary and Ditt were there on their honeymoon in 1944. Noah took them fishing as a wedding present. Beaver had built a dam across the outlet. I'm tickled to learn your friend found the rotting remains of Noah's raft last summer. I recall we managed to give it a shove out across the pond but by then it was quite waterlogged and beginning to fall apart...

Have fun. Good luck, Helen

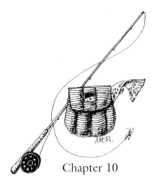

Chapter 10

Madeline Dodge and the Hermit

Madeline Dodge said, "Noah had a humorous way of saying come to his mountains on vacation and avoid the highway carnage."

Noah: "It doesn't take 400 dead people to celebrate a holiday in here."

Madeline Dodge's voice was one of Noah friends I always recalled when used to bathe in the deep pool that made a great swimming hole in the wild river on the downside of the remains of the log dam. When I described the once deep washbowl and how very cold the water felt brought eighty-eight year-old Madeline's wonderful hermit memories to the forefront. She acknowledged that the cold I had felt was cold, but assured me it could not have been as cold as what she had experienced back in the 1940s. Madeline stressed it was *really* COLD!

Madeline Dodge was an early 20th-century mountain climber and member of the Adirondack Mountain Club. Over the years she dropped by to visit with Rondeau at his digs. Many years later, after he left the woods and resettled in Wilmington, New York, Noah made her home a stopover. They both believed in economy. Both reused coffee grounds and tea leaves. When Noah brought a can of tobacco along and pulled his pipe from his pocket, Madeline wasn't opposed to filling her crusty old briar pipe right along with her house guest. With both sitting in rockers by the kitchen range, Noah would lean down to the wood box, open the door, light the end of a splinter of soft wood from the hot coals and turn the burning end to ignite their tobacco. Silently both then drew several deep puffs, savoring

April 10, 1949. Madeline Dodge and Noah outside her Village of Wilmington home.
Courtesy of Madeline Dodge

the aroma of the flavored tobacco. A smoke. A nip. They enjoyed their necessary vices.

In time Madeline talked with me about her friendship with Noah and how he coaxed her into the water the first time she met him.

> *Madeline: He was a gentleman of the first order; he could hold his own with anyone—king, queen or president. The first time I hiked in I hadn't the faintest idea of what to expect but I had made up my mind. After walking fourteen miles I was going to say, "Move over kid, I'm going to stay" if there was any opposition to his having company in camp.*

The fussing wasn't necessary. Mary and "Ditt" Dittmar had assured her often throughout the hike, "Oh, you'll like him." That was the truth.

> *Madeline: We were younger than him but that made no difference. He was wonderful and free at camp and on the trail. He was so intelligent—the type of person who had a reason for everything he did. He would explain everything. He'd pick up a leaf and tell you what kind of tree it came from. He could talk at length about contemporary events, but he was more concerned with other things. He would do anything for you. 'Course he also had no feeling about being polite to people he didn't like. If he didn't care for you, you might as well just be dead because he would just ignore you. Period.*

The Dittmars were always prepared to swim because of one of Noah's favorite sayings whenever they departed camp. It went like this: "Bring your bathing suits the next time. The water's cold but you'll feel like a million dollars after the long, hot hike."

> *Madeline: I remember the first time I arrived in camp with the Dittmar party. Noah greeted us with, "My friends." He then waved toward one of the wigwams and said, "I'll put a sweet grass*

*mat down and throw a blanket over it for you. It'll be restful."
Then he pointed to the river and said, "Now Mary, Ditt, Madeline, I want you to put your bathing suits on and go down and
cool off. Just walk right into the water." I knew the **Cold** River
had to have gotten its name from somewhere. The air temperature
on the long hike had been very hot, but the water was cold, cold,
cold! Well, I'm here to tell you that water was like ice—and I was
only up to my knees! I didn't care much for swimming and
thought even less of being numb. When Noah saw me hesitate he
instructed, "Walk into the water right up to your neck, then turn
around and come right out." The coming "right out" was no problem! I wrapped my shivering body into a towel I wished had been
a large terry cloth robe. Noah remarked, "You don't need to worry
about catching a cold, you'll be perfectly all right."*

**Noah's Singing Pines home in Wilmington, NY. "Noah was my official gardener.
He came to help me tend to my flower beds and vegetable garden. He was a true
friend."** —Madeline Dodge. *Courtesy of William J. O'Hern*

Noah outside Maggie Dodge's Hazelton Road home.
Courtesy of Richard J. Smith from Noah's photo album

Following the introductory dip, which proved to be Madeline's first and last plunge into Cold River, the entire party shared in cooking supper. The food was simple fare but there was plenty to go around. The mountain-climbing trio had brought in fresh baked bread, potatoes and corn on the cob. Noah supplied the fish and greens. In her mind, Madeline questioned the source of the greens, but in the end ate them without inquiry. "I didn't die," she noted.

> *Madeline: Oh my, but did he know his weather. Oh how he did! "Well," he would say, "we're going to have showers but they won't last so long. You can go out in them and you won't even get too wet." It might have been clear and sunny when he predicted an oncoming storm, but sure as anything later in the day it would pour. I always thought he preferred animals to humans. He respected black bears. And, underneath all his guffaw he was a religious person. "No animal would ever hurt you if you didn't bother them," he held, "but people—now that's another story."*

Following Noah's move to Singing Pines in Wilmington, he became a standard fixture in Madeline's kitchen rocker by the large wood-fired cooking range. Her laughter (and the incessant cigarette smoke) still filters through my mind as I think of her delight in telling me stories about the times they shared.

> *Madeline: Noah used to come to my house quite a lot. The bus would let him off in front of the house and then, about 5:30 P.M., the driver would return, toot, and Noah would leave for his Singing Pines home.*

She pointed to the rocker.

> *Madeline: That was his chair. Sometimes he'd come to go walking. We used to do that an awful lot. He loved walking. We'd have cookies and coffee or tea. Sometimes he would come just to sleep.*

There were times when he would walk in, sit down and he wouldn't be in that chair any longer than two minutes and he would be asleep. He'd just sit down and the first thing you'd know he was dead to the world. I'd go about my business. When he heard the bus horn toot he'd wake right up, stand up and go outside. Sometimes he never said a thing! Just like he belonged here. He was a wonderful, wonderful man.

There were Adirondack Mountain Club chapter meetings to which Madeline would take the old hermit. She related the old man would sit "fairly still" and listen.

Madeline: Sometimes it was boring. He'd let you know. He'd say, "Well, how are you enjoying it?" He would never just say "Let's

Lt. To Rt. Old Friends gather. Maggie Dodge, Noah, Mary, Adolph and David Dittmar. April 28, 1951 Tahawus Sportsmen's show. *Courtesy of Richard J. Smith from Noah's photo album*

go." I got his drift. On the way home Noah would turn to me and say, "Mag, I don't know what I'd do without you." And I would answer, "The same thing you did before you knew me." Lord, he was very special to me.

"Girls," Ditt summoned. He never announced it was time to go or asked if everyone was ready. It wasn't his way. Rather, in a pleasant, easy-going voice he would finish with the challenge, "On your toes." At that, all members of his party would know that for their own good they'd better be moving out. Goodbyes were said. Packs were readied. Supplies anyone cared to leave behind for the hermit were dropped into an old wooden box Noah kept propped up on two legs against a tree. Rucksacks were shouldered. "On your toes," and off they would go.

As they trailed out of camp on a well-worn dogtrot toward the main trail, Noah called after them, "Don't forget to bring your swim suits, friends," Ditt and Mary always brought theirs along, but Madeline never again did.

Noah's Secret Code.

Ϙθθ×| ℘℩ ×θ ×+−×θ Ϙℙ×θ−ℙˋᛐ ℙ|θ ✓ᛐ−+|℘ ⅄
ℙᴼ−ᛐ+℘ |ℙ×θ−θ+θᴏ−θ⸚ ×+−×θ ⟋ +ℙℙ−ᴏ ℙᴏ− ⟋ ⟋+−ᴏ−⟋×θ⸚
⅄ −ᴏᛐ××θˋ ℙ|θ |+−ˋθ ℙᴏ℘ ℙ|θ −θ⟋ᴛ ⅄ ℘+θ ℙ℘+θᴏ−
|+−ˋθ ⅄ℙ℘+θᴏ− −θ⟋ᴛ ℘℩ ×⟋×θ ⟋ ℘+×℘ ℘℩ ℘+θ |⅄|⸚ ⅄
|θ℘ +℘ ᴏ−ℙ℘⟋ ℘+| +| |−ᴏ⟋θ□

"...seems to me like Somebody once caught an orbit somewhere, like a hoop or a circle, and pulled one side out one way and the other side another way to make a tilt to the sun, and set it rotatin' in space—that's the Earth." *—NJR might have imagined the hand of God reaching out and setting the world in motion.*

Chapter 11

Earle Russell's Hermit Connection

The idea of a hermit living in your locale is an exciting notion for some people who would like to believe that when you walk away from society's mainstream you can actually live freely and independently. But it's foolish not to consider all the necessary ties to civilization that are needed for survival regardless of where a person lives. Hermiting might sound appealing to some people who idealize only the personal reflection, a.k.a. "the spiritual side" of the equation. There are many ways of living in the circle we call life.

I shared with Earle this thought as we talked about the hermit of Cold River. "Earle Russell's Hermit Connection" relates the remembrances of Earle Russell; his mountain home; his family's Adirondack background; anecdotes gleaned from his mother, Blanche Russell Graves Shippee; and his father, Lou Russell, who last worked as a forest ranger at Shattuck Clearing's interior outpost along the Cold River.

Earle's ancestors' roots are embedded deep in the Adirondack Mountains. He is proud of his hometown of Long Lake and his boyhood memories of growing up in the mountains. Earle thought highly of his parents' hermit-friend.

I told Earle that I understood his cherished days-of-youth-in-the-Adirondacks feelings, and explained my empathy for anyone who holds fast to the value of open space, protection of wildlife, enjoying and valuing the natural world, and leaving a wild heritage for future generations. Many people, young and old, take a mental look far beyond the physical boundaries of the life around them. They might see sidewalks, wood and stone buildings snuggled close with narrow alleys separating each towering structure, taxis, buses, trains, and cars streaming along streets and highways, and masses of people crowding stores and sidewalks. There is little to nothing natural—wild—as far as they can see. Then a mental picture comes to mind—a far-off desert or mountain range, a great forest, tundra, or expansive plain—and their spirit pulses with the excitement of that faraway place.

The idea that a person would walk away from society because he thought he could get a better deal in life, would be willing to chop a large supply of firewood to heat a cabin during long cold mountain winters, would catch fish and shoot wild game and do most of the cooking out of doors, as well as deal with so many other things including isolation seemed curious to Earle, especially considering the vast shortages of basic food items the country faced during World Wars I and II.

All the same, World War II confirmed Rondeau's long-held convictions about society. The war also forced the hermit to come out of the woods in order to register and then "wrangle with the Coreys ration board in order to get my food supplies." Complained Rondeau, "This brush with

Lou Russell at Noah's abandoned Cold River City in 1953 on a parole upriver during the period of time of the lumbering operations following the Big Blow of November 1950. *Courtesy of Earle Russell*

"My father's [Ranger Lou] donkey used to carry supplies to Shattuck Clearing. Dad often brought in Noah's mail and other things he needed. Dad found one of Rondeau's bear traps. He also has a chair that came from Rondeau's camp. It was quite a conversation piece." —Earle Russell. *Courtesy of Earle Russell*

civilization (he'd had a number of earlier hostile encounters with government regulations) was enough in itself to drive me back to my wooded Utopia for keeps."

"And at the time...well...," Noah resumed after a long reflective pause like the storytelling barber and spinner of philosophical theories some say he was, "...the country was never any good. It was no good then and never will be until it's overthrown. That's the only remedy for a thing like this, is to overthrow it completely. That's going to be done, but it's slow."

The man who withdrew physically and emotionally from society to ensure that he got away was not beyond humor and compromise. In the forest, a majority of Noah's visitors (beyond mountain climbers and anglers and hunters) were noisy raccoons, snoopy white tail deer and big-footed bears. He nailed "Town Hall" to his hut and lived up to the label. He was mayor, councilman, trustee, treasurer, town clerk, official bird watcher, weatherman, and animal control officer in one, and he governed as an absolute monarch, even if he did dispute New York State conservation laws and make his own game laws every now and then in the name of survival.

Boundaries were something Earle understood. It is important for everyone to create boundaries in their lives. An example that Noah felt he owed it to himself to draw was his explanation about the wildlife he allowed to remain outside his arrow's range—his oftentimes binding compromise with the forest critters—which meant that he often allowed himself to be content with a more prosaic meal of old-fashioned flapjacks.

Those who knew Noah in the early 1900s when he was barbering in Lake Placid held that, like many barbers, he was seen as a homegrown philosopher. Local, state and world happenings were hammered out while he was cutting hair and shaving customers. Perhaps he was soured by seven years of barbering "in shops all around Lake Placid" and hashing over the same political issues again and again. His various other reasons for "taking to the woods" have been explained.

His first attempt to get away from a job and society he found unacceptable was to funnel his talents into being a highly respected sportsmen's guide, but he quickly grew critical of the lack of sportsmanship many of his clients exhibited. He also did not care for the fact that many spent more time drinking and merrymaking in camp than they did in the field. So he quickly began to reevaluate this new career. He looked outside the box of answers society offered. To my way of thinking, that is what good judgment is all about.

Thirty-one years following Noah's trading in of society for a hermit life in the Adirondack Mountains, Earle's father, Lou Russell, took over the interior ranger position at the post far back at Shattuck Clearing. Earle explains, "My dad was assigned to Shattuck Clearing at Cold River in 1944. A forest ranger earned between $1,200 and $1,800 a year back then. There was a pension when he retired. Dad knew of Noah and although he had heard that the hermit was not overly friendly, he nevertheless wanted to meet him."

Ranger Russell was a practical man. He knew the question was not, "How will Rondeau and I get along?" but "How do we see each other co-existing?" Earle said, "After two visits, Noah warmed to the overtures of friendship, and on the third visit, Rondeau returned with Dad to Shattuck Clearing and spent the night with him in Buck Horn" (Lou's cabin at Cold River). "It was the beginning of a good friendship, as their visits continued and they shared some pleasant times together."

I imagine Earle stared out the window that overlooked his Queensbury, New York, backyard on November 22, 1994, when he penned his last letter to me. Our correspondence had spanned almost six years to the day. Surely he looked around at the neighborhood, then reflected back to 1914, the year he was born in Long Lake and one year after Noah Rondeau trekked into the mountains to live. Following Earle's discharge from the United States Army Air Corps at the end of World War II, he relocated to a down-state location where he worked at the General Electric Company until retirement in 1979.

"Oh, the Adirondacks I once knew."

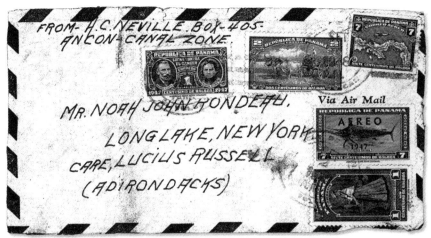

Noah marked this letter as received and read 09-13-48. It is typical of the mail that was addressed to either Noah or "Noah's Hideout" in care of Ranger Lucius Russell. *Courtesy of Earle Russell*

His eyes studied the proof of the second volume of a privately printed book he was finalizing. Earle titled it *A Glimpse Into The Past, Memories of an Adirondack Town*, then returned his attention to the letter he was ending to me.

"Noah and my dad used to talk about all the game that was once around Cold River." There were once trophy bucks and an abundance of wild brook trout.

Lou felt Noah had changed after he returned from a Sportsmen's Show in Madison Square Garden in 1947. "He was taken up with the city and movie stars." My slant is the experience overwhelmed him.

Reading between the lines in Earle's letters, I sensed a feeling of nostalgia for the mountains of his youth and his ancestors' past days—long before the modern improvements that came, slowly at first, following World War I.

By 1994, the once wild environment that girdled Long Lake Village had become the place where hardworking residents "once wrestled the improvements seen today" from a backbone economy of guiding recreational hunters and anglers, timber harvesting, contracting and caretaking summer cottages. Many natives were engaged in all four vocations.

So much of the "nucleus" that had surrounded Earle's youth had changed, perhaps the single reason why Earle's strongest memories were of his childhood and one of the reasons why he held tight to the stories and remembrances of his grandparents and parents.

★ ★ ★

Having a heart attack can have odd effects on the victim's mind. It casts a light on things that makes what is important and relevant in life blindingly clear. The reality of Earle's last medical emergency was beginning to sink in. He went to his notes: "I will try and answer a few more of your questions, Jay, and put together the pictures you want copies of."

Earle was generous. He was diligent in writing his manuscript "in my own hillbilly style" but still willing to share information I was seeking.

Anyone who knew Earle also knows family and local history were his favorite topics of conversation. He had a clear appreciation of how

Noah at Plumley's Point House dock, August 25, 1947. A flood of mail
to Noah arrived at the Long Lake Post Office following his return to Cold
River at the end of his appearance at a sportsmen's show in New York
City in 1947. "Dad would bring it to Shattuck Clearing for him. One of the
letters was from a couple who wanted to visit him and renew an acquaintance of many years past. Unfortunately, the man died before the trip
could be realized. After Noah's persistent invitations, the widow finally
agreed to visit. ...Noah asked my mother if they could stay overnight in
her home at Long Lake. She told him his visitor could stay, but that he
should find lodging elsewhere. The lady came by bus from Albany, where
she had been visiting friends. She was a very nice person, but appeared
nervous about the visit. It was such a long hike into Cold River that Mom
advised her not to go. She did agree to go with Noah on the Long Lake
Mail Boat as far as Plumley's Camp, where the trail starts. She returned
to stay at my mother's home another night, and relatives arrived the
following day to take her home." —Earle Russell. *Courtesy of Jim Plumley*

firsthand stories dovetail with the history of a region. His dad suffered his first stroke in July, 1946 "while returning to camp with Victory Baumister and son..." Noah learned of Lou's misfortune on July 13 from a visiting conservation officer.

In "Remembering Dr. John Gerster," Earle tells about the noted surgeon who summered at Long Lake who he credits with "arranging for my father to be taken to the New York Hospital," and then looking after Lou's mother until Lou returned, following two operations that "extended his life by ten years."

"Noah had a lot of photographs he liked to show." The photos Noah liked showing, the ones to which Earle referred, were taken in 1947, after the hermit had returned from his first Sportsmen's Show. Earle observed that Noah "returned to Cold River elated and very happy. He brought with him pictures of movie stars and celebrities and some of the ladies had their arms around him. This boosted his ego immensely."

Earle Russell reported that the publicity and notoriety the hermit enjoyed "brought a small flood of mail to Noah..." The letters were addressed to *In care of Long Lake Post Office*. "Dad would bring bundles of mail back to Shattuck Clearing" for the hermit.

The following remembrance of Earle's mother provides an interesting wink at what the "old boy did during one of his visits to Plumley's Point House near the head of Long lake. It is one of the countless little stories that have surfaced which I consider to be little gems for anyone who wants to learn priceless details of the Cold River hermit's life.

"One of the letters was from a couple who wanted to visit him and renew an acquaintance of many years past. Unfortunately, the man died before the trip could be realized. After Noah's persistent invitations, the widow finally agreed to visit. This was in 1952, and Noah asked my mother if they could stay overnight in her home at Long Lake. She told him his visitor could stay, but that he should find lodging elsewhere. The lady came by bus from Albany, where she had been visiting friends. She was a very nice person, but appeared nervous about the visit. It was such a long hike into Cold River that Mom advised her not to go. She did agree to go with Noah on the Long Lake Mail Boat as far as Plumley's Camp, where the trail starts. She returned to stay at my mother's home another night, and relatives arrived the following day to take her home.

"A Sportsmen's Show at Tahawus also featured the hermit with a display of animal skins and bows and arrows that he had made. One large bearskin was the background for a tall tale of an encounter with a bear. My mother's sister was among the crowd being impressed, and she told Noah that it looked like the skin from the bear my dad had killed. He didn't reply, knowing it would have spoiled his tall tale."

Many of Earle's memories lay in the life of the mountains just as thirty-seven years of Noah's nights were spent on Cold River Hill, thirty-seven years of living his dream in a secure place he called home.

"I saw Noah John Rondeau for the last time between Tupper Lake and Saranac Lake just off the highway near some cabins. He visited with anyone who stopped to see him and he was selling his 'eyebrow pencils' made from sticks with charred ends. He netted twenty-five cents apiece."

Three years following Noah's Madison Square Garden appearance he removed himself from yesterday's Cold River wigwam skyline, the Town Hall and Hall of Records huts, neighborhood critters, and deep woods flower beds and vegetable patch. The woods person still enjoyed seeing and talking to people, but the meetings were miles removed from his former hermitage.

Noah's Secret Code.

⊙θ´∘ ♂´∧₸⁰⁸ ⊢† ×₸ ´∿ᴩᶅ+∘´∘⊢ θ+×× ×´×θ ⊚ᶅ∿
⊢´∘∘₸⧧θ∘θ ´∘θ ᵢᶠ×θ ᴩ∘θ+ᵢᴩθ` ×+⁻ᶅθᵢ ∧` ∠∿∘∿θᵢ□
+⊙ᴩᵢᵢᶅᶦθ+ᶦ+ ⊢θ∘θ ´ᴩ Ⓠ´∘∧´, +⊙ᶦᶦ ᴩᶠ∨₸□ +⊙ ⊢´∘θ
ᶦᶦᴩ ⊢+⁻ᶦθ`´ᵢ ₸θᴩ⁰⁸ ∿∿ᴩ θᶦθᶦ +⊙ ´ᶠ →ᶠ +⊙ θ´ᴩ ᴩᶠ
´ᴩᵢ⊢´Ⓠ+⊙θ+ ♂∘⊙⁸Ⓠ♂´□

Dear Lady,—if my autograph will make You happy-here are some twisted lines and curves. It's snowing here (at Saranac Inn) today. I have not fished as yet, but when I do go I want to catch a BIG TROUT. —NJR to Mrs. B. Strauss on April 29, 1947

Chapter 12

Dorian's ABC's Microphone

In 1991, while seeking out Clayt Seagers, or an offspring connection, I met Dorian St. George, a close friend of Seagers who enjoyed a long and interesting twenty-odd year career as a reporter-announcer for ABC and NBC. St. George recalled, "In the 1940s and early '50s I was an announcer at ABC in New York City. I was assigned to attend the 1947 Sportsmen's Show...and find something of interest for a late evening sports program."

It was a simple, yet challenging assignment. "New York was (and is) a pretty blasé place, and for any one person to be a media event one would have to have done something outrageous to merit any great attention."

Dorian, long retired and enjoying fly-fishing in Meridian, Mississippi, had interviewed notables ranging from Ted Williams and Dale Carnegie to the Duke of Windsor, and Lowell Thomas—band leaders, singers, journalists, actors and politicians. His experience had swung far and wide over so many celebrities, media magnets, public figures, famous persons and stars, and yet St. George's mind locked on one character who was none of the above.

"The New York State Conservation Department had as their presentation that year a replica of Noah John Rondeau's 'camp' in the Adirondacks... complete with Noah himself dressed in furs, complete with beard and a sharp native sense of humor. Clayton B. Seagers, who was Director of Conservation Education and the editor of the *Conservationist* magazine, was in charge of the exhibit. I thought Noah might be just what I was looking for and invited him (and Clayt) to come to the studios that night for an interview."

Dorian St. George describes Rondeau as a man of unflagging originality and Seagers as a man with whom he became good friends.

The studio was what was called a "speaker studio." A room with acoustically treated walls cleverly concealed behind a porous rice wallpaper. A side was decorated like a comfortable study in a moderately wealthy man's home. Some large wing chairs, a handsome leather-covered table for Joe (and me) and Joe's guest.

An early appointment was to give Noah some time to relax… to chat a bit about his life in the Adirondacks, etc. Thus the interviewer (me) could learn just what sort of questions would elicit the more colorful aspects of his life…and avoid treading on embarrassing subjects. For example, we wouldn't have wanted Noah to mention his sanitary arrangements (if any!) in his bailiwick.

There were, as I remember, the usual questions of "What made you want to become a hermit?" etc. And then the usual explorations into how he managed, where he got his food, clothing, medical care, and so on.

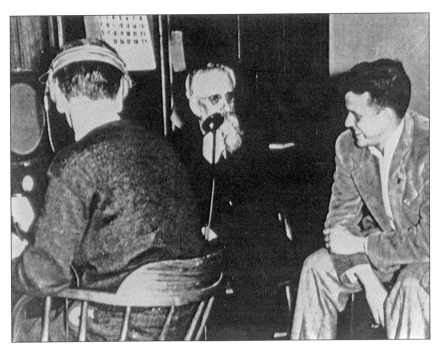

March 1947. Rondeau at the microphone as senior Leslie Farmer interviewed him for a radio station KSLU of St. Lawrence University in Canton, N.Y. report.
Courtesy of Leslie G. Farmer

Noah explained how he'd been a barber in some Adirondack village and had decided that he'd about had it with civilization and so went into the deep woods to be a hermit. I gathered that he was the recipient of the bounty of his summer visitors and that he, being no fool, worked that angle as far as he could. Apparently, the people who came to visit understood this very well and were willing donors!

Well, our program came off well and I, because I wanted to talk to Clayt some more, asked them to come down for a drink or two. Clayt said he liked a "taste" on occasion and so did Noah!

St. George did broadcasts from each succeeding Sportsmen's Show until the mid '50s. "I left ABC but continued with an outdoor program on NBC until about 1960."

At ABC, as the man in the field, Dorian took on Noah, saying he did not consider the hermit to be among his most challenging assignments.

I surely wouldn't want to flesh out that one evening session with Noah from a faulty memory because it would be all too easy to imagine conversation that never took place and that surely wouldn't be fair to Noah's history and to his person. He was surely a colorful individual but I couldn't tell you if he possessed any extraordinary wisdom or not. What was unusual, to me that is, is that he tired of the "rat-race" and decided to go off into the woods and live off the land and any gifts that came his way was just so much lagniappe (a southern expression meaning something extra).

Dorian offered a series of recommendations for me to follow up, among them a search of the New York City newspapers' morgues to learn if Noah was interviewed by anyone else. He defined the short time spent with the Adirondack hermit as "interesting." There was a connection because of the men's mutual outdoor interests. Rondeau was simple, and he didn't think that "Old Noah was a media event. Not in New York!"

Chapter 13

Clarence and Stacia Whiteman Meet the All-American Hermit

Cold River has always been a place where men and women find freedom, as Clarence Whiteman found out in 1946. Being mindful that the best experiences are often found in the humblest of quarters, Clarence and his fiancée wandered up the spur path, off the main Northville-Lake Placid Trail, and passed under a makeshift entrance of long poles bent over the foot trail. There they saw a threadbare banner stretched across the path, pronouncing GATE TO THE CITY. They saw on one of the wigwams pointing skyward a sign that read MRS. RONDEAU'S KITCHENETTE. Tacked over the doors of the two low-roof cabins were the signs TOWN HALL and HALL OF RECORDS.

Clarence called out, asking if anyone was in camp, and thus began the part of his Cold River investigation that most excited and disappointed him. The hermit of Cold River Flow had been the subject of a recent news story. Clarence didn't remember exactly which newspaper it was.

"I do remember it was sometime during the winter. A reporter from New York City snow-shoed in there with a state forest ranger. It was either the *New York Mirror* or *New York News.*" Whiteman, a Schenectady, New York native, had learned a little information about the hermit from interviews that had appeared in other papers. Each article provided a few more sought-after bits of information. Each news report Clarence read about Rondeau seemed to whirl the facts he had previously learned about the fascinating man like an autumn wind whips up leaves. The stories, reports, and photos were like colorful leaves that swirl before you, and Whiteman told me that when he closed his eyes, he could see himself being lifted back to the isolated valley where Rondeau lived. "I told Stacia, we had to meet this woodsman. I was an avid outdoorsman myself. Meeting him and maybe discussing his life in the backwoods of the Adirondack Mountains became a goal for me." Clarence often imagined he heard the voice of Rondeau in his dreams. Certainly it was an imagined voice, but it woke him up one time. Clarence said he did as the voice directed. Soon after the ice cleared from Long Lake that spring, he and Stacia launched their boat on their maiden voyage toward Cold River and the hermit's abode.

Like other fanciers of the long time mountain dweller, Clarence would learn about more of the problems that persisted into Rondeau's teenage years and young adulthood as word of his rustic life spread following the publication of Clayt Seagers' biographical sketch in the New York State *Conservationist* magazine.

Clarence could not help hearing the voice of Noah as facts about the hermit's life unfolded in many published interviews. The woodsman's printed voice seemed often to be focused on some of his life's shortcomings, and what he did to escape a world he did not always feel comfortable living in. If his parents seemed to have failed in their parental duty, one only needs to remind oneself that times were very different then. After all, Noah had been a miner's son and lived at a place called Jackson Hill, four miles from Au Sable Forks in the Adirondacks in the last decade of the 19th century.

All children are sensitive to loss and sadness, but most are flexible enough to deal with whatever circumstances life hands them. Feelings of not fitting in persisted throughout his childhood, but he had an alternative world to immerse himself in: The family farmstead and the surrounding forest. Noah had been a rebellious and sensitive child, and displayed patterns of resilience and change that exist in all humans.

Clarence, who spent countless hours afoot in Cold River during deer hunting season between 1946–1949, had been surprised when Noah revealed that venison was not a main staple for the mountain-living Rondeaus when he was growing up. He had also tried to imagine what Noah's childhood had been like—the hardscrabble little farm, his father tired and grumpy from working too many hours in the mine, and Noah's fondness for escaping to the woods even back then.

★ ★ ★

Clarence reflected on all of this as he looked around the wilderness yard. Rondeau's camp was a model hermit's dwelling. Rustic, weathered outdoor furniture. Buildings and structures with utilitarian purposes. An untreated deerskin target for bow and arrow practice. All sorts of odd bits of remains from the former Meigs and Meigs logging camp lay scattered about. A number of large iron kettles filled with soil were suspended from pole tripods around the yard. (The suspended cauldrons made perfect holders for hanging flowers.) Small plots of freshly turned dirt outlined the location of flower and vegetable beds. A large can of rendered bear fat and the mashed leaves of wintergreen stood on a shelf inside the Beauty Parlor wigwam. (It was Rondeau's medicine for blisters and bruises.)

There have always been a handful of male and female hermits, all strong-willed and strong-minded people. Survivors. Men and women who've experienced a failed romance and lived with a broken heart make good hermit candidates. Draft dodgers were good candidates in the past, and people evading the law in other ways still are. Other hermit aspirants are those who see themselves as victims of some sort, those who reject society or authority or dislike the constant press of changing technology or are sickened by ultra shifts in political and cultural ideas. Certain attitudes make it easier to profess a willingness to walk away from everything they know, replacing former ways of life with simpler ones that fit better with their beliefs and behaviors.

Clarence calculated correctly that Noah had suffered "some sort of jolt" that caused him to disassociate.

The idea that the grounds he was standing on were those of a true recluse wasn't exactly accurate. Another person who knew Rondeau, a former newspaper writer and for twenty years Editor and Head of Publication Branch, Office of Naval Intelligence, Vincent Engles wrote of Rondeau in his book *Adirondack Fishing in the 1930s* and gave his slant on the term *hermit* in connection with the Cold River recluse when he camped at the hermitage during a June trout fishing excursion:

"Our host was a pleasant man of the woods... Webster defines a hermit as 'a person who retires from society and lives in solitude, especially from religious motives; recluse; anchorite.' Mr. Rondeau was clearly a recluse, but although he was reading The Western Christian Messenger *when I first came upon him, he was no more a hermit of the devotional type than Natty Bumppo or Henry David Thoreau. He lived in the woods because he loved nature and detested the towns, and particularly the presence in the towns of people who might set limits to his independence—mayors, sheriffs, and the administrators of the fish and game laws."*

"You always feel free in the woods if you know what you're doing" is the standard explanation. Rondeau going off to live alone "didn't seem irresponsible to me," but, Clarence pointed out, "knowing anything can happen and living miles from any assistance is particularly tricky."

1946. Lt. to Rt. Unknown man, Noah, and Clarence Whiteman posing with a trophy buck. The story of "Noah's Lickety-Split Ride on Clarence Whiteman's Buck" is told in *Life With Noah*. *Courtesy of Clarence Whiteman*

Experience and the weather were on Clarence's mind. "I was concerned about the new movie camera I carried in. I planned to take pictures of Noah and his diggings. But the spring day in 1946 when Stacia and I walked in there the weather grew less favorable for moving pictures.

"Well, by the time we reached Rondeau's," daylight was as gray as the palest shade of an April day, and "it started to rain. The movie film back then required you had to have sunlight in order to get any nice footage, so I kept the new camera wrapped in a canvas sack and resorted to taking black and white photographs as you see here," my host for the day said as he pointed to a group of poor-quality snapshots in a photo album. "They're all I have of the first attempt. Too bad they aren't better." The images were a clear example of how overcast the day had been.

The uninhabited, rugged individualist setting held an indistinguishable force, Clarence recalled. It kept "tempting me" with the image that it was the home of a commanding and consequential person. "I was disappointed" and bitten with a burning desire to pay another visit. The next time he hoped to find the hermit home and arrive on a well-lighted day. A return trip was needed to satisfy two bittersweet desires.

"I remember taking one last look at the tent-like City of Wigwams. It seemed a wild spectacle, but it was two o'clock now," Clarence continued to recall of his first effort to see and film the all-American hermit. The daylight muted, suggestive of endless rain. "Stacia was uncomfortably damp" and the couple's pack baskets had been left at Ouluska Pass lean-to, "a good distance down river." Clarence recalled that decision had come about for a good reason. "We had left them there to lighten our load."

"I told Stacia time was marching on. 'I think we better start getting back.' We ran all the way. We were young in those days."

Throughout summer Clarence planned, and looked forward to, their next Cold River adventure. As he and Stacia planned their future house, looking at floor plans and talking about carpets and colors for drapes, Clarence's thoughts often wandered to Rondeau's sparse possessions. Everything the man owned in the world was standing right on the little hilltop. No fancy clothes to wear. Certainly no mansion on the hill. Clarence could not wait to once again be among the spruce and hemlock, pine and cedar trees, and hike along Cold River, sometimes with his thoughts embellished in visions more common forty-six years earlier, when Cold River City was founded and few people were guests.

A bright September brought an end to Clarence's oftentimes dreamy weaving of past and present images of Rondeau's camp. On the first day of the month the couple set off on their second attempt to film the hermit's encampment and to meet the man Clarence had read so much about.

The couple would not be famous historical visitors such as the Rockefellers and Meigses. But the Whitemans' ordinary call encapsulated in a few precious frames of 8 mm film the life of this often misunderstood man who had captured the imagination of so many people.

The motion picture filmed that day was not high quality or lengthy. However, Clarence told me, it might ultimately be one of the only film clips that have survived.

I sat with 87-year-old Clarence in the fall of 1992, and we viewed together the short clips, a moving portrait so to speak, of the motor boat ride down Long Lake, backpacking through the woods, crossing the still standing suspension bridge, and the Big Horn ranger station that once stood at Shattuck Clearing where the picturesque MacKenzie Mountain provided the perfect wild country backdrop. There were snippets of the hermitage, Noah holding Stacia's hand as he led her around the yard and stopped to look at a pot of hanging flowers he was proud of cultivating, and more. There is Noah holding an oil painting of "The City," lots of pans of the surrounding scenery, and clips of later day trips when Clarence arrived at Harper's Clearing on the mail boat where a teamster he dubbed only as Farr was waiting for the deer hunters with a wagon and a fine team of horses. The home movie, made in November, showed snow and the rough winding tote road the teamster had followed—a far cry from the more direct and well-maintained foot trail backpackers follow today.

With nostalgia and honesty, Clarence revealed to me the longings for his deceased wife and the connections that drew him to "Cold River City." The aged man's memories also show us that it doesn't matter what we might individually think of our experiences. For within our everyday living there is historical value that will enlighten another generation who can only learn from those who lived during an earlier era. In my interviews with Clarence, I was the happy recipient of his knowledge about Noah and about life in an earlier time in the Adirondacks.

Clarence recalled that the tall woodpiles first appeared as specks, growing as they advanced up the pathway. They entered under the entrance banner and "...found Noah sitting at a little table in the Town Hall eating." The door to the building was open. "When we walked in there he was eating a few little fish he had caught. He looked up, greeted us, and remarked 'it was hard to make a living.'" Following a friendly exchange that caught them up "we were taken on a complete tour of the city."

From what I saw and learned from Clarence, Noah was friendly and talkative. Perhaps egged on by Clarence's sincerity, the hermit stood with a bemused expression as he told of being hired to haul in a wagonload of traps for some trappers and of the lumbering men who moved out in 1921, the same year he was given written permission to occupy the abandoned Big Dam lumber camp. [Vincent Engles reported Noah told him the early game protectors "...doubted the authenticity and validity of the scrap of wrapping paper on which the head of the lumbering firm of Meigs and Meigs had scrawled a deed, giving the hermit title to the camp buildings and the ground on which they stood..."] He said the winter cold did not bother him, "Not the least." His two rough log cabins were about ten feet long and eight feet wide with assorted bits of canvas for roofing. The first of September was "a beautiful day," Clarence reported. "I took moving pictures...and found Rondeau was not queer at all. He was a smart old man. He invited me back to deer hunt that season."

Clarence's first trip to Cold River had been a disappointment since Rondeau had been away on his spring migratory circuit and the day had been gray. Film images taken on his second visit in September of 1946 show the beauty of the area and Noah's warm welcome. The film preserves the lasting impression Noah made on the couple. Stacia sat on a stump stool in front of the Beauty Parlor wigwam as Noah fussed comically to freshen her

"It was not unusual for there to be several inches of snow at Rondeau's during the white-tail deer hunting season. Noah would sweep snow paths between his hut and the various wigwams." —Clarence Whiteman. *Courtesy of Clarence Whiteman*

face after the long hike in. "He even had a can of face conditioner. The 'beauty cream' was made of charcoal and bear's oil. A soap dish made from the skull of a bear set above the 'wet sink,' nothing more but an old hollow log. He had them all labeled for fun," an excited Clarence recalled of the trip with his new bride.

The couple found themselves in the presence of a spry hermit living among a collection of castaways, surrounded by deer and bear bones, strings of animal teeth, fur and feathers, and clever homemade fishing lures. Rondeau had a .35 caliber Remington automatic rifle and a .22 caliber rifle, a shotgun, and a homemade bow and arrow. Clarence's initial reaction was a lack of words when Noah "invited me to return to Cold River and set up a deer camp," having learned he enjoyed hunting. "I clasped his hand and shook it," with a fixed gaze into his eyes. "I felt like I could leap ten feet high. Was I ever *excited!*"

EARLY WINTER. NOVEMBER 13, 1946

Clarence and five hunting buddies returned to Cold River in 1946. They set up a deer camp near the Big Eddy.

Several unusual events have never escaped Clarence's memory.

"The first time I went in there Farr stopped at Shattucks. We ate lunch while the packer fed his horses there. A ranger was still there in November. He had of late had a heart attack. We asked him about signing up for a permit to set up a semi-permanent camp on state land but he told us 'Oh you boys don't need no permit. I know where you are going.' So the next year we went in, nobody was in the camp at all so we went on without a permit. We didn't leave a note or what. Farr didn't neither. So when I come back in [to camp] at night from hunting the boys said a game warden and ranger had dropped in and they told us we needed one to avoid a violation so I walked down after dark that night and got the permit. I remember that clearly 'cause he couldn't spell Schenectady. I also remember him telling me he had been out with Rondeau putting on a little drive." Whiteman thanked him for the alert and assured him "Clarence Whiteman don't violate."

Clarence was sketchy on the years of the following recollections. Time blurred the years. I concluded from a combination of listening to Clarence, reading Noah's entries, and viewing his film, that he was referring to events that happened in 1949.

Clarence remembers. "You want a deer for camp [meat]? Noah asked." The day was November 6, 1949. Whiteman's party had come upriver for a visit and some fun. "We rapped on his door. He was eating corn bread muffins dunked in a bacon and bear grease mixture. A recycled four pound Daisy Ham container that had a colorful label showing dancing pigs in various ballet poses stood nearby. It was used to store drippings. 'Come in, boys,' he said. When we poked our heads in to greet him he surely saw our stare at the sparse meal. He looked up and said, 'Hard Times. Hard Times to make a living.' I thought of Stacia's earlier remarks when we left in September. She had suggested we ought to give him some money but I didn't think any other of it until we started to walk back and by then it was too late."

"'I'll go along with you,' Rondeau told us. He had planned to spend some time at Big Horn Camp the next day. We looked forward to the prospect of him taking some time to hunt with us. We knew he did the same with Doc Latimer." The Whiteman party's camp was not far from Dr. Latimer's Camp Seward. Rondeau told Clarence that he had hunted yearly, since the 1920s, for the doctor and cut wood for the camp. "Made sure there was always a good supply of dry wood in camp."

"We respected the hermit's skills." One "didn't usually set eyes on a person like him." Whiteman's party also knew in the case of a deer hunt, "the deer could never beat the hermit at his best game." They had heard Rondeau talk about his early days of killing deer and bear with a bow and arrow. "Once," as Rondeau told it, a "bear kept going with the first shot but I got a second arrow into it and he didn't go any farther."

"So we went out and hunted around," Clarence continued. Deer hunting back there didn't require fine-tooth searching. "Oh Lord, he didn't have much for boots on his feet. Oh those shoes weren't much fit for walking.

Well, out we went. Oh geez, there were deer signs all around. They was just like cattle. Deer was thick. You couldn't walk through the woods without seeing them, they was so many."

Later that day, following the hunt, Noah moved on to Shattuck Clearing and his ranger friends who were hunting out of Big Horn Camp. A few days later, "On Rondeau's way back home he stopped by our camp. We had previously talked about him staying with us to break up the trek to the hermitage but he decided against it. Noah notified me of his decision in a note he left. There were five of us in that little tent." The men joked they would plan to tip up a table to make a comfy sleeping quarters but Noah saw it differently. "He penned, 'There is no room for me. I'll make my way up home,' and off he went toting a heavy pack of supplies that we would have helped him ferry the next day."

The early winter trail conditions, cool temperatures and snow, a heavy pack, the worn bottoms of his rubber-bottom boots, a short stop for a breather and to eat a doughy flapjack from his pocket and a wind that

Whiteman Party's tent site in the vicinity of Natural Dam. *Courtesy of Clarence Whiteman*

came down High Banks Pass into the clearing by the river, then rushing on to beat total darkness were just the kind of conditions Rondeau did not find uncomfortable. The "man was tough."

"I heard from an old lumber man, Joe Jock, a story about Noah," Clarence shared. "It was about the time the fellow first came in there. Joe was one of the loggers from Tupper Lake area who cut timber up and down—lumbered that whole mountain range off in 1918. He remembered the first day he met Noah. Joe had just gotten a deer for which he had not retained a license. He had planned to use some of the venison for camp meat and jerk the rest of the meat. As he was bent over dressing out the animal, he spotted a figure from a long distance off coming along the log road. Joe said he looked different from all the men he knew. Everyone else wore lumberjack clothes back in the woods so when Noah came walking along, he knew he wasn't from these parts. Jock and his crew carefully kept an eye on him. In the fullness of time they saw he wasn't a game protector but still wondered who the person could be. He was wearing clothing Joe called 'dressed up clothes,'—a big overcoat on and a hat.

"Drawing near hollering distance, the figure called out, 'I see you got a deer.'

"Joe replied, 'Yes, that's so.'

"'I spec you plannin' to put in some full-time hunting later on till your licenses are filled,' he called back. The brief exchange was enough of a cue to reveal to Joe the approaching man was 'all right'—he understood about illegal meat for a larder.

"As he came up close, Joe said, 'Without a word he pulled out a big pocket knife and started to help skin it out and quarter the deer. After the deer was dressed, he offered, 'I'll show you something.'

"Joe said the older man took each quarter. The snow was deep, and he tossed 'em out in different directions. 'I just stood and watched the meat disappear in the snow.' When the fourth quarter landed he turned to me and spoke. 'Now you see those trees where they landed. You marked them spots in your mind so if sometime in the future a stranger comes along you can take off. Later on you can return, pick them up, and you see you won't be bothered.'

"'That was the first time he came in there to find work in the lumber camps,' Jock said. Joe Jock told me he didn't know nothing about lumbering; the Frenchie had done work around camps but he said he could sharpen steel and file saws and such. He was a little bit of a feller.

"After the lumbering was over he stayed back in there—living here and there at some of the camps that were back in there and running trap lines. The camps were built for the deep snow—there was usually six feet on the level and more, you know. Eventually he claimed the Dam camp as his base."

These accounts and others affirmed Clarence's idea that Noah was a genuine hermit and his 'Cold River City' a mecca for sport and adventure, as well as a place of beauty.

Of course it was just nostalgic imagination for Clarence as he talked about Noah, his close hunting connection, and their Adirondack wilderness days. Each question asked helped Clarence peel back the mental layers to his final season at Cold River.

My impression of Clarence Whiteman is of a generous man who made time to talk with me even though he was having a real struggle with his health. At the end of our meeting, he gave me a letter Noah wrote him and an 8mm home movie he filmed back at Cold River. I offered him a photocopy of the pages I had transcribed from Noah's 1949 journal. Richard Smith then owned the actual diary. I had a feeling Clarence would enjoy reading the hermit's daily annotations—especially since he was mentioned. The following "Footprints" constitute the pages I left with Clarence.

In 1949, on what was Noah John's 66th birthday, the self-disciplined recluse mailed this handwritten letter to his Schenectady hunting friend about the possibility that Whiteman would not find him in camp.

The correspondence was written on stationery announcing it belonged to…

Noah John Rondeau
Mayor of Cold River
Coreys, New York

October 25th, 1949

Mr. C. S. Whiteman
11 Canton Street
Schenectady, N.Y.

Dear Mr. Whiteman:-
Today,- I got Your letter at Saranac Lake; I came out from Cold
River City Saturday; I have a bunch on my Arm-due to a fall on
the ice last winter.
    First,- I must see a Doctor- then if I find I can return to Cold
River shortly, I will drop you a card.
    Chances are I will not be at C. River much more this season.
    On the other hand—I may see You. And if You chance up to
my City in Snow Storm-go in Log Cabin and build you a fire in
Box Stove.
    You will find Deer more plentiful this season.
    When I came down River Thurs.- Fri.- a party setting up near
Yancey's and one at Moose Creek-Dr. Latimer is due to day-
    Yancy is due last of month.
    At Saranac Lake a Bob Cat hangs on Main St.
    I take the next Bus for Au Sable Fork.

    Noah John Rondeau

Reading that October, 1949 communication and the hermit's journal entries helped revive Clarence's memory. The diary record also suggests the swelling on Rondeau's arm was not as aggressive a symptom as he might have anticipated at the time he posted the notice.

October 30 - November 1, 1949
Saranac Lake- Calkin Creek- Jungle Lodge-Chattock Clearings
Nice late Autumn day; Clouds and showers Park car 3 mile
mark. See Hunter on Rondeau's Hill. 11 A.M. at Peek-a-Boo

Cabin. Noon: Look for Bear Trap on top of Hill. 3:30 P.M. at
Camp Wild Cat. Fancy Supper in 2 Tin cans; and Fancy Bed by
Calkin Creek. Rain during night 3 miles through wet Spruces.
At Dark (5 P.M.) set up camp in Jungle. Night: wet, cold
snowed- 1 inch. Up at dawn in snow Jungle (code). Walk to
Chattock Clearing by compass. Dinner at Twin Bridges cross Cold
River at dusk. Supper and Lodge at Big Horn Camp.[2]

Noah's entries for Sunday through Tuesday did not read like meaningless destinations to Clarence. "I know the course he took that brought him back from Coreys to the interior station at Cold River. Big Horn was the name of the ranger's camp. I frequently walked a portion of that route," Clarence said.

Sometimes when I was talking with Clarence, his eyes, facial expressions and voice had a look and sound that told me he saw the long years disappear and he was young again with Noah. He used to enjoy doing camp chores with the old hermit—not so much because Noah needed his help, but because he welcomed every opportunity for them to be together. He breathed a long sigh and sat silently for a time, lost in his thoughts of long ago. Then he said something along this line of thought: "It's comforting to think of the years that have come and gone."

Thursday's-Sunday's entries tracked the hermit from Shattuck Clearing to his camp. Clarence enjoyed reviewing the hermit's postings. It gave him another perspective on the man he used to know and he was glad indeed to have the opportunity to share nostalgic longings and learn what Noah had been doing in the days prior to the arrival of the Whiteman party.

November 3–6
Frost last night. To Day: calm and Sunshine
At Chattuck Clearing - Town Hall I carry pack from Chattock to
Cold River Town Hall. A flock of Snow Birds call at Cold River
Garden. I dump 2 pails Pebbles in my Ash Tray. Pebbles collected
from Cold River Bed July 6th. I put wood and food in Hall of
Records for possible winter travelers. Hunter's from Big Eddy call.

The mountain Scenes are winter like; and the feel of Valley Air varifies "winter like."

Clarence said he had an even greater interest in Noah's writing now than when he had been going up to the mountains. There was something comforting about the stolid segments. War had come and gone, past visitors to the hermitage were grandparents, and Noah had died, but nothing changed the diaries. They lay on shelves in a climate-controlled and fireproof vault. They would always be there to preserve the past that Clarence and so many others held dear, a treasure of information that provided transport to earlier days.

Monday–Sunday, November 7–13
Very cloudy–driz, rain, snow Cold River Town Hall–Big
Horn Camp.
 I carry pack to Big Horn. I hunt 5 hours on Sugar Bush Hill.
4 men carry 6 Point Buck to Rightmyer Camp. 3 men put roof on
Big Horn wood Shed. Ranger Manley take my Rifle and kill a 3
Point Buck to trim new wood shed. I hunt between Chattock and

Buck Horn camp, Shattuck Clearing. The interior ranger cabin was a gathering place for sports until it was removed in the early 1980s in the belief man-made structures had no place in the wilds. *Courtesy of Clarence Whiteman*

Sullivan's P.O. I saw a Chickadee, a Rabbit and a small Deer. I carry Bill Petty's Basket to Jack Ass Gate.

Sunday night as the hermit bore gear to Jack Ass Gate, the Whiteman party passed through Shattuck Clearing on their way to the men's customary camp site near the Big Eddy and within sight of High Banks.

Old Whiskers learned from Ranger Manley that Clarence had stopped to obtain his camping permit. On Monday he headed out to Big Dam loaded with supplies. The Whiteman campers were young, agreeable and very charitable men. Rondeau would have been looking forward to seeing them again. Unfortunately the hunters were anxious to deer hunt Tuesday morning. By the time Noah reached camp they were off in the mountains. He could have tarried at camp but he knew the combination of the weight in his pack basket, the temperature and the snow depth all took its toll as he always seemed to be struggling a bit more this year to get over the towering High Banks section of the trail.

November 14 – 15, 1949 Monday – Tuesday
7:45 A.M. about 90 wild Geese go southwest
Big Horn Camp to Town Hall
10 A.M. to 4 P.M. I carry 40 pound pack from Big Horn
Camp to Town Hall. Leave note at C.E. Whiteman's camp.

On each yearly hunting vacation, Clarence noted something new. Noah's connection made the Cold River back country extra special. Confabs with the hermit helped him to see Nature's aura. White tail deer hunting was much more than following deer trails and sitting on watch. It was Noah's often "poetic gaze" that changed how Clarence saw the natural world around him. Ideas the hermit fostered began to affect the hunter. Heavy frosts. Awakening to find a drizzling rain falling or seeing the terrain as a carpet of dazzling white. A bright sun shining on evergreens loaded with slush and water as he followed tracks that led into a deep swamp.

"We would oil our rifles, fill the magazines, pocket a good lunch, and go up there on a ridge. The snow made it easy for a person to move about noiselessly in the woods," Clarence remembered. The cushioning effect of the snow made it possible that there would be a good chance of tracking some buck to its hideaway.

"It wouldn't be long after we left our camp, maybe ten minutes and we would see tracks—deer and other animals." Animal tracks never fail to interest a hunter.

"Once when high in the mountains Rondeau pointed out the country roundabout had been lumbered, and showed us an old roadway near the head of a pond on the mountainside. Many years ago a lumber shanty had stood in a clearing near a beautiful spot of evergreens.

He recommended we best eat our lunch 'to keep up strength,' because the valley on the south side of the Seward range had windfalls and dense growths of balsam and spruce which held the snow from the ground and made tracking difficult."

> *November 16. Wednesday*
> *Ice last night. Today: cloudy, cold. Mountain tops are*
> *white. At Cold River Town Hall*
> *2 P.M. 1 eye at Alexander's stand. 3 P.M. A good shit in*
> *Fancy shit wigwam. 10 A.M. 3 hunters call from (Clarence)*
> *Whiteman camp. I hunt 3 Legged Swamp. 2 to 4 P.M. I watch*
> *at mouth of Seward Brook.*

On Wednesday's drive the party got a particularly "large buck." Clarence filmed the drag back to camp. "The hunting party played the part of Santa's reindeer while Noah, grasping a switch in his hand, circled it over the heads of the men as if he were Santa as he encouraged his steeds to pull back their ears, dig in, and pull as he hollered each man's name: 'On Clarence,' and so forth...'to the top of Cold River Hill, now onward you go.'"[3]

Clarence knew the "vittles" his party brought along lasted "...very well. We had more on hand than we ever anticipated needing. We knew Noah didn't have an excess of food in storage for the long season. We wanted him to have the extra but didn't want to offend him by just handing it over so we planned a farewell meal in his honor."

That evening five hunters all bowed their heads at the table before beginning to pass the platters around the table. "God bless Cold River bucks and our guide" was part of the meal's prayer. At the end of the invocation, Noah's attention was directed to a canvas sack that was for him. 'Yes, sir,' he nodded, 'everything's goin' to be all right this winter.'"

In unison the Whiteman camp replied with a saying Clarence first picked up from Noah, but often repeated in friendly fun: "Yes sir, it sure is hard to make a livin.'"

Snow was piling up on the brims of the party's hats. It was cold that last November day when the men walked down the tote road following behind Farr's wagon, "We walked a fair measure of the distance to Harper's Dock."

The fact that they walked when there was a wagon wasn't any surprise to me. It might have been miles to Harper's Dock on Long Lake but they would have been harder miles had they tried to stay atop the wagon. The driver handling the large draft horses and wagon over a muddy and rutted route on Whiteman's film looked very uncomfortable.

Noah, Stacia, and Clarence got together the following year in Wilmington. They met at The North Pole amusement park along the Whiteface

Lt. to Rt. Clarence Whiteman, unidentified man, Ranger Lou Russell.
Courtesy of Clarence Whiteman

THE HERMIT AND US

Mountain highway. They sat in a tight circle, nibbled on some refreshments and shared their stories. It was "our way of catching up as well as recapturing a little of Cold River's spirit when we couldn't be there."

Noah was working at the newly opened children's theme park. "He was dressed as Santa Claus. He insisted on having his picture taken with Stacia because, as he put it, 'of her pretty hair.'"

This gathering would be the trio's last.

"There were not many letters of correspondence between myself and Noah over the next few years because I was building our home at the time. When I received a note (and often a handwritten poem) from him I would answer it as best I could, so you see we seemed to slowly lose track of each other."

When the Conservation Department finally reopened the Adirondack Park after the Big Blow, Clarence and his buddies established a new deer camp in another location. Cold River would never be the same without Noah living upriver.

"I used to buy a package of Noah's 'little back breakers,'" Clarence made known. It was a small act in honor of a man he admired. "I'd tuck them in my pockets until we'd set up camp. Noah always told about how he would set up more and more of them. 'You have to keep after that stuff,' he would counsel us. 'I'm always up against them mice. They're mischief and they're everywhere.'"

As I packed up to leave Clarence Whiteman's home, he pressed a metal film can into my hands. It was his copy of the film he had taken back at Cold River.

"One more thing," he said. "Some people would come up [to Noah] and want to know how to be a hermit. They wasn't so much interested in the land, and the animals, and plants, and so forth, as they wanted to just be a hermit—as if somebody would give 'em a job and pay 'em to sit somewhere and look agreeably curious."

Clarence was always right on the money. Noah never wanted anybody's sympathy when he set off into the woods. He just got sick of civilization.

"I was born and brought up in the woods," he would simply say. "When I was a youngster, I used to chase chipmunks and rabbits."

"I guess Noah just grew into hermiting that way," Clarence concluded.

Chapter 14

The Trials of Youth

Saturday, September 14, 1946
At Beauty Parlor.
A perfect September day. 4 men call
(3 Schenectady and 1 Michigan). I see
Venus 40 times in 3 hours before sundown.
　　　　　—Noah John Rondeau's memorandum

Fred R. Studer was one of the youthful backpackers Noah referenced in his 14 September 1946 entry. In Studer's 1991 interview, he told me an interesting observation he made during his group's end-to-end Northville-Lake Placid trek. "The natives of the Adirondacks had a different outlook on life than the partners in my group." For example, "The average native [of the mountains] couldn't understand why anyone would take their leisure time and climb mountains."

Studer continued his recollection of September 14, 1946:

> *We were lacking many of the conveniences available today. Dried potatoes and dried eggs were unavailable...in short, camping took a lot more planning, ingenuity, effort and so forth than it does now. In like manner I feel sure hermiting then was far more of a challenge than it would be now...*
>
> *We knew very little about Noah John Rondeau. As we approached his place we had no idea of what to expect. We did expect him to be sort of a backwoods, native, Adirondacks type.*

Earlier visitors described the hermit's yard as a "pig pen." It was unjust and false. When Fred Studer and his three college-bound friends approached the entrance to Rondeau's bailiwick, which had become an almost legendary destination in the Adirondacks down through the years, they first spotted the tall wooden teepees on the horizon, then the tattered banner over the spur trail's entry that announced *Welcome to the City.* Iron kettles planted in pansies hung from the center of pole tripods on each side of the proclamation. The man-made beauty on a semi-wooded sand bank aside the edge of a water waste—the flow ground—additionally greeted guests to the municipality. The host extended his typical hospitality. His greeting "had an air of formality." On first reaching his cabin, the men were asked to "sign my guest register."

So imagine the excitement of the four backpackers, raised in an urban environment, when they happened upon Noah just prior to his grand media exposure.

1946. Bill White, Fred Studer, Bill Barzler and Phil Rumbolt. The backpackers talked about their future the entire camping trip. They had an opportunity to make a living in the civilized world or, kidded Fred, "We could become hermits. We might even make a name for ourselves." Courtesy of Fred R. Studer

Their level of anticipation grew as they passed the cut over to Dr. Latimer's camp followed by High Banks, and further upriver, Natural Dam. As they passed over Ouluska Pass brook, "...we knew we would soon be approaching the hermit's domain."

It wasn't long after crossing the logs that spanned Seward Brook outlet as it tumbled into the Cold River near Ouluska Pass lean-to that "...we came upon the entrance to the hermit's place. It was a rather worn side trail curving off to the right and up a hill toward Cold River from the main trail. Large green lettering painted on a canvas streamer stretched between the sapling poles pronounced that this was the doorway to Cold River City. It was eye-catching. It was quite obvious the hermit had gone to some pains to keep this spur trail discernible where it left the N-P trail."

"As we approached his place, we had little idea what to expect. We did expect him to be sort of a backwoods, native, woodsman type. Since it wasn't all that easy to cope with living in the wilds by using what nature

Fred Studer, Bill White, Bill Barzier and Phil Rumbolt said they talked about their future the entire backpacking trip. According to Fred, "We had an opportunity to make a living in the civilized world. Or we could become hermits like Noah. We might even make a name for ourselves! We might do any number of things."
Courtesy of Fred R. Studer

made available, we were very interested in how he did it. Because we had planned, prepared for, and undertaken our two-week trip on the N-P Trail, we had a hands-on feel for the problems of existing away from the amenities of civilization." Observations they were later to make led them to surmise that there was much ingenuity on the hermit's part.

"We were quite taken by the ways he had set himself up to pull through. It showed he was truly a remarkable man."

Rondeau was an inviting host. "He was quite cordial to us." At first he was all business. The party was required to identify themselves and certify their presence by signing a bound roster. Following a charade of formalities, their arrival "necessitated a guided tour of the facilities." His two cabins, half buried in the ground, had signs designating the structures. "One would not only have to *step* down to get into these buildings but also *bend* down. Posted on the door of the Town Hall was a written list of gripes against the New York Conservation Department. In addition, the many teepees had been given names.

"Right from the first face-to-face meeting, Noah did not fit my concept of the native of the Adirondacks," Fred confided. "His signature was written in a flowing Spencerian calligraphy! I didn't think that style handwriting was normal for the typical native of the woods."

The ground around the small cabins was hard and dry. He had bones and skulls hanging on the outside walls. The summer season was almost over. Fred envisioned the bits and pieces of small animals and fish skeletons that lay spread about, with bits of hair and hide attracting bees and bluebottle flies in warmer weather. Noah John extended his usual hospitality, inviting the boys to eat out of his pot and sleep in a wigwam on a downy balsam bed. The foursome, however, declined. They had brought their own food and planned to reach Duck Hole before evening set in.

Noah John extended his usual hospitality, inviting the boys to eat out of his pot an sleep in a wigwam on a downy balsam bed. The foursome, however, declined. They had brought their own food and planned to reach Duck Hole before evening set in.

"Upon completing our rounds, Rondeau disappeared into one of his dog houses [teepees] and brought out a bear skin rug, draping it over a

Resting on the remains of Big Dam, Cold River. *Courtesy of Fred R. Studer*

small hand-fashioned log bench at an outdoor table for us to sit on." He had practiced the same great formality when he asked them to sign his guest register.

I'm sure the reason the hermit experience stands out so clearly in Fred's mind (he said he could still see that old man sitting in his rocker on Cold River Hill) is because his early college days were spent in such a happy, carefree, secure environment. When Fred looked back on his pleasant mid-'40s years, he said it disappointed him to admit those trails of youth are gone forever—not just for him but for most children and young adults growing up now.

Fred and his friends, Bill White, Bill Barzler and Phil Rumbolt, had enjoyed a leisurely month of vacation backpacking "at a dignified pace, enjoying the mountain air, seeing wildlife, and climbing high to sit on bare mountain tops." The electronic media—the Internet and the entire array of desktop and handheld gizmos—with all its benefits and potential for learning, has also stripped children of their innocence and preoccupies people's minds so that they enjoy less physical activity than his generation engaged in when he was in college.

"Today people often grab a day or two of climbing for a quick week-end," Studer said. He grew up in a more stress-free world, but not one wholly innocent of the evils and wickedness in civilization. I think one of the reasons Fred found Noah had so many fans by the 1940s is because The Hermit retained some of this upfront, uncomplicated innocence in his openness to most strangers. The whole make-believe "city" was his play-ground. He had ranged everywhere, investigated every hill, mountain and valley. He knew the terrain backward and forward and offered bushwhack-ing advice when asked. He "gave the impression to welcome anyone who came to visit." At least that was Studer's experience. Rondeau looked as if he "had a wonderful time doing whatever it was he did in camp. We really enjoyed the time he spent with us."

Later, Fred learned from newspaper stories that life was harder for Ron-deau once he moved out of Cold River, but at least he had someone to help him create a delightful resemblance to his former life. Of course he was referring to Smith's offer of his Wilmington Singing Pines Camp.

Today Fred looks back with regret that he did not do more "camera hunting." His photograph album is empty of any snapshots of himself with Noah. It wasn't that he wasn't any good with a camera. He was a young man and could not afford many photos. Life is short and we all have re-grets. Fred never had another chance to return. On the other hand, he did meet Noah the following year at a Sportsmen's "show in New York City. As I recall, he seemed very commercial and not at all like he was in his [former] home."

★ ★ ★

We humans often try to transform ourselves in an attempt to bolster our egos after a perceived failing in everyday life. Psychologists might refer to our actions as coping mechanisms to avoid destructive behavior.

It's a fact we all experience loss and confusing pain in our lives. But what do we do to bring balance? To manage?

Some of us listen to some inner voice that rejects the traditional response. We create an alternative world. Make bold decisions. Experiment with alternative ways of life. Each individual reacts to influences in very different ways. Some move in a direction opposite from what might be expected, or they close down completely.

The hermit was dead serious when he spoke about his trials and tribulations—"Big Business" and "Education." He connected "Big Business" to enslavement, or what he called "industrial slavery." He viewed physical labor as an oppressive yoke. He saw education as an essential part of any human being's life. He recognized that knowledge allows a person flexibility and freedom.

Rondeau often ran off on tangents. The recollections of his friends, Dr. and Mrs. William L. Gregory, help keep the hermit's arguments in focus. Noah told them he ran away from an abusive father (a "taskmaster" might be a more accurate term) at the age of twelve. Rondeau was taken in by a Presbyterian minister in Vermont. "From his years living with the minister, Rondeau picked up his courteous manner. He is the most courteous man we ever met. He's almost Chesterfieldian," said the Gregorys.

Rondeau told his inquisitive visitors that he had come on "Hard Times" as he lit up and began "smoking incessantly" a great meerschaum pipe given to him years ago. The pipe's nickname was "the goose egg" and witnesses said "It goes comfortably with a large bear rug he draped over his chair. Mr. Rondeau is 'in state' when he sits on the 'bear' and holds the 'goose egg.' He looked a true venerable of the mountains. A patriarch among long beards."

He kept up to date on current events. He said he read a variety of dated newspapers and magazines that passers-by brought him and questioned his infrequent visitors about the news of the day. [In those days hiking in the Adirondacks was not anywhere as popular as it is now, particularly in the Cold River region.]

He admitted he had developed a personal philosophy of life: "Nothing is worth doing unless it brings some good and desired return, with interest."

His philosophy could go for war, hunting, reading or woodcutting. Living up in the Adirondacks' most secluded vastness afforded him long periods of time to acquire a somewhat non-technical knowledge of the atomic bomb. "I feel the atomic bomb hastened the end of the war. I've read up a good deal on atomic power, and in a way I was sorry they made an instrument of war out of it. But the way it saved so many of our boys' lives I guess it was a good thing."

Regarding international relations, he was by no means a political isolationist. Nevertheless, Noah believed America was "...too concerned about other countries. Take Russia. I've been reading where some of the folks have been deploring the fact we can't seem to understand Russia. What do we want to understand them for anyways? We can't even speak their language."

He stayed up late to peer at the stars through his homemade telescope, which stood on a birch stump in his front yard, and one of his chief ambitions was to paint the Seward Range. He had never experimented with oil paints but believed he knew the mountains so well that he surely could reproduce them on canvas.

Suspension bridge over Cold River near Shattuck Clearing. *Courtesy of Fred R. Studer*

Fred admitted, "We were a little timid about asking too many questions of a fairly personal nature. The hermit seemed to be genuinely interested in talking to us. I was very impressed at how well read he was and how well he expressed himself. He appeared to be quite learned."

Having peered at the lengthy bookshelf in the Town Hall, Fred shared, "It seemed to me that Mr. Rondeau had quite a collection of books. Surely they helped him to make use of his isolation and to teach himself many things. It wasn't clear where he got the books from, but it was very evident he had the ability to teach himself complicated matters—a talent in itself. He was quite well versed in astronomy and other scientific, political and religious subjects. He conversed quite knowledgeably, and quite effortlessly switched from one topic to another, although he was decidedly opinionated when it came to politics.

"One interesting aspect that really impressed me was that he had retained the ability to see other people's points of view (perhaps not totally) in spite of his isolation."

Scenic Cold River. *Courtesy of Fred R. Studer*

Lots of yards have litter scattered about, and Fred could understand why a place like the hermit's was given to such rumple. An untroubled and often earnest man who never had much money and never seemed to care, Rondeau found comfort in his camp arrangement. "I wish we had climbed down to the river to see the remains of the Big Dam and the small pool he told us he had designed along the side of the river so he was sure of a meal if necessary," Fred wistfully confided, " but we became caught up with his stories. Much to our surprise, he related how a fellow hiker, Robert Hall, who we all knew and who lived just five houses from me in Schenectady, tried bushwhacking down the back side of Couchsachraga Peak a week or two before our arrival. Hall started out in shorts and a shirt, but his clothes were pretty ragged and he was all scraped and torn by the time he reached the hermitage. When later talking to Hall, we were able to ascertain that, in at least one instance, the hermit did not embellish his wild tales."

The fellows figured they spent "...two or more hours with Noah John Rondeau." He inquired about where they were from and listened to Fred's story about his closest wildlife encounter when he was a youngster living in Madison, Wisconsin.

Talk about a fracas. Fred used to pride himself on his stealth "each time I approached the skunk house at the neighborhood zoo without being sprayed"... until one day. Noah laughed at this stranger's story. He knew from experience one can't stand against the force of a skunk's will.

By late afternoon the travelers began nodding to each other. It was time to leave. Never one to turn away friendly folks, the hermit told them, "Come back again." The men knew Noah meant it.

As they hiked upriver along the trail toward their evening's destination, through a mushy swale that skirts the flow and runs past several lumber clearings and distant ponds, they talked of a number of successful, well-off people in their community who had all the money in the world and just as many troubles. "Is the hermit better off?" one traveler asked.

The group had no more than finished discussing how few backpackers traveled the winding Cold River Trail through the valley when they came upon an "older ranger who had set up camp in a large canvas wall tent," Bill White remembered. They halted their advance and exchanged greetings with the state employee. "Welcome," he said, addressing the group. "I'm happy to see someone else in the woods."

His eyes appeared to be following the reactions of the troop. Bill thought he might have been lonely and wanted to talk. Apparently he had not seen anyone in the woods for a couple of weeks. It wasn't long before the topic of conversation centered on the hermit. With a deep-throated chuckle, the ranger shared a recent experience. It seemed that a newsreel company (Bill believes it was Pathe News) arrived at the upper Cold River lean-tos with their cameras and recorders to interview the hermit. They asked the ranger to walk in to the hermit's camp and request that he walk out for an interview. The ranger gave Noah the message but returned alone. "Rondeau told me to let you know he was too old to walk out for such a purpose," he related to the crew.

The cameraman was clever as he turned to the groaning crew members and told them to be patient. "Tell you what," he said to the ranger. "Go back to his camp and offer the old guy twenty-five dollars to walk the six miles up here." The crew was not trying to make more work for the ranger. "For pity sake," the ranger replied, "I'm not the enemy. I don't mind going back. This is the most excitement I've had so far this summer." The ranger did as was asked. To his disbelief, Noah raised an eyebrow and grinned at the offer. Instead of flatly refusing to talk with the news, Noah looked forward to the interview. He not only came out, but outdistanced the ranger on the trip back to the crew's camp!

Bill figured the old hermit didn't mind a little buttering up. "I guess money talks."

That evening the young men sat around a campfire and regaled themselves with recollections of the day's events and an indulgence in a weighty religious discussion, similar to the philosophical conversations they enjoyed with Rondeau.

FRED'S FINAL REMEMBERANCES

A gnawed wooden picnic table in the grassy clearing at the hermitage was heaped with lightweight foodstuffs, while four backpackers and a hermit

Fred crossing Cold River. *Courtesy of Fred R. Studer*

ate peanut butter and jelly sandwiches. "It was our first visit to Cold River City, shared Fred Studer. Bill White, Bill Barzier, and Phil Rumbolt and I had left the ranger's station at Shattuck Clearing with heads swimming with hermit stories." For days during their end-to-end trip on the Northville-Lake Placid Trail, the college freshmen talked about their hands-on outdoor experiences. The hikers didn't figure a man living a full time woods life would have opinions about higher education, politics, and almost any other subject under the sun, but they learned quickly the hermit did. "Noah told us he 'lived in the woods half the time' because he liked it and half the time because 'Hard Times required me to.'"

Fred's backpacking party preparing to start out on their trek. *Courtesy of Fred R. Studer*

Hard Times, reading and *scholarship* were all-important words in Rondeau's vocabulary.

Studer recalled Noah telling them, "There's a multiplicity of brooks on the Panther [Mountain] Range. It's possible a few trout may be found in any of them."

"He said it with an assurance that he knew something about the country. It was also evident he was happy to be living free from the 'distempers of human civilization.' He said there were plenty of examples: hotel fires, icy sidewalks, influenza, airplane crashes, World War, and so forth.

"His manner was courteous and polite. When he addressed us, it was in a soft voice and picturesque. A lack of formal education was evident when he spoke. Yet his phrasing was so unique we found ourselves imitating the jargon when we left camp.

Noah was willing to answer questions about his way of living. He seemed to enjoy having his picture taken.

"Term paper distemper!" Bill White would say after the fellows left the hermitage as they continued their trek. "We thought Noah's lingo so clever that we all began to imitate him in playful banter. We weren't mocking Noah," Fred assured. "We admired and enjoyed his good humor."

Forty-hour work week distemper, someone else would reply. The buddies would nod thoughtfully, their eyes reflecting for a moment to consider all that it meant. Farther along the trail someone else might advance, *Yard work distemper*. Then from someone else's graphic mind would come *Hard Times. Hard Times. My boots are making my feet sore. Yes sir. Hard Times.* The witticisms were all in good fun.

What hard times? someone else quizzed.

We are surely free of hard times.

Noah John is the philosopher, not you, another quipped.

They all nodded in agreement.

The trails of youth had taught them some valuable lessons and rewarded them with a memory they would carry throughout life.

Chapter 15

Youthful Boy Scout Callers

A long-time mountain-dwelling hermit with a long grey beard who stood about five feet two inches and dressed in much-patched clothes and a floppy, green-painted hat is not like any other model a scoutmaster could point his charges to as an example of how to survive. But Noah lived the skills taught in the scouting *Handbook for Boys*—just as he could have written the *Handbook for Hermits*.

For the troops of Boy Scouts who took a walk in the woods to reach the hermitage, most found the long day hike a modest distance even with the weight they packed on their backs. Cold River Hill was not a random destination. The Cold River Valley was not the cultivated urbane orb of paved streets, smelly buses, crowded housing developments, school playgrounds, and city parks. On camporee weekends, scouts usually pitched their tents on the outskirts of such cities in former orchards and on pastureland that substituted for the wilds. Meeting a most curious mountain man must have seemed a novel and worthwhile goal.

Long before Noah's rise to prominence in the media, many scoutmasters from Vermont, Pennsylvania, New York's Capital District, the Southern Tier, central New York and points beyond had learned of Rondeau's digs. Cold River City was a first-hand example of a man's successful attempt to survive in the wilderness.

Scoutmasters might have described a hermit as a person who is usually anti-social for numerous reasons, and becomes isolated by preference. As they led their young charges toward Cold River, they might have qualified that definition, joking "He might even offer you some of his 'Eternity

Tea' or 'Everlasting Stew,' which if made from a blue-jay, might be heartier by leaving a few of the feathers and what-not intact."

The former campers and scouts, now elderly, enjoy their easy chairs and memories of their favorite wild places.

Caution tossed aside, youthful visitors found Noah John "warm and friendly," according to H.P. Donlon's remembrance, "with merriment that was joyous." He entertained his scouting visitors with stories and fiddle music, in a fashion they would almost certainly have found unique.

They also heard Noah's salty commentary about his dislikes and learned about various facets of his life, including his long romance with the Cold River country, starting with his first hunting trip there in 1902. His choice of words was of special interest. Noah was inclined to throw big words into the conversation. Many did nothing for the subject, but considering his lack of formal education, his vocabulary made fascinating listening.

Along with whimsical weather and nature notes and a record of the hermit's daily "doings," he managed to work off steam on most of his pet peeves—the game protectors, politicians, "big fool American business,"

May 1951. Rotary Fair, Malone, N.Y. From Noah's photo album. *Courtesy of Richard J. Smith*

and officialdom in general. No target was too big, as witnessed by some savagely caustic references to Franklin D. Roosevelt.

The hermit's journals record the crowding on dusty Deer and Main Street.

> *August 13, 1941 Wednesday*
> *Cool. Hall of Records. 11 scouts from Vermont camp came. (Come [and] go.) 400 cents [they paid] for guide. Hail Hitler.*

> *July 21, 1944 Friday*
> *Rain last night. Cloudy and showers today. At Town Hall, Cold River. Six Scouts and a Scout Master from Riverdale called. At dusk- castor- 99 fish.*

And in 1945, he spent two summer weeks finalizing the "Ash Ground"—a grave site at the Hermitage—which he hoped would be his final resting place.

> *July 21, 1945 Saturday*
> *Clouds and sunshine. A nice day. At Big Dam. Sam Walls and five scouts called. Fred C. Mc Lelane dropped note twice (looking for plane-lost July 18).*

> *June 23, 1946 Sunday*
> *Beauty Parlor. Nicest Ever June Day. 16 men and boys come, go (Penn. Scouts).*

"Rondeau was a great talker."

"I heard him go on for 45 minutes without any 'an-uhs' and he was interesting in everything he said."

"He was fascinating."

"He played a mean fiddle. He loved to entertain with the violin and join in dancing and other highjinks before the campfire."

"He was an excellent marksman with both rifle and bow and arrow."

These are some of the dozens of comments gleaned from former scouts' stories of their contact with Noah. The scouts who remember meeting

Rondeau had never been so simultaneously impressed and thrilled. "We spent a whole afternoon poking through his buildings," Edward Miller would recall decades later. "I met him in the summer of '46. He seemed quite talkative and friendly. Not my idea of a hermit. The next time I ran into Noah, he had been invited to participate in the Sportsmen's Show in Schenectady. It was in 1947. Post 38 BSA under Erwin H. Miller, sponsored the show."

Edward Miller continued:

I had been active in scouts before the war and on my return from the service I became scoutmaster for a group of crippled children confined in Sunnyview Orthopedic Hospital. We met once a week. I organized activities—mostly games and fun things, since the kids were in casts and bed and traction. When I heard Noah was in town for the Sportsmen's Show, I asked him to come around to the hospital to see the boys, who I figured would be thrilled to see a genuine hermit. He was friendly and outgoing. That gave me the confidence to ask this favor. Noah didn't let me down. At the appointed time I picked him up, [he was] all furs and woods trinkets and he looked the part of a hermit. What excitement! Noah told the kids about Cold River and life in the woods—he probably embellished it a bit and passed around his furs and articles of clothing…The meeting was a complete success! Or so I thought.

Next week I showed up at the hospital to find that the kids had broken out in a mysterious skin infection, and all the boys had their heads shaved. The ward was quarantined until further notice. No more scout meetings for a while. I expressed my sympathy to the head lady and silently walked away. Shortly thereafter my work shift was changed to days and that was the end of the scout troop. I don't know if anyone at the hospital ever understood the cause of the problem, but I never had any doubts, nor did I have the nerve to go back to the scene of the crime…

I do want to emphasize that my recollection does not imply any lack of personal cleanliness on Noah's part. For his appearance at

the hospital, he was dressed in clean woods clothes. If the scouts got
their skin problems from Noah's visit, I suspect it was from the
skins. Of course, the whole episode could have been coincidental to
Noah's visit too.

John Hasenjager recalled the day Noah visited his Boy Scout Camp Borton on Cayuga Lake in 1948. "He asked me what I had to do in order to earn two of my merit badges. My father introduced Noah to me. He talked to me for some five minutes or so. He arrived at camp in the early evening. It was too dark to take pictures. He had to leave early the next morning. I don't think many of us young scouts were up to see him off."

August 19-27, 1949 Friday - Saturday
Cool Atmosphere - Perfect Sun. At Mrs. Rondeau's Kitchenette. Half
the Leaves on Spreading Dogbane are Yellow and Brown. Raccoons
make tracks last night in Kitchenette and they scatter dishes. Two
Scout Masters and 14 Scouts from River Dale at Cold River,
Town Hall and camp. 34 hikers arrive (this week). Half a dozen

Studio photo of Noah. One of several pictures he commissioned. Rondeau sold them at venues he attended including Boy Scout jamborees. *Courtesy of Earle F. Russell*

Deer and 2 Raccoon raise hell all night. Big buck gazes at me near
Artist's Studio- later get Salt and Macaroni at Beauty Parlor.

Noah was always glad to have adult leaders drop by with youngsters from Camp Riverdale on Long Lake. Paul Wollner called to mind that he had "worked as a trip counselor from 1948 to 1952." He took pleasure in "first meeting the hermit on a camp canoe and hiking outing when Rondeau was still living along the Cold River." He felt time spent at the summer camp in the mountains gave the boys an "idea about how to slow down and LIVE." One camper felt he "walked higher for weeks after getting home." No kidding. He sensed something had changed in him after setting foot on a real hermit's doorstep. With his paddling experience and his trek from the outlet of Cold River to Rondeau's, he was "hooked like a trout"—never to live right without at least an annual Adirondack Mountain return. "We had solitude, we saw hardly a soul for days during our time at the hermit's and along the Cold River."

John Hickey was "one of a group of thirteen who visited the hermit at Big Dam in '43 or '44. Noah offered us dinner, but surveying his cooking utensils, we declined." Apparently John, or someone else in his group, felt "Noah's utensils were never washed. They hung on nearby broken branches, covered with grease and flies."

All the youthful visitors recalled the constant sound of the river flowing over what remained of the log dam. The pleasant endless background sounds of nature were locked into their minds and put on hold so that just by concentrating they could once again hear them. As with spring peepers in April and May and crickets in the grass in August, most of nature's sounds are soothing. The former campers and scouts, now elderly, enjoy their easy chairs and memories of their favorite wild places. "I like to think on this kind of thing," Donald "Jack" Anderson shared. He isn't alone.

You can imagine the joyous reunion scene when troops from Camp Riverdale arrived over the years. They came with their own tents and had good food to share. They often stayed a week, chattering about different woodland animals, learning about Noah's marginal yet successful survival effort, investigating the corkscrewing river above the dam, fishing mountain streams and ponds, and climbing mountains. Evenings were spent in the city's yard, with everyone gathered around the outdoor fire pit. The boys listened to delightfully detailed information about the problems of curling a bear's mustache, identifying edible plants, trout-fishing tips, hearing adventure stories of getting by alone in the mountains, and one touching story from Rondeau's childhood of a girl and her doll. Rondeau told the poignant story "simply and to the point." It went like this.

> *To a little girl in the 1800s, a doll, possibly brought to her from Canada, was her only plaything. She treasured it, cared for it, and when she grew too old to play with dolls, she prepared a box, lined it with colorful cloth, and covered it with glass to make a niche. Then she hung it on the wall, a reminder of youth and a decoration for the house.*

The object of the simple story was perhaps to teach a lesson. Compared to the late 1800s, the late 1940s were days of affluence when children had more toys than they could ever play with or appreciate. Perhaps Noah was hoping that his listeners would realize how lucky they were.

Rondeau's fiddle playing was also part of the happy nighttime celebration of being in the company of a real hermit. It didn't take long before the boys' minds were teeming with dizzy dreams in which they were armed with rifles and Bowie knives and Colt revolvers, and were dragging deer and bear.

As host at the hermitage, Noah offered one morning to prepare flapjacks for Riverdale's troops. It didn't take the boys long to take an interest in the hermit's culinary methods. Wielding a large, two-handled frying pan that held about twenty medium-sized pancakes, he wowed the boys by shuffling all the cakes on the surface, flipping the entire contents into the air, and deftly sliding the flat, hot cooking surface under the entire batch, with each landing cooked side up.

"We all stood wide-eyed with mouths agape," reported one scout. They were in awe of this ace woodsman, and even more astonished by Rondeau's batter and the maple syrup on a hot summer day. One of the scouts noticed that several flies had been stirred into the batter. When he pointed it out, the hermit set aside the boy's apprehension with the reassurance that "flies are good for you, like currants you know." Then he poured maple syrup from a ketchup bottle that still "housed some dried ketchup!"

One scout confided to his scoutmaster that he couldn't believe it when the hermit opened a can of vegetables, bent back the lid, wrapped the scout's bandana around the sharp lid and took the time to instruct him as to how to use it as a handle when warming food in a can over the fire. When the contents was heated, Noah stirred his butter knife around the can, loaded the tableware with lima beans, drew it out holding the knife flat side up and proceeded to line the beans up with his fingers "like soldiers on parade," ready to eat each individually.

In short order, the entire assembly was engaged in a primitive, culinary ritual—the eating of food with the blade of their scout jackknives. In a short time, all were talking and laughing and rejoicing in the feeling people often

Noah autographing a picture for a wide-eyed youth. *Courtesy of Richard J. Smith from Noah's photo album*

experience being together outdoors. Rondeau, true to his reputation as a hospitable and entertaining host, patiently answered all questions. His smoothness with children, his warm humor and sharp wit kept the troop lively and in "big laughs" well into the wee hours of the evening.

On another occasion, just before dark, another scoutmaster and three raw recruits accepted the use of a wigwam to sleep in. The boys were unpacking their rucksacks and separating gear. Sleeping bags were not yet in widespread use; those that were available were expensive and beyond ordinary means, so the boys were spreading out their rubberized ground cloths and blanket rolls over old deer grass, pine needles and balsam bough litter that covered the interior of the cone. Suddenly they leaped back, nearly jumped out of their skins, and barely missed falling backwards into the evening campfire that was blazing outside the wigwam opening. Noah was amused as he watched the antics from his rocking chair by the open fire. The meat wigwam, which hadn't been used in a year, was full of snakes. When disturbed, some slithered out between the poles around the cone base. The scouts joined Noah around the fire to give the rest of the snakes ample time to make their way into the forest. Upon deeming it safe enough to go back into the shelter, the boys scrutinized every inch as they "cleaned house." Then Noah watched the crew do a quirky thing. They opened a bag of salt and spread it around the outside perimeter of the wigwam. "Curious thing," he remarked about the salting, as he tended a well-filled iron pot of stew that hung over a bed of coals. Enthusiastically, the scouts shared that the information had been gleaned from an old woodcraft book. "Interesting," was the only comment Noah made about the act.

He had a slightly different attitude toward the boys' snake prevention. Much later, with a twinkle in his eye but with a certain degree of seriousness, he proclaimed, "Given the circumstances, the scouts showed an interest in applying what they had previously learned. 'Course they practiced imperfect information, yet they reflected some intellectualism. I don't know what book taught snake chasing with salt, but it sure wasn't a wilderness academic text."

According to Scoutmaster Miller, once Noah treated his scouts to a woodcraft experience.

Come morning, following a late breakfast, the hermit and scouts located a white ash log and carried it down to the river where it would soak in the pool below Big Dam. Later in the week, they peeled the outer bark off the water-soaked log and rolled it to ensure the entire surface was well pounded. The purpose of the pounding was to loosen the fibers between each growth ring—the yearly cambium layer put on by a tree for every season it lives. Next, a sharp knife was used to score the desired width of strips, followed by gentle pounding that would help release each splint as someone lifted and pulled each strip off the log's surface. By carefully following Noah's instructions, each scout left that week with a souvenir, a miniature pack basket, woven by their own efforts, a memento of their time with the Cold River hermit.

As our interview drew to a close, Erwin shook his head in wonder, then looked for a moment as if he had another thought. He then shook his head again confidently, and started a last recollection.

"In the late 1940s my Explorer Post was looking at projects, fund raisers, for a log cabin meeting place we planned to build. Some of our committee had visited Noah at Cold River and thought it would be a hoot to see an old friend at New York City's Madison Square Garden for the February 1947 Sportsmen's Show.

"We could not help to notice how Noah's lifestyle and social status had taken a considerable turn because of that show. Newspapers heralded his airlift from his wilderness hermitage by helicopter. Rondeau was set up in a simulated forest environment at the Garden. He turned out to be the show's main attraction. Although paid a $100 fee for his appearance, the enterprising hermit placed his large pack basket at the edge of the display into which the crowds could contribute coins and bills toward a poor hermit's well-being. He also sold pictures of himself (for which he paid one-half cent each) for twenty-five cents apiece, fifty cents if autographed. He loved signing his name. We heard his ire, though,

Oscar Burguiere's father received this special Christmas offering from Santa Noah, taken when he worked at the North Pole in Wilmington, N.Y. *From Noah's photo album.*
Courtesy of Richard J. Smith

when he talked about the light-fingered gentry who occasionally made off with one of his photos at the show.

"It was then we decided that it would be a great experience for our explorers to run such a show in Burnt Hills. We started organizing the show months in advance. We requested the Conservation Department to make Noah available for our local show. They did so and he stayed at my home for two nights.

"We had a great exhibition with all the attractions expected at an outdoor extravaganza. My daughter was about three years old at the time and she sat on Noah's lap in a rocking chair. His long beard fascinated her and he seemed to enjoy entertaining her. He was soft-spoken and very clean—not a rough and gruff backwoods creature. His language proved he had some education and enjoyed literature. My wife remembers our daughter believing that he was a Santa Claus. He was a salesman and loved to push his photographs, etc. He enjoyed our conventional breakfast.

"The following year, 1948, we learned Noah received five hundred dollars for appearing in Boston's Sportsmen's and accordingly jumped his picture rates to fifty cents and a dollar."

And with that last recollection, Erwin H. Miller, former Scoutmaster and Explorer advisor, found himself heading for Cold River Hill in his mind, listening to the soft rushing waters of Cold River, to the crackle of a campfire ringed with delighted scouts, and perhaps to the haunting sound of an old hermit's fiddle.

Noah's Secret Code.

"How did you happen to become a newspaperman?" —NJR's redirect *when a group of reporters and photographers from* The Knickerbocker News *asked how Noah happened to become a hermit.*

Chapter 16

What I Remember About Noah

In 1991, Stephen Klein Jr. wrote about his first meeting with the hermit and a gesture of kindness.

> *"I've admired Noah ever since I shook hands with him in New York City when they had his set-up in the Sports Show in 1947. I was 17 years old then. Me and two of my friends went to the Grand Central Palace. We had to wait in line [to see the hermit]. I...got his autograph on the show program..."*

The next summer Klein visited Rondeau at Cold River. Forty-two years later, Klein duplicated that trip twice for the express purpose of commemorating his idol.

> *"...I hiked back twice that year [to Rondeau's site] in one day. Each time I took my boat to Plumley's Landing on Long Lake. From there I hoofed it over the N.P trail. It was eleven miles one way. I hiked 22 miles in 10 hours ... There wasn't much left there from when I first dropped in on the hermit. I saw the sign needed replacing...so I returned with a handmade one with the type engraved into the wood and then filled in with paint...I go to the [Adirondack] museum every year to see Noah's display..."*

John Hickey of Burnt Hills remembered Rondeau after first seeing him at Cold River, then at a Sportsmen's Show, and then much later in the hospital.

"…I was one of a group of thirteen who visited the 'hermit' at his camp at Big Dam on the Cold River in '43 or '44. He offered us dinner, but surveying his cooking utensils, we declined.

"His housekeeping, or lack of it, was apparent…the cooking utensils apparently were never washed. They hung on nearby broken branches, covered with grease and flies…

"The last time I met Noah John was in the Lake Placid Hospital, where my mother-in-law was also a patient. His appearance was markedly different—clean and combed. He gave each of my children an autograph—in a very fine copper-plate script.

"I still have an old hand-forged ax head I salvaged from the gravel bank at the base of the old dam structure…I should donate it to the Adirondack museum…"

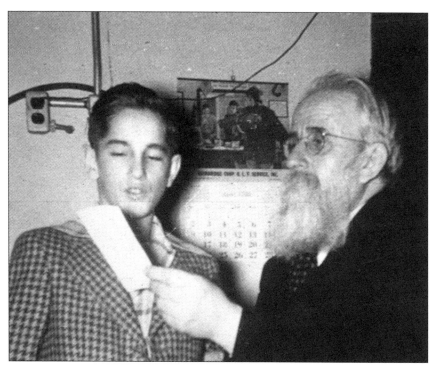

Young and old alike enjoyed meeting Noah. Stephen Klein Jr. said, "I used to beach my boat at Plumley's Landing, hike along the N-P Trail to Cold River Hill and return to my boat all in one day—22 miles in 10 hours." *From Noah's photo album.*
Courtesy of Richard J. Smith

Noah John Rondeau. 1946. *Courtesy of John M. Harmes*

Richard Benson's family lived next door to Clayt Seagers. The Seagers boys, Tom and Murray, were chums with Richard. Their father wrote the blockbuster "The Hermit of Cold River" article that appeared in the October-November 1946 New York State *Conservationist*. Benson wrote:

"…Between listening to Mr. Seagers's [outdoor] stories and my incredulousness when I read the breaking news in the *Knickerbocker News* that a hermit had been discovered in the wilds of the Adirondacks…I was tremendously impressed by the discovery of Noah, and what a name—Noah—Biblical in nature and certainly of visage. I can still picture the photo of his Cold River site…and my meeting him in either the Washington or New Scotland Avenue armory. I can't recall which it was.

"I was ecstatic. My visualization of a hermit included an individual whose hair was greasy and tangled, whose beard was huge and unkempt, whose fingernails were incredibly long and dirt-encrusted, whose clothes were fashioned from animal skins, whose ability to communicate was minimal, and whose aroma would prompt one to stay upwind.

"Needless to say, my father and I…[met a much different figure]. Two impressions remain after all these years: Noah was clean and he was very articulate! I cannot recall the timbre of his voice, but I vividly recall how shiny he was, and think I remember how soft-spoken he was as he responded to the questions hurled at him. I was tremendously impressed that the man had lived quite comfortably on the Cold River. I was also struck by the tragedy of his 'discovery,' and this tragedy was evident to an adolescent. I really felt very sorry for him, for I had received the distinct impression that he had lost control of his life and that if he ever returned to the Cold River he would never regain the beauty of what he had experienced…"

Benson, who I think is the best overall representative witness, was talking about a feeling he sensed behind performer Noah's eyes. He knew Rondeau had lived his life in the backcountry. The famed Cold River hermit's period in the limelight just didn't feel right. Benson tried to explain that the amount of time it took Noah to feel acclimated to the Outside gave him the feeling that Noah John's real life was still in Cold River, but he was no longer there. He said that from what he saw and felt, Rondeau had undergone an extreme conversion. Noah John Rondeau, a proud man, surely felt his disorientation increase because he was now performing for the public and depending on income from show promoters and donations that spectators left him. Once a survivalist who had always managed to earn his own way, he was now society's stepchild.

In some ways Benson was not wrong.

Noah John's success at Sportsmen's Shows brought him offers to attend future expositions. Invitations to speak about living in the wilderness also poured in from various clubs, organizations and groups.

Perhaps the outside world provided a good deal of fun for an old hermit as well as an attractive purse for his effort. Surely the numerous clippings pasted in his scrapbook testify he had many engagements. But Richard Smith would have agreed with Richard Benson that Noah did change. He determined that had happened the day Noah asked him if he would please fashion him a briefcase (of metal) to "securely hold materials for my lectures." Smith also pointed out that Noah "spent hours improving his display before each new show."

The deserted Town Hall. Winter 1961–62. *Courtesy of Peggy and Wayne Byrne*

THE BYRNES REMEMBER "NOEY"

"Noah definitely kept himself busy," Peggy Byrne remembered during the first of several interviews I had with her and her husband, Wayne. "After Noey came out of the woods we would have him come to visit us in Platts-burgh. He would address the local chapter of the Adirondack Mountain Club and other groups—this was after 1947—after the Conservation Department took him out of the woods in the helicopter [to attend the February Sportsmen's Show in New York City]. He had a change of life once he was lifted out of the Cold River country. He began to see what fun it was talking to all those people. The vision of a quiet little suspicious hermit was baloney to begin with. This man was just gregarious enough so that he had a tremendous sense of drama. You've seen his handwriting. He had a huge idea of being center stage all the time...even though he lived alone [in the mountains] he was center stage for the birds and animals and anything else. He WAS the Mayor of Cold River, just as he was center stage when he went to Sportsmen's Shows, where he sat mending snowshoes and whittling sticks near a pseudo replica of his little cabin, dressed in deerskins and smelling of bear grease...He was not a modest, quiet little hermit. He was an actor... He became famous overnight."

In May, 1961, Noah promised Peggy he would loan her all his journals just as soon as he gathered them together. Peg was working on an article about Noah's early feud with Game Protector Earl Vosburgh and her father's involvement in it, but she also had made arrangements with Noah to act as his official biographer. [Peggy never found the time to write the life of Noah John Rondeau that the two had planned.]

Had Peggy written a biography about her old friend, it would have included remembrances that had never appeared in print. She said, "Noey was enthusiastic about the prospect of my writing projects." She shared a letter he had written her in May 1961. The correspondence was chatty and ordinary, ending with "...come anytime next week. Stay as long as you wish. I'll be hunting up my albums, scrapbooks and etc." To guarantee she didn't make a wrong turn, he even enclosed a hand drawn map "so I wouldn't get lost."

Here are a few examples of the memorabilia Wayne and Peggy shared with me. Wayne recalls that when…

> Noah would do a show for an organization he would talk about his observations there at Cold River country, his trapline, how he'd get along until spring. In the spring the birds would come back, that type of thing. It was all good material for Peggy's book…and he entertained a lot of questions. …He certainly surfaced as a luminary.

Wayne and Peggy Byrnes' recollections continue:

> He would probably not be as well received today. Perhaps people are too sophisticated. He wouldn't be a surprise anymore. We would have a Downtown Day or Rondeau Day in Plattsburgh. Anyway, he would sign autographs. He'd walk down Main Street and be here at 10:05 a.m. and sign autographs and maybe the merchant would sell an extra shirt or something like that. The crowd really followed him because he was so different. He looked so little in his shiny black suit and his rounded out felt hat. We fed him and housed him when he came to town. The town didn't pay him.
>
> He never ate too much; he was too frugal. He thought that it was terribly wasteful that I would make him a huge stack of pancakes— allowing the excess to go uneaten…250 pounds of groceries is all the food he bought for all year—that's not too much. He told me he got a 50-pound bag of flour and sugar and whatever he could carry since he only came out once a year with his beaver skins…

Wayne Byrne recalled a story that I found interesting for two reasons. First, Peggy read me the woe-is-me letter Rondeau wrote Mr. Inverarity on April 28, 1962, having to do with his problems with the Essex County welfare department and the $228.70 rifle he bought. Next, Wayne filled me in with additional background.

...when Noah came to Plattsburgh that year...we were in the gun business along with other things. In fact we sold him that gun that he talks about in the letter.

The other thing he wanted when he came to town was a new felt hat—this was during his Sportsmen's Show era. I would take him into a men's clothing store, a haberdashery, it had to be a place where I knew he could get the best bargain and, of course, men's hats were big deals in those days. He wanted a good felt hat, and to test it he would get hold of the hat and push from the bottom up and made it look almost like an Abe Lincoln hat, straight up like that. In that way he pushed the crease out of the hat, leaving it completely round. Then he'd put it on top of his head and look at himself in the mirror and try to decide whether he would take the light gray one or the dark gray one. I was right by his side and I recall him saying he wanted a very good hat because that was the thing to have then. And if there was not a good hat, one was not worth buying. I was always amazed that after paying a good price for the hat, he would punch the crease out of it. Some things he was frugal about but when it came to his hat he would pay top dollar.

"There were several standing wigwams the winter we snowshoed back to Cold River Hill. Wayne propped up one of Noah's notched poles, what he called premeditated firewood." —Peggy Byrne. *Courtesy of Peggy and Wayne Byrne*

Chapter 17

In Edwin Reid's Footsteps

My mental tape recorder played back Rondeau's words on the first morning of a planned three-day backpacking trip in to Cold River valley, following my reading of a fellow author's visit to the same destination point. The commentary on the hermit's character had been written from notes Edwin A. Reid had made decades earlier. Once retired from New York State's Conservation Department, Reid became a local self-published writer, or "a dedicated woodsman of the Adirondacks," as he called himself in lectures.

Back in the late 1960s and early 1970s, Reid was working as a forest ranger. The Cold River country was part of his district. It was a part of his job to make sure the site of Rondeau's hermitage was marked with an appropriate New York State historical marker. The wooden sign informed hikers of the exact site and provided a brief historical significance.

Ed, authored several small books he called "Adirondack Reidings." Following are his commentaries about a trip he took to visit the hermit of Cold River when he was a teenager.

"September 15, 1949, was my first visit to the hermitage of Noah John Rondeau...It is one of my most interesting Adirondack memories. The small swamp maples were afire on this chilly fall-like...day. I wore an army field jacket and my companion, Jack Andrews, a heavy sweater, though we had hiked several miles with packs to get there.

"We reached Rondeau's clearing high on a bluff upriver above the Big Eddy and High Banks that afternoon and passed under one of his entrance teepees. I felt as if I had passed into another time. Before us stood what appeared to be an ancient, little village of small log structures, some close to the ground and others pointed skyward like the many-pole wigwams, or 'teepees.'"

Ed described it as "an enchanting scene." At first glance he thought they saw "no sign of recent human habitation scattered about. The weathered logs blended perfectly with this wild land." He has never forgotten the scene or the feeling he drew from the rustic setting. "Here," he murmured to himself, "a humble man has lived in peace with the world about him for many years. How did he do it, and why?"

He called out from the entrance, "Hello?" No one was in sight.

Reid questioned whether they had arrived only to find the hermit not at home. Then he caught "a long, snaky column of smoke [that] reached upward from one of the cabin's chimney pipes." At the same time, he wondered aloud to Jack if the hermit would mind an "unannounced intrusion, and if he did, would he bolt from his hut and fire a few shots to drive us away? Were we trespassers of his domain? We took the chance anyway, counting on this possibility as being improbable." He assumed Noah was "in this little hut; I wanted to meet this hermit. I wanted to see what kind of person could live in such an austere, people-less land without the support of society in its many forms at his front door."

Reid's companion did not feel the magnetism that Ed did. "My friend, Jack, was rather lukewarm about visiting Rondeau, if I remember correctly. He had come along for a hike and not for an interview with a hermit." For Ed, however, meeting and talking with Rondeau was one of the two reasons for making this trip. The companions were also planning on climbing several of the major peaks in the area. They planned to make camp at the Duck Hole, six miles to the east, their destination that day.

No words can easily recreate that soul-renewing time for Ed. "Over the doorway of the tiny building puffing smoke from its chimney, a sign read Town Hall. So, the hermit is a politician and a frustrated one at that who resides at the seat of his democratic government of one," he gambled. "I bent forward and tapped politely on the door. No response. I waited. Should I knock again? Then the door opened slowly with a slight squeak. Instantly, the doorway transformed into another chimney from which a cloud of white smoke rushed for freedom." As the wood smoke gushed out from inside the log building, a foggy figure "emerged" in the opening, where moments before an old-fashioned plank entrance door had held the dry heat and smoke inside. Perhaps Ed could have described this materialization as bringing ecstasy or joy into his life. It was, he wrote, "a bearded, little man wearing a heavy wool sweater. He immediately greeted us in a high pitched but gentle voice."

This could have been the low point of the young men's trek, but for Ed it was the beginning of a connection with a true Adirondack character with whom he had longed to connect. "With a wave of his arm, he invited us to join him inside. [Rondeau] quickly realized, however, that the thick smoke [that continued to bellow from the wood fire] was too much for his visitors, so he stepped outside to continue his salutations. You might say I permanently fell in love with the little old hermit right there—could it have been any other way?—for he treated us like dear friends who had just dropped by to share a few moments with him."

The hermit was humble and generous in welcoming the strangers. He "was cooking when I knocked," Ed said, "so as the smoke thinned I gladly accepted his invitation to join him inside. I could not resist the opportunity to sit with this rugged [individual], this man of the wilds. Such a man is one out of many millions." Ed was more than willing to accept some private time with Noah. He thought it would give him time to learn about how the hermit felt about living in the wilds, maybe learn about the environment, and the man's years alone in nature. "On the other hand, Jack would have nothing to do with sitting in the smoky hut, hermit or no hermit." Jack preferred to take a rest break outside, eat a snack, and circle around the village while his buddy, touched with joy, bent low and entered the tiny cabin.

"As I sat on the low bunk, Rondeau attended to cooking his meal. Now and then he checked food cans resting on hot coals in an open, cut-down oil drum about a foot high and imbedded in the ground in the corner near the door." How," Ed wondered, "could a man live like this from day to day and year after year?"

Ed was filled with curiosity and happiness—two of humanity's most precious gifts. "I'll never forget the can of corn niblets. He opened the can, bent back the lid to use as a handle, and placed it over the coals. When it was heated up [and began to gently boil], Rondeau invited me to share [the vegetable]... I took a spoonful or so just to complete this primitive, culinary ritual...of sharing food." Rondeau had not lost contact with food and where it came from. Ancient Ayurvedic philosophy teaches the importance of touching food and forming a spiritual bond with it. That image remained with Ed over a lifetime. "And so there we sat [side by side] on his bunk eating corn niblets out of a can." And to boot, the smell of the cabin's interior, the personal gesture of friendship, and the offering of surely hard-earned food always came back. "A hospitable and entertaining hermit, was he."

Sharing time with a legend was fascinating. "In the short time we were together, we had a lot of big laughs in that tiny hut. My open enthusiasm must have entertained him, for he patiently answered all my questions with gentleness and humor and a few sparks of wit thrown in to keep things lively."

The longer the old man talked to the young man, the closer Ed was drawn to Noah. I liken it to dropping a pebble in a quiet pond. The circle starts small but continues to ripple out from the center as it makes wider circles. The hermit of Cold River was having a similar effect on Edwin.

"...Rondeau...invited us to stay for supper. He would prepare something special. We could even stay for the night in his guest teepee where there was a big bed of hay. That we did not accept this generous invitation has always been one of my lasting regrets. Had I been alone, I would have stayed and probably for more than one night, had the invitation been so extended."

Noah pressed Ed to get Jack to come into the smoky cabin. "I knew Jack, and I knew he would stay outside. I think Rondeau realized that if my companion did not join us, I would soon have to leave and he did not want this to happen just yet. We were having too good a time. Did he see me as a kindred spirit? ...Our conversation rolled from one topic to another."

For example, Rondeau explained how he felt when he first started his wilderness journey.

"When you're young, you've got ambition on something, and my ambition was good, but it was too good to succeed under the

Washing dishes. Noah's legendary tales of the exploits of the "Clan of Knaw-It-Runabout-Us"—pesky field mice that inhabited the wigwams and cabins—were a favorite topic to share with guests. *Courtesy of Dr. Adolph G. Dittmar, Jr.*

circumstances. That was the trouble. I done painting, and then I could do carpenter work pretty well in time and some masonry work, and then I was a good barber at one time, but a barber is like music, no matter how good you get, if you drop out of it for four or five years, you've just about got to start over again."

He was about thirty years old when he decided to go back into the woods to live as a hermit.

"Of course before that, in the fall, I'd get me some supplies, and I'd hire a man with a little Ford car to take me up in the woods, and I'd guide in time. At the same time I drifted to Axton or Coreys in there, and from there I drifted to Cold River. Well, it didn't take very long, and I knew the woods well enough, even in them back sections to take [fishing and hunting] parties in there."

Ed knew the isolated spot the hermit chose to put down new roots was getting into the heart of the wilderness. Noah shared that view about the country.

"Yes, as much as you can in New York State. And it pays to go there if parties think that; of course some parties come there, they drink a little liquor at the hotels, and finally they buy a deer from a guide and go home."

Both of the men laughed at that observation. As natives of the mountains, they knew from experience that a number of city sportsmen found the challenges of physically pushing back into the wilds as difficult as solving a puzzle that had a thousand pieces. It doesn't always go together that easily. Ed continued on with his standout memories of a hermit and his canvas-roofed cabin in the mountains.

"I thought, maybe, it was just a matter of conversational exercise, a letting loose after not seeing anyone for a number of days, for Rondeau was not a hermit out to avoid all contact with people. A taciturn hermit, he was not.

"Rondeau might even be labeled the talking hermit. Yes, he loved to talk, but on his own grounds and about what he wanted to talk about, such as his life as a hermit. After Bill Petty shuttled him out to the world as a bona fide Adirondack hermit, he spoke to small clubs and groups or to thousands and even millions when he talked on radio's 'We the People' program."

"In the woods," Ed presumed, "Rondeau was a good neighbor, if you were not one of the law who harassed him for years, and made fools of themselves doing it. 'What's the use of being a hermit if you don't meet a lot of people?' was Rondeau's stated attitude. Maybe this was what he enjoyed most about his lifestyle. He knew he was different and even special in his own way and people would seek him out for this reason.

"As we talked I thought of the many derogatory terms used to describe the way he lived. Terms such as lazy, and crazy, and dirty—all relative terms because people tend to compare another's ways with their own and in so doing, close their eyes to individuality and uniqueness if it does not fit their code. Primitive self-reliance means nothing. On the other hand, how many would talk so openly and intelligently to a stranger as he did? Hermiting, no doubt, taught Rondeau many vital things about himself and people. For one thing, he did not force his ways on anyone and expected the same from others."

Other visitors to Noah's camp had found the proprietor of the hermitage to be "a loquacious, friendly little man," and now Ed found himself many long miles from the nearest town, laying between the Seward Mountain and Santanoni Mountain ranges. It was about (and still is) as wild a section as you can find anywhere in the Adirondacks. He was seated face to face with the practicing, real life hermit who had charmed so many others.

And Reid was just as much taken as those others with this man who turned from society and walked into voluntary exile. In Ed's growing years, it had been common for him to relate to outdoor stories. He had been raised in the mountains. He saw the Adirondacks as a special place. He also valued the philosophy of Henry David Thoreau.

"From my middle teenage years, I had self-Thoreauized myself—so now I needed a little real-life Rondeauizing to give balance to the bookish ideas as to what a hermit is really like in the wilds. Rondeau was a primitive Thoreau, a Thoreau gone to the wilderness instead of Walden Pond."

"With this in mind, I could not help but bring up the subject of *Walden* and its author, Henry David Thoreau. Rondeau said he had read Thoreau but did not think much of him as a hermit. Then, in a short diatribe, he blasted the sage of Walden Pond. To a young disciple of Thoreau, this was embarrassing and unnerving. Though his acid criticisms seemed unjust, I listened. 'You call Thoreau a hermit,' barked Noah, 'when he spent less than two years at Walden Pond and walked into town almost every day to see his folks. He may be the most talked-about hermit, but to me he was a phony.'"

Noah admitted to reading quite a bit. "Back here I would take a kind of course, like something—astronomy, religion, philosophy or something like that just on my own authority. I'd get a few good books and when I'd get through with it, I'd know more than when I started."

Seeking seclusion from the rest of the world changed him. He developed an increasing distaste for civilization in general. "I got so I hated the most of the government, and a lot of it I didn't get over and I don't want to. I see it that way. There's too much pressure and too much put on. You know what the taxes are now, and they keep taxing it so that now it's no better than it was fifty or sixty years ago when I was a boy when people worked for ten to fifteen cents per hour."

Noah drew a "line of demarcation" between the government and people. He didn't try to offend people "for nothing. ...maybe in error [he did] as much as anyone else. But the way it is, there's so many of them. There's a hundred that could be picked out that they all see that the other fellow is wrong and themselves generally right."

The men's conversation shifted, and turned, and returned to a familiar subject throughout their confab.

Ed said, "I considered Noah's words but did not know if they had anything to do with Thoreau. If people considered him a worthy hermit, that was one thing, but the fact is Walden was a part of Thoreau's deliberate experiment to put transcendental theories into a life form and he did it. Noah had a firm and narrow concept as to what made a hermit authentic. Evidently, it was not what he [Thoreau] accomplished, but how long he stayed. So, Thoreau was verbally excluded from his fraternity of hermits.

Nor would he give him any credit for sublimating the solitary life. His fiery criticism of the 19th century sage assured me, however, that Noah was probably one of Thoreau's most unusual and most avid readers.

"In my mind, I began comparing the two hermits. Both were of French descent. Both were 'of short stature, firmly built, of light complexion with strong, serious...eyes and a grave aspect,' and each had a 'face covered in late years with a becoming beard.' Such was Merson's description of Thoreau. How well it fit Rondeau—except that his eyes were brown and Thoreau's blue. Maybe Noah had a less 'grave aspect' than Henry and he was probably a more jovial fellow.

"Neither of the hermits ever married. It is said...Thoreau gave it some thought but then turned his back on it."

Noah said, more than once, he had no room for marriage. I'm "too busy living alone in the woods all alone. So I never got married."

If truth be told, when pressed about any thoughts of finding someone to share his solitary life, he owned that when some female mountain climbers did begin to come along the trail he was in his fifties and figured there was "no hope."

"At the time of my visit with Rondeau there was talk around Long Lake about his interest in a spry old gal, though nothing came of it. The lady just laughed it off."

Edwin's thoughts swung back to comparing Thoreau and Rondeau. "Both hermits were good with their hands in repairing and building things. This basic skill of self-reliance appears to be one of the prime requirements for a successful hermit.

"As far as formal education went, Rondeau, an elementary school drop-out, had very little. On the other hand, Thoreau grew up in an atmosphere of intellectualism, in close contact with such great minds as Ralph Waldo Emerson.

"Talking about Thoreau with a real, live hermit deep in the Adirondack wilderness was a great experience. There could not have been a better classroom for such a discussion. In this environment, however, Thoreau seemed at a terrible disadvantage, not only because he could not represent himself, but because he seemed tame and academic, and not the man of the wilderness often depicted in books by his modern-day admirers, but a man of the gentle, pastoral scene.

"In his own right, Rondeau was a frustrated intellectual. He thought about life beyond himself. He looked to the sky and the stars, to nature and the woods, to books, and to people to whom he talked of many things. For example, when he finished with Thoreau he moved on to Darwin's Theory of Evolution. I had no doubt that somewhere in one of his little huts was a worn copy of *The Origin of the Species*. All I remember, however, is that we dealt with the subject for sometime. I concluded Rondeau was definitely a disciple of Darwin, whom he had enshrined in his mind.

"From Darwin, he took on Christianity with considerable skepticism. 'All this talk about Jesus Christ is a lot of nonsense. He was just a man.' Anti-Semitic sentiments were also expressed. 'Who wants to go to Heaven just to sit on a cloud and look at a Jew?' This sarcastic remark I'll never forget. His apparent bitterness disappointed me. Did not the wilderness have a sweetening effect on those who loved it? Was it real or put on for effect? Was he too long in the wilderness? Maybe.

"Can a cynic have a twinkle in his eye and still be serious?" Ed asked, and then quickly answered. "Rondeau did. You never knew exactly where he was on certain subjects. Was he merely tossing verbal jabs to see what kind of reaction he might get? Even friendly hikers who often left him miscellaneous gifts and food staples were not spared. 'All they care about is climbing a lot of mountains. They get on top, look around, gulp down a chocolate bar and head for the next one. They do it so they can join a special club. They think they can learn to know the mountains with candy bar snacks.' A typical attitude, perhaps, for a hermit who believed in long association with an area before claiming it as country you know like the palm of your hand."

Seated in the small, snug cabin made partly of logs, partly of rough sawn boards Noah salvaged from a deserted lumber shanty, Ed thought of his buddy waiting in an adjacent wigwam that provided a camping place for hikers, fishermen, and hunters who came this way and wanted to bed down on the bluff above Cold River. Jack was no doubt studying the pole structures and had discovered they served as Rondeau's woodpiles, as Ed was gearing up to learn a few things that were still on his mind.

"Now it was my turn to inquire about Rondeau's writings. He certainly had ample enough opportunity to give Thoreau some stiff competition in the literary-hermit field—if he wanted to work at it. Rondeau claimed he made almost daily entries in his diary. I was dismayed when he told me that much of his writings were in coded hieroglyphics.

"Next, Rondeau brought out one of his coded books. I looked at it and wondered why anyone would spend so much time writing something no one else could decipher unless it was to describe the location of a hidden treasure. So I asked what the purpose of writing in code was if its value dies with its creator. 'It's so no one else can read it,' was Rondeau's curt reply. Evidently he did not think it an onerous and senseless way of keeping things to himself. Maybe they were not worth reading. On the other hand, maybe they were directions to cached traps and overnight camps, great fishing holes, set locations for taking fur bearers or special deer hunting watches. Maybe, it was just a game he was playing with people so they could always have something to talk about. He also mentioned that he was working on his autobiography. Of course, he would want others to read his autobiography, so it would not be coded. That he would produce a finished literary work of any kind in this primitive environment would be highly commendable, I thought.

"Twenty years after my visit, part of Rondeau's literary legacy became known to the world when Maitland DeSormo of Saranac Lake published the book *Noah John Rondeau, Adirondack Hermit*. The book contains Rondeau's "Recollections of Sixty Years," excerpts from his journals, and some of his colorful poems, all more or less untouched to preserve the rustic flavor of the self-educated man. I promptly bought one. It is still one of the best-selling Adirondack books about a genuine lover of the wilderness.

Before leaving the hermitage, Rondeau gave us a final tour of his tiny municipality in the wilderness. The many bones and skulls hanging from buildings or laying on the ground he identified as those of deer and bear and various fur bearers. Unlike Thoreau, this hermit was a hunter and trapper, a good rifle shot and something of a bowman who crafted his own bow and arrows. Thoreau, however, had a good eye for finding ancient arrowheads on his many walks."

Noah's method of drying firewood stacked into wigwams added to Cold River Hill's mystique. Each mass had a name: Beauty Parlor, Mrs. Rondeau's Kitchenette, Meat Wigwam, Pyramid of Giza, Summer Wigwam. *Courtesy of Peggy and Wayne Byrne*

When the teenagers were guided to the door of the Hall of Records, Noah gave the fellows "a glimpse of his many diaries, coded manuscript, and other items. He opened a large ledger book which he requested us to sign. From the many entries it appeared this was hardly a lonely hermit at certain periods of the year. 'Why not stay for the night, boys?' asked Noah as we took one more look at his guest house teepee.

"As we stood by the Town Hall preparing for our leave, we took a few pictures to document our visit. I also asked the hermit to sign a page of a tree identification book where I had opened to a sketch and write-up on red maple. He cheerfully agreed without hesitation and promptly disappeared into his hut for his 'special pen and ink.' On his return, he took the book in his hand, and sprawled his sweeping, artistic signature across the page. In addition to his signature, he stated who he was, 'Adirondack Hermit,' as if it were his trademark, and his alone, which he was proud to bear; and lastly, he dated it. Another perfect document of proof. Apparently Noah was glad to give his signature, for though it cost him nothing, he knew it would be held as a precious gift to many receivers."

Ed, like many other hikers, liked the friendly, bearded hermit. He was proud of the pictures he snapped and the page in his tree identification book that Noah signed. They were reminders he would carry home to show his friends.

"Finally, we shook hands with the hermit, said good-bye and quickly left. As Jack and I walked briskly down the trail, I looked back for an instant as Rondeau waved and then dipped forward to enter his low hut and disappear in a gray cloud of smoke.

"Now, at an accelerated pace, we turned our attention to getting as close as possible to the truck trail east of Mountain Pond before dark—a distance of several miles. Though we made it to the Duck Hole lean-to, there was some fumbling in the dark. All the way, however, I wondered why I had left the old whiskered hermit. My only consolation was that we would return in a few days by the same trail to visit with Rondeau again.

"On the day of our return, however, Noah was nowhere in sight. Where was he? His Hall of Records, the building where he kept his keepsakes, such as his violin, pipes, books, and manuscripts was padlocked. Had he gone to the outside world, or was this just the way he left things in any absence from the hermitage? Without him, the site was just another lonely clearing in the woods. The place even had a kind of spookiness about it. We loitered around, hoping the hermit would eventually show. We relaxed and ate a late lunch near the edge of the high bluff overlooking the ruins of the old dam. We dallied as long as we dared to and still make a leisurely trip back to the Ouluska Pass lean-to.

"The next day, on our way back to the cached canoe, we stopped at the skillfully constructed log cabin ranger headquarters that blended so well with the scene at Shattuck Clearing. I wanted to chat with Lou Russell to let him know we were on our way out. Russell was not a stranger to me, for I had visited here before and even shared a meal of beans and hot dogs with him.

"'Well, how did your visit with Rondeau go?' he asked, with a smile in his voice as well as on his face. 'Quite a character isn't he?' Russell apparently liked his rustic neighbor. I told him about our long conversation. 'Noey likes to talk all right if you hit him while he is in the right mood.' The ranger said there were some little annoyances with the hermit in regard to the lean-tos, but nothing serious. Obviously, this ranger was not out to harass Noah. After all, Rondeau was not only a novelty but something of a celebrity since the outside world had gotten a glimpse of him.

"Noah's alleged attempt at courting a lady in Long Lake also had reached the ranger. So the hermit's heart was still open to romance in the autumn of his years. Maybe that's where he was that day in September long ago when we did not find him at home," Edwin concluded.

Ed was thankful for the hermit's companionship and for the opportunity he had to reach out and touch the life of one of the Adirondacks' most celebrated figures.

Noah's Secret Code.

ʘ∘θ⅃∽∘×θ †⟋∿⁄θ ⁹ ×⟍∘⁄† ⟩×⟋×× ⟩∘⟍†† ⁹⎮ ∘†θ†∽∘ ×†⎮⟍⟩
∘†⟋∘ ∘†θ⟙ ⟍⁹⎮ ∘ ∘††⊢⎮× ⁹† ∘†θ⎮θ ∿†∽†θ∘∽ ∘††⊢⎮†⎮□

"**People have so much small stuff on their minds that they don't think of these bigger things.**" —*NJR when philosophizing about the formation of the solar system.*

Chapter 18

Eleanor Webb's Memories of an Interesting Man

I remember my first reaction to Enoch Squires's February 3-6, 1959, broadcasts. "What an interesting job," I thought. "You do live interviews with celebrities and talk to unconventional people. A broadcast journalist can meet and talk to interesting men and women from varied backgrounds and all walks of life."

To me, WGY's conversation with first-class eccentric Noah John Rondeau was extraordinarily interesting. After I listened to the first segment of the seven-day series, Squires's first recorded interview with Noah played on my mind. I could hardly wait for the next broadcast. The media world was quite different in the 1950s, and local live programming was the backbone of radio and television then. As a kid, I listened especially to a lot of radio.

The subjects of autobiographies, biographies and stories of adventure have long been favorite reading sources for me. I was intrigued by Rondeau's parley about his mountain life. His story touched on one of my early interests, one of which I have never tired. Family camping trips in the Adirondacks paved my way into the mountains, but hearing Noah John helped mold me into a die-hard backwoods wanderer. Squires's interview also triggered my interest in reading more New York State history as a youngster. I'm positive all this led to my adult hobby of gathering Adirondack memories.

By December of 1991, I had developed a friendly relationship with Richard Smith. I gave him a copy of Squires's 1959 interview. He said he had heard the broadcast "long ago," but appreciated owning a cassette tape of it. He looked forward to hearing Noah's "actual voice again after so long a time." He wondered aloud how much attention Noah would garner if the interview was aired then, in the 1990s. He said something like, "I wonder who would be interested in listening to an old hermit tell about his dislikes and running off to the woods to listen to the hum of bumblebees and songbirds' chirps?"

I assumed many would, and assured him plenty of people were still interested in unique characters, wholesome people and things that showed what life in the mountains used to be like, all exemplified by Rondeau. Maybe today's teenagers wouldn't care much for the decades-old program, but there surely were still many folks who would find fascination in an opinionated hermit. They might even find his story spellbinding enough to want to strap on a backpack and romp over a rolling trail that would take them back to Cold River Hill, as I've done again and again.

I felt the account of how Noah's hut came to be saved was a particularly important slice of Adirondack history. Following my December visit with Smith, I decided to learn more about just how the WGY Rondeau program came about.

Lt. to Rt. Mary Carr, Monty and Eleanor Webb sitting in the Town Hall.
Photograph by Harvey Carr. Courtesy of Harvey Carr

My search started with a telephone call to the WGY radio station and a 'help needed' advertisement in a North Country magazine. Ronald E. Brindle, then vice-president of programming at WGY, politely listened to my interest in his station's old recording. "Enoch Squires was his real name," he said. "No, he didn't use a nom de plume." But I hit a brick wall when he shared, "No one here has a clue of how to reach him. His last known address was in Amsterdam [NY]." I never was able to find the whereabouts of Squires. On the other hand, the station V.P. wished me his very best and granted me the station's permission to use the entire text of the program in my Adirondack publications.

Eleanor Webb read the ad I had placed and contacted me. This chapter is built on a combination of four letters received from her dated between March 11 and March 27, 1991.

Eleanor and her husband "Monty" were residents of Blue Mountain Lake. Eleanor described them as an Adirondack couple whose time is "fully occupied owning and operating The Cliff Hanger resort for a longer season than most in the Adirondacks…" She added that they were also "concerned with protecting the wild character" of the Adirondack Park.

Eleanor reported that Monty and she "…personally knew [Rondeau]. It is our opinion alone, unadulterated by anyone else's—as we never…have had the privilege of talking with anyone who truly knew him…. Indeed, we did not think of him as a celebrity but just an interesting old man who had led an unusually independent life, resorting to, for the most part, his own ingenuity…. We know he was a spirited man, which some people found irritating, and somewhat hard to cope with, especially for those whose job it was to interfere with his independence. Yet there were those among those very people who became his good friends. With us, he was unfailingly courteous. Whoever shares his memories with you, I hope each one will be kind."

She wrote…

We met Noah John eight years after the Big Blowdown had driven him out of Cold River. That was in 1958. At that time he was living with a family in Wilmington…He greeted us courteously and talked mainly about the terrible hurricane force winds during the 1950 blowdown he said had 'driven him from his home on Cold River.' He knew, by daylight of the next morning, that he could never live there again. The terrible tangle of fallen trees made hunting impossible. Therefore, there would be no meat supply. We understood him to suggest his garden had been buried under the crisscross logs and tangled limbs. He gathered together a small pack basket of survival supplies and started out for Ampersand Park and Lake Placid, never, he thought, to return. Climbing over and under the fallen trees, dodging and fighting his way through the mass of tangled branches was exhausting and danger-ous. I remember commenting that the shaking and rattling of his little camp had to have been terrible throughout the height of the storm. The sound and vibration all blended into what Monty and I said sounded like a speeding freight train at a grade crossing. We couldn't imagine being in the middle of a forest as the elements raged on.

Listening to Eleanor, it was clear to me she held that Noah John was a rare individual. He was someone who could mix with the socially privileged as easily as he mixed with the working class. She emphasized, "He actually liked honorable people who appreciated his good qualities and made many long-term friends of the people who visited him during many hiking sea-sons. His feelings were just as strong in the opposite direction concerning those that he felt he could not trust or who he felt were harassing him."

"Incidentally, he told us that the story commonly circulated that he had become a hermit because he had been jilted by a woman he loved was 'nonsense.'

"One of the many jobs he had engaged in during the twenty-seven years he had spent alternating between going to school, as long as his money held out, then working to save more in order to return to school repeat-edly until he finally graduated, was guiding people in the woods. The longer he did that the more he liked the woods until he finally decided he would try to stay there.

"On another day…when we drove to Wilmington…we took Noah John for a little ride. I remember we stopped and walked around the lawn, admiring the beautiful view at St. Hubert's. I noticed that his blue denim jacket and pants were all neatly patched and clean. I picked three or four violets and handed them to him. He said he would press them between the pages of his diary. He also came to visit us in Blue Mountain Lake. It was July 2nd, 1959. He came for lunch with Mr. Roy Lash, who drove him from Wilmington. We had an interesting 'confab,' as he called it. Then the two men left to talk with Dr. Inverarity at the museum, where I believe the details of his exhibit were discussed.

"We only saw him once more. It was years later. By then he was living by himself in a small house [Singing Pines] on a side road near Wilmington. The place was tucked among the many trees surrounding the house. He had planted vegetables which could tolerate partial shade. I remember mostly the large, healthy artichoke plants.

"As we started to leave the old man said, 'Wait just a minute. I want to get something for you.'

"He disappeared into the house, then came out with a jelly glass of plum preserves. Scratched on the lid was a label in his own code…it was illegible to anyone but Noah John himself. 'It's my own homemade,' he said. 'I want you to have it. I remember you were good people.' A compliment we have never forgotten nor ever will…"

Eleanor returns to recounting her involvement with the WGY Rondeau interview and Harvey Carr's salvaging of the hermit's cabin:

"Harvey Carr was another Blue Mountain Laker. He worked as a logger for a spool company. His company had either bought land in the Cold River country or the timber rights, I don't remember. I don't think Harvey knew anything about us knowing Noah John until he approached Monty and me saying it was 'a shame' Rondeau's cabin was about to be bulldozed. Harvey had been living back there, staying in an established lumber camp. He hoped that we could help him to rescue one of the cabins. Although we really had no idea on how to go about it, we agreed to at least try. One day shortly after we agreed to help, Harvey took his wife, Mary, and us into Rondeau's old camp site on top of Cold River Hill.

The hermitage before the Hall of Records was removed. Once removed to the Adirondack Museum, the building was converted into a replica of the Town Hall.
Courtesy of Harvey Carr

After seeing the little dwellings and having talked at length with the grand gentleman Noah John was, we felt that the Adirondack Museum should indeed find it an interesting exhibit. By the way, thinking at the time the cabins would almost certainly be bulldozed, I took Noah John's big white coffee cup as a reminder. It is now on the table in the cabin at the museum.

"As I said before, Monty talked to Mr. Bruce Inverarity. He was the first director of the new museum. Inverarity had heard of Rondeau. He felt that the Adirondack hermit, because of Rondeau's appearances at the Sportsmen's Shows, was commercial and a fake. He also assumed that Rondeau had made a small fortune out of that. Quite the contrary was true. Actually Noah John had been taken advantage of. The sporting goods manufacturers only paid for his expenses and one hundred dollars for each show appearance.

"At this time, Enoch Squires was broadcasting stories of New York State over WGY out of Schenectady as the 'WGY Traveler.' It occurred to me that he might be interested in Noah John's story."

Eleanor was a fan of Squires' *WGY Traveler* stories. Picturing the places he visited brought her feelings of serenity. The Adirondacks was her pastoral playground. She was pleased the land she loved was getting positive attention. It also satisfied her to know of the positive acceptance of the listening public toward Squires's program. She continues…

"Since I enjoyed listening to the 'Traveler' stories on the air, I simply thought a 'Traveler' episode that included Noah and one about Harvey Carr's effort to save Rondeau's Town Hall hut would make an interesting program.

"None of us personally knew or had even talked to Enoch Squires. Therefore, I wrote Squires and invited him to stay at our home. Enoch Squires needed no further urging from us beyond my first letter. Apparently he was happy to have the opportunity to do the story.

Noah's abandoned Town Hall stood as a ghost town in the wilds of Cold River until the early 1970s. *Courtesy of Harvey Carr*

"In fact, he underscored it, saying he 'was *very* interested in Noah's story.' So we invited Squires to stay with us."

Eleanor recalled, "Some of Enoch's audio recordings were taped at our winter cottage only as a gesture. WGY and Squires wanted to give us and Harvey Carr 'a credit line,' so to speak. We were not prepared [to be tape recorded] so our comments were inept, really meaningless, except that we…emphasized it was Harvey's idea to save the cabin as well as it would be his hard work and devotion to the project that would make rescuing the artifacts a success.

"After our discussion with Squires, Monty had another talk with Inverarity about seriously considering Harv's wish to save the Rondeau relics. Carr sincerely felt the hermit things had historical value, but I know Inverarity still expressed his skepticism to Monty."

At the conclusion of the initial taping of Harvey telling about his interest, logger Carr invited radio personality Squires to go with him into Rondeau's country. Eleanor recounted:

"Following the taping at our home, Harvey and Squires left to go to Cold River immediately after breakfast the next morning and only arrived back in time for dinner that night. I do recall that Pat Collins did some of the work in assisting Harvey and Enoch.

"The next day Enoch and Harvey left early to go to Wilmington to interview Noah. They returned to have dinner with us and to tape some harmonica music performed by Harvey. The evening broke up. The Carrs went home. The rest of us went to bed, and Enoch left for Schenectady the next morning.

"When Enoch was done, he figured he had made enough tapes of the story to fill a fifteen-minute program for seven consecutive days. I felt the best part of the entire story would be the fascinating interview with Noah John himself.

"It was, perhaps, the most successful of all of the 'WGY Traveler' series. WGY sold copies of the reel-to-reel tape for $35.00 each.

"I remember when I listened to it on the air. I had thought at least our comments would have been deleted. They weren't! Monty sounded all right and so did Mary and Harvey Carr. However, I have a tricky voice.

It almost invariably fails me when I am tired, as I was then. Indeed, I remember a listener from Indian Lake, when he came to work the next day, asking me, 'Why didn't you speak up so a body could hear you?' The simple fact was, I couldn't.

"If I remember correctly, it was not until after the success of the Enoch Squires story that Mr. Inverarity rather grudgingly consented to accept the cabin into the museum grounds where it became, if not the museum's most popular all-time exhibit, certainly the most popular at that time.

"As soon as that permission was granted, Harvey Carr took on the arduous job of moving the cabin to the museum. He painstakingly numbered each log, each board, and each item, carefully dismantled it all, prepared it for travel the long way out over the rough logging road and then was almost defeated trying to get some help and some way of transportation out [to the museum]. I think one man [Paul Crofut] helped him after he had gotten the consent of the museum to send a truck. Then Harvey put it all carefully together again on the farthest-out perimeter of the grounds."

Eleanor ended her last letter by bringing the cabin placement up to date. "Unfortunately, exposed log cabins do not last too long. Therefore, several years ago, under a new director, the exhibit was moved indoors."

Richard Smith would probably have been right had I placed a bet with him. A hermit in the 1940s and '50s would have been more popular than he ever would be in the 21st century. But, as late as the 1980s and '90s, when I was presenting historical slide programs for Adirondack Discovery throughout the Adirondack Park and for the elderhostel program at Sagamore Institute at Raquette Lake, I realized that the majority of people in attendance still wanted to learn more about the Adirondack hermit.

Noah's Secret Code.

⌀┼Θ ₋◦╱◦₋ℓ◦₋┼ ╲┼Θ ╲Θ◦◦₋Ŧ ₋◦⁹⁹◦₋ ┼╵ ♭╲╱╱ℓ◦┼₋ℓŦ𝕚

╲♭ℓ ₋◦◦Θ╱┼⁹╲| ┼╵ ♭╲╱╳┼₋ℓŦ ╱ ╳┼₋ℓℓ╳Θ ℓ┼╵Ŧ |╳Θ╳╳𝕚

╲♭ℓ ℓ┼Θ |ΘΘΘℓΘ|ℓ ℓ┼┼╵┼ ┼╵ ℓ┼Θ ─Θ⁹⁹╲|

"The partridge berry...poor in quantity, but precious in quality; a little tiny smell, but the sweetest things in the woods." —NJR *said when questioned about his favorite of all the flowers.*

THE HERMIT AND US

Noah was pleased to know his past way of life would be preserved in the Adirondack Museum's display of his hermitage. *Courtesy of Ruth King*

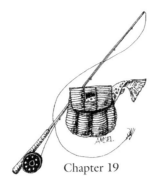

Chapter 19

Ted and Eleanor Hillman on Noah

The morning sky was a uniform grey, infused with light snow flakes that amounted to nothing more than a pleasant taste of the upcoming winter that would slowly creep over the Adirondack forest throughout November 1996 I was pleased to be back on the road. Bette and I had left Camden early, after breakfast. The day promised to be overcast, cold and rewarding.

For days I had been anticipating meeting the Hillmans. Ted wanted to share some early connections they had had with Noah John. He had kept those memories close to his heart as someone would protect a favorite snapshot when only a single print remained.

The Hillmans were in their mid-eighties, old timers—perfect candidates to share recollections of the old days in the Adirondack Mountains.

I was on a historic trail to track down and talk to folks who had known Noah during his early years. The search had started as an avocation sparked many years earlier by Maitland DeSormo, a noted Adirondack history author, when he mentioned choosing not to include in his book much detailed first-person information about people who knew Noah. "Who really wants to read particulars about Rondeau's trap line, or being back at his camp or for that matter what his life was like once he left Cold River?" he asked me.

"Well, I would," I replied, and I found folks who knew Noah also enjoyed simply reminiscing. Yet, I also knew Maitland was looking at Rondeau's history from a practical and economic point of view. It was not possible to afford to include everything about the hermit in the biography he published in 1967. As a result he avoided including the ruminating stories I sought from North Country people like Ted and Eleanor "Sis" Hillman.

Adirondack narratives were not something professional journalists sought out until deeply interested researchers and writers of local history, most of them North Country amateur historians, began to recognize the value of collecting and storing the vanishing histories of natives. Stories and experiences of the pioneers, hermits, early camps and guides, lumbermen, and community characters began to be saved. Now, years later and approaching my own old age, I'm sharing what I've learned in permanent form for interested readers of Adirondack history.

Ted and Sis built and had operated Hillman's "Stoneyland" cabins on Lake Colby Drive (Route 86) one mile north of Saranac Lake for decades when I interviewed them in 1996. They had lived in the mountains all their lives. Their roots went back generations—back to the days of the stagecoach. Ted enjoyed revisiting the bootlegger days when "men in black cars would come down from Canada in the small hours of the night to pay cash to fill up trucks" at the gas station and store his father operated. Ted didn't ask any questions. He knew better.

Elenore and Ted Hillman cherished their friendship with Noah.
Courtesy of Miriam H. Kondroski

Ted and Sis loved the outdoors. Their daughter and son-in-law, Miriam and Mike Kondroski, said the loving couple "were true pioneers who embodied what it means to be an 'Adirondacker.'"

Ted was like a good number of young boys growing up after the turn of the nineteenth century in the Saranac Lake-Coreys section of the North Country. Stories of hunting, fishing and fur trappers with lucrative surreptitious trap lines accounted for, and filled, a special spot in their desire to be actively engaged outdoors.

Ted's older brothers, Frank and Richard, filled him with stories of his own experiences; they taught Ted how to recognize animal tracks and showed him how to place a thin sheet of parafined paper over a fox trap, before brushing snow over the set with a bough snapped from a limb. Then as the youthful trappers left the scene, they would brush away their tracks. This was the way it was done back in the early 1920s. Such a set was never certain, yet the boys had learned from oldsters that intense cold would soon freeze out what little human odor was connected with the set, and the chances of being successful increased.

Canvas tents were a common sight along the Raquette River. Noah Rondeau lived in a borrowed one during the early 1920s. Ted Hillman's brother's Axton camp was typical of these temporary sporting camps. *Photograph by Richard Wood. Courtesy of Inez Wood Buis*

Ted learned about the professional local nomadic trappers who set down trap lines in the Sawtooth-Cold River country. Over time he visited many derelict lumber shanties early sportsmen had turned into temporary shelters and picked up a few stretching boards hanging on log walls that the porkies had failed to reach.

One crude temporary remains of a camp he chanced on held a particular interest. He said, "It was constructed of cedar logs set vertically over a brook, an outlet from a pond. A trap line outpost no doubt. It was convenient. The occupants only needed to lower a bucket on a rope to draw water. I come on to a number of crude shelters. All simple and used through hardship."

Ted figured the humble log hovel over the outlet of Blueberry Pond might have belonged to trappers or meat or hide hunters. That region had once been a real wilderness. Without doubt the country had teemed with bear, deer, lynx, fisher, otter, beaver, fox, marten, other fur-bearers and perhaps some moose. That would have been in the glory days of the hide and meat hunters. Lumber companies had their own hunters to supply the camps with wild meat. Hide hunters butchered game merely for the pelts, leaving the carcasses to rot.

It might even have been one of Noah Rondeau's early shelters before he settled at the Big Dam camp at the far end of the Cold River Tote Trail.

Ted's repertoire of stories included interesting yet vague recollections of a Lake Placid guide called "Old Tom" who was reported to carry "an overload of booze under his belt;" a Long Lake trapper referred to only as McCarthy who "got up the [Cold] river quite a ways; a lumberman known as Pelcher; an unusual woodsman Tupper Lake folks referred to as Louie, not to be confused with "French" Louis Seymour, who had a "fur nest" staked out in the Seward Mountain territory a safe distance from Rondeau's range; and Noah, whose territory fanned out from Peek-a-boo Mountain to Blueberry Pond to the central portion of Cold River.

I had heard other stories about "Meestaire Pelcher" and Louie.

Pelcher was reported to have had a logging camp in the Cold River wilderness. Early trappers had reported they'd seen a rough board nailed on a sapling along a woods road that pointed in heavy pencil marks the direction to "Pelcher's Camp."

Louie had tried to put a stop to Noah when he first moved into the region. Upon finding the traces of a rude camp with a cheap sheet metal stove in what he maintained was HIS province, Old Louie declared to the community of Coreys, "Sacre bleu! Louie will put an ax to who ever built 'is wigwam in my territory." That had been years ago. Since then the men had met, developed a mutual respect, and stayed out of each other's way.

"The first time I saw Noah was at my brother's camp. The next time was when he was at the dam camp; the third time was at the New York State Sportsmen Show; the fourth time at my fish and game club dinner; and then in the 1950s," recalled Ted.

"My older brother had a camp up in the Axton area in the 1920s—it was a tent platform affair with a legal permit. There were others up there. It was in July and we were about to have dinner. It was nice warm weather. [Ferris] Meigs was still lumbering up there back then. I was tickled to death. I came up in a car. I was a teenager. We had steaks but no bread. Somebody suggested we go over to the lumber camp and talk to the cook—see if he'd sell us a couple loaves or three. The cook was alone and agreed. About that time I saw this little man coming along. Well, he looked little to me. He was coming out from the Cedar Bridge trail right out of the woods near my brother's camp."

At this point, Ted's calling to mind a memory of seventy years ago became confusing to me but I didn't interrupt. It was interesting just hear him talk about an era that had long vanished. I felt the gist of it was more important than absolute accuracy of location.

"It was behind Ampersand. Along Ward Brook at #4.

"What are you doing over this way," someone called out. The little man answered, "I heard some noise and come to investigate." "Well come on in," my brother invited, "we were just about to have dinner."

"Oh he had a short beard and mustache. Black. He told us he had stopped back near the bridge and ate some cheese. It wasn't much to make a lunch. He'd had it stashed in a spring hole. Well, he sat around and we talked and talked. And later we hunted together. I remember seeing him pull up his rifle and shoot when we hadn't even seen anything. He shot with accuracy. 'What you shoot at?' we asked. At that time he shot a .35 automatic

"I saw Noah only once, I believe. It was when he was at the North Pole, and I was so dumbstruck I couldn't think what to say. I had so many things I wanted to ask him about that I got tongue-tied and just stood there, staring at him. I think that annoyed him, so he said something like 'You don't want to talk to me,' and that scared me so I took off. Blotched my only chance, as it turned out." —Neal Burdick. *Courtesy of Neal Burdick, Adirondack editor and writer*

Remington. 'A buck,' he replied. And our jaws dropped. There was a buck. He had sharp eyesight. I found out later how good he was as an archer. He was simply an all-round good a marksman. Fast and accurate.

"Rondeau said he had several camps, one called Cedar Bridge Camp near Cedar Swamp; he had another near Pickerel Pond and Blueberry Pond. All temporary shelters that game wardens looked for. Built using simple brush or green timber. He kept the places in big spruce and always left the top [foliage] alone. Said he'd stayed in them even at twenty-four below zero.

"Aden Lawrence was a hunter from the Axton area. He knew Noah—said Noah would take a good size buck, bone it and pack it out. Lawrence said he only had to help him [Rondeau] slip the pack back straps over his shoulders as he hefted the pack. It took a big deer to make a hundred pound of meat.

"Aden Lawrence said to me, 'How would you like to go in and see Rondeau? I was maybe twenty-three, oh maybe twenty-six. We put some gear together and went to see him. Went in down Moose Creek outlet. We stayed overnight in a clearing. Next morning we followed the river to the big dam."

The partners followed a winding old tote road route downriver. Old lumber roads looped off the main trail. One of Rondeau's trap lines for marten made a big loop around Mountain Pond before coming back to the main trail. Around all the old lumber buildings he ran lines for weasels.

By the time Ted and Aden went, Noah wasn't as guarded about folks approaching. Just the same, the men took Noah John Rondeau seriously. While both men were cautious entering camp, they were also respectful. They did not make light of the solitary man who was using the site seasonally at the time.

"He was glad to see us," said Ted. "He remembered me as a younger fellow. My brother had told him I was a crack shot."

Noah was very hospitable. He wasn't about to let friend or stranger go hungry or without shelter.

"We planned to sleep that evening inside a teepee on a grass and balsam bough bed," Ted continued. Noah tossed in a bear skin, saying that would be better, and we had a couple blankets. I was tired and thought of taking

234   THE HERMIT AND US

a nap. Bugs didn't seem to bother us but when I pointed out a snake that just come slithering out between the poles I had second thoughts of laying down. Noah said, 'They ain't going to bother you. I even have deer go in there.' He joked about not knowing we were coming because the telephone didn't work."

The drop-in visit called for a tour around the grounds.

"'I'll take you down to my storage room in the river there,' Noah said, pointing to a spot near the dam. We climbed down the bank on a set of very narrow stairs. The incline was very steep. It led to what you might call a beach, really a shoreline filled with small rocks and pebbles. It wasn't anything like a sandy shoreline. Close to the back of the log cribbing was a hole where Noah kept burlap bags filled with canned food. All around the top of the hill were pin cherry trees."

I asked Ted if he remembered what he did during the day back there.

"We talked about the possibility of investigating the country across the dam but he said we'd waste our time trying to cross the bridge and whatever trail was over there. We'd just come out at the Duck Hole.

"What did I do during the day? I napped.

"Noah was willing to talk with us. Said there was a trail that would take us to Long Lake. We left camp but only walked down the trail that crossed Ouluska Pass brook.

"We talked a lot. He was interested in what was going on in the news. He was glad to be away from the game protectors. He underscored, 'They had a road into Axton and Duck Hole.' We took it to mean he felt the law had easy access but we never questioned it."

"He seemed to be able to live practically free. Said he lost his money one time. There was a cabin fire at Coreys. He'd gone off trapping. Said he had twelve hundred dollars in a trunk. Lost it and all his diaries and personal effects.

"I was somewhat familiar with the Axton-Coreys area. I used to stop in to the Woods Hotel in Axton [Axe-town]. The hotel was near the iron bridge. It was popular with hunters and fishermen. I never saw so many pretty girls than I did right there in one place. The attraction was fishing and hunting and a carry for the Upper Saranac."

I thought Ted might be mixing up the Woods Hotel with the Rustic Lodge, but either way, it was the recall of all the "pretty girls" that was most important in his memory.

Ted's reminiscing swung back to Noah. "Ferris Meigs owned the gore [that Rondeau lived on]. He could manage anything; he was a survivor.

"Noah didn't complain neither when he ran out of smoking tobacco; he said, 'I just scrape off some nice maple bark, dry it and have me a smoke.' He got a taste of the tobacco and I suspect it was something to do.

"He'd talk to himself like a lawyer. Aden told me he'd heard him preaching, carrying on a conversation on his own.

"I'd heard Meigs and Mr. Rockefeller were always nice to him. Ferris Meigs allowed him the freedom to pass over his property [Ampersand Park], even gave him a key to one of the outlying camps. He could go in anytime he wanted. Avery Rockefeller allowed him that same freedom.

"Sometimes teamsters transported things for him. That was during the lumbering years."

Following the November 1950 deer season, Noah left the woods. He stayed at 4 Alpine Terrace, the Saranac Lake home of his friends, Phil and Helen McCalvin.

He noted in his yearly journal that he "Attended a Moose Venison Dinner at the Fish and Game Club" in town. Ted was in attendance. He told me, "As I recall, Ed Worthington was the fish and game club president at the time. He had invited Noah down to talk. And oh boy, did he ever. He talked about his life. He'd say right out he didn't want nobody to ever feel sorry for him. Somebody piped up and asked, 'Rondeau, how long did you ever stay there alone without seeing a human being?'

"'Well sir it was thirteen months. You know I looked down the trail and I saw somebody coming and it was none other than five women.' And he laughed. 'You know they was the nicest people. You know I was getting kind of low on supplies by then. When they left, they gave me everything. They were mountain climbers who wore the red-green-and yellow emblem [of the Forty-Sixers of Troy, N.Y., climbing club]. 'I lived on the top shelf for a spell after that.' He had a colorful way of expressing himself.

"Noah was very much at ease fielding comments. There were many questions about the number of deer, size, fishing—he seemed to appreciate telling people how he lived." He welcomed people and they in return received him into their homes.

"Arlen Branch was a farmer in the Saranac Lake area. Noah occasionally stayed with him. Sometimes when he was in the area, he'd stop by Stoneyland during the day or when Arlen took him places.

"Typically, Noah would stay with us, on occasion; it was the middle of the winter. He never had a chance before coming to town."

One day when Sis was over at Mrs. French's house, Noah stopped by. Sis spoke about that day: "Noah asked Mrs. French if she had a lemon. I heard him talking from where I was standing back off in the pantry and I wondered what he was ever going to do with it. Well, she gave him a lemon, he took it, pulled out his pocket knife, cut it in half and squeezed it. As the juice began to squirt he caught the liquid in the cup of his hand. Next thing I knew he bowed his head, took a big inhale and snuffed it right up his nose. He said the juice was a preventive to ward off colds. You'd a-thought it would have choked him or something. He had no reaction. It couldn't have been new to him. He might have got the idea from Mrs. French herself. I know she used to rub it on her hand and let it absorb into her skin. She said it was a good remedy for the pain from arthritis."

Mrs. French was the Hillman's neighbor. Sis said, "She lived in her house next door till she was 96. She'd work in her garden, bake donuts and bread. She grew the most beautiful flowers. She'd sell bunches of sweet peas. She'd set them in glass fruit jars and place them by the fence to sell for twenty-five cents a bunch. People would stop and buy 'em. Noah and she enjoyed talking about flowers and all things that had to do with the beauty of nature. She lived till she was in her hundred and first year and was still making donuts then."

While Rondeau was known as an entertaining speaker who could keep a capacity audience "chuckling throughout an hour's talk," Ted said some of his behaviors were odd and begged for an explanation. One example Mrs. Hillman pointed out took place when she worked at Montgomery Ward's: "I was a clerk in the order department. Helen McCalvin was another clerk

Ted Hillman recalled fond memories of Noah. *Courtesy of Miriam H. Kondroski*

who worked in the same department. Noah lived with her family. I was always under the impression that somehow Noey was related to the McCalvins but I know now he wasn't. They were just very close friends. I remember there were days she would come in simply fuming. It always had something to do with Noey. Well, this one time she had put him in charge of taking care of her little boy, Gary. When Helen returned from work, she found Noah and Gary sitting at the kitchen table. Noah had opened a can of dog food and was feeding it to Gary out of the can. Well did she ever bristle about what he had done. I don't know if she ever got any kind of reasonable explanation. You know he had lived so long without needing to read labels at Cold River, or he might have figured it was edible for humans—go figure."

Ted and Eleanor both remember seeing Noah walk down the Lake Colby road during the winter. "He was a very recognizable figure," said Sis. "He always wore a black, heavy winter coat that went down almost to his knees. He had it buttoned all the way up the front and wore the collar in a stand up position. His grey beard drooped on the outside. He looked like Father Time. He wore a fur hat on his head. It had long ear flappers. He wore black buckle galoshes on his feet. Dressed in that outfit and beard, you would recognize him immediately.

"That was back in the '50s when he stayed with Harley and Sally Branch for a while at The Branches on the Trudeau road," Elenore said. Miriam Kondroski, Elenore and Ted's daughter, remembered Harley and Sally from her childhood days. "I used to go to their house when Mom and Dad has something important to do and couldn't take me with them." Her parents always referred to their friends and their house as The Branches. Elenore continued, "Noah was a walker—went everywhere on foot. He was as good on snowshoes. He'd tell us about the days he would make almost a twenty-mile hike through deep snow carrying a forty-pound pack basket," prompting him to remind Ted and Sis, he wasn't that strong any longer. "That was thirty years ago."

Chapter 20

Enoch Squires'
Making of a Legend

Saturday, January 31, 1959
Cold atmosphere and breezy.
At Wilmington, N.Y.
Melvin Peck moved Bantams from Town Hall replica to hen coop.
Enoch Squires call on me most of afternoon. We make three tape
recordings. Big visit about Hermit Life, Adirondack Mountains,
Vallies, Flora, Fauna, Fishing, Hunting, Trapping and Wig
Wams and Cabins; And Astronomy overhead (Cold River Style).
                                                        —N.J. Rondeau

"Hermits in the real sense of the word are aloof," Enoch Squires, a popular
WGY Schenectady radio reporter commented during his February 1959
radio show, Traveler, the seven-day interview series that featured former
Adirondack hermit Noah John Rondeau.

   At the heart of the interviews, was the radio journalist's interest in learning Rondeau's reaction to the possible fate of the camp the hermit had
abandoned in November of 1950.

   WGY: *I've heard some talk lately that your old woodland camp is*
   going to…may be demolished by a bulldozer. Now, how do you feel
   about that?

   NJR: *Well personally I…er, in a way I don't like it, and on the*
   other hand I might say I don't give a darn. I can't go back there

much. I had planned to go to Cold River and spend the month of June and fish the river from one end to the other, see, and write it up —"Cold River In June." Well, I still got the idea, but I'm getting too old. I might try that next June, but there is a lot of other things to do and I don't get around too well. And of course I would be three weeks, you know, fishing the river from the Duck Hole clear down to the Raquette River."

WGY: "There's one other thing. I know there are people who are interested in taking your shacks, and cabin and teepees, or at least one of them, out to civilization so that a lot of people can see the very buildings you lived in as a hermit. Now, what do you think about that?"

NJR: Well the idea is all right and personally of course I lived there, I built them cabins and what's left of the camps. Personally I might say that I don't care. I'll probably never go back to Cold River; if I do it would only be for three or four weeks in June.

Harvey Carr and co-worker during the removal operation. *Photograph by Harvey Carr*

WGY: Of course you must realize that it is so far back in there that a lot of people couldn't possibly get back.

NJR: Oh, it's just one in a few thousands at the most, you know.

WGY: So you think it would be a good idea to transport your old Adirondack wilderness home out to the highway where a lot of the visitors from down in the populated areas can have a good look at it and see what the buildings were actually like?

NJR: I think the idea is grand, and that idea comes from a good class of people too. Ah, as far as I'm concerned it's up to them. I don't own a thing up there.

The relocation of the buildings at Cold River and the *WGY Traveler* series quickly renewed reporters' interest in the well-known hermit. Staff writer C. R. Roseberry of the Albany *Times-Union* newspaper tells what happened to cause a resurgence of interest in the hermit's life.

Rondeau, who had been "spending his sunset years back in cahoots with the civilization from which he fled as a young man, came down from his present comfortable home as a boarder in Wilmington…to inspect the installation."

The "installation" to which Roseberry's July 26 article referred was the Adirondack Museum's "newest acquisition…The museum stepped in just in time to save…" [Rondeau's Town Hall cabin]. The article continued with the saga of Rondeau's resuscitated digs.

> *The cabin [of] the last authentic hermit of the Adirondacks…was set up on the landscaped museum grounds within recent weeks, along with one of the firewood 'wigwams' which were the hermit's own labor-saving invention.*
>
> *…Now age 76, he is still spry and keen-witted, his long beard liberally sprinkled with white. He still makes like a naturalist-philosopher. "I love the flory and the fauny," he opines.*
>
> *The Great Northern Lumber Co., completing a contract cutting in the remote Cold River basin which spreads between the towering Seward and Santanoni ranges, has made a shambles*

of the site known familiarly to mountain climbers and sportsmen as "The Hermit's." It was about to bulldoze the deserted cabin into oblivion when an employee with a sentimental feeling for mountain lore informed the Adirondack Museum of the impending catastrophe.

"We were tickled to death to get it," says Dr. R. Bruce Inverarity, director of the museum. The cabin was dismantled, its pieces carefully numbered, and trekked out over ranger trails via Shattuck's Clearing to Long Lake with the cooperation of William Petty, district forest ranger. Harvey Carr, of Blue Mountain Lake, supervised the reassembling.

Personal belongings and utensils of Rondeau were obtained to furnish it, including a bearskin for the bunk. The whitened shoulder bones of beavers are nailed over the doorway, as the Hermit used to have them.

In March of 1991, Harvey Carr told me about how Noah John's cabin was brought out of the woods and became part of the Adirondack Museum's collection. Carr was instrumental in making the ramshackle shack one of the museum's most popular exhibits

"The whole story went like this," Carr began.

We [the logging crew] went in to Cold River the fall of 1958. I was working for Paul Crofut. He was the logging contractor. He was working for the Northern Lumber Company and the U.S. Bobbin and Shuttle Company owned the property—they're the company that made wooden spools and such I guess.

We stayed in there during the winter at the lumber camp. We cut the hardwood and brought it out and sometime during the late winter or as it was going toward spring, whatever, somebody from the U.S. Shuttle and Bobbin Company came in to camp and told us, before we got down toward Noah John's camp, they wanted us to take the dozer down, smash it up, bury it and get rid of all the lumber and everything because they were afraid of hunters moving in and causing a forest fire. Of course that wasn't a bad idea, but you know, there was brush and weeds and a lot of slash...Anyway, they wanted us to destroy it completely.

I sat there in the logging camp that night and said to the boys, "I hate to see it go...Gee it's too bad. It should be in a museum or something." Then I hadn't even thought about it for two, three, four days and then I got to talking about it again. You know, like it would be a shame to tear it all apart, bury it and everything. And about then, Jack Swancott, he was one of the truck drivers, he give me the idea. Real casual like he says, "Well you got a museum right there in Blue Mountain Lake."

I said, "Oh yeah, but I don't know if they'd be at all interested or not. Naw, I doubt they'd want it."

Jacky said, "Well maybe they would."

'Course we stayed in there [at the lumber camp] all week and it would come and go on my mind. So...I stopped up there [at the museum]. Oh it was late January or February '59.

Mopping up operation in the Cold River country by the U.S. Bobbin & Shuttle Corporation. *Courtesy of Harvey Carr*

I mentioned how I felt about it [his wish to save the camp] to Monty and Eleanor [Webb]. They liked that sort of thing—old stuff, antiques and all. I also went up there [to the museum] and stopped to talk to Ralph Raymond. Ralph was the custodian up there. He lives up there year round and takes care of the place. I explained all about Noah John's camp and so forth but he didn't get too enthused about it. He didn't know much about it…

Now I know Eleanor and Monty say it differently, but I remember Ralph saying to me, "You ought to talk to Dr. Inverarity about it." The museum was about two years old by then…

Sometime soon afterward I told Eleanor and Monty about the old hermit camp; I took them into Cold River. We drove up in my truck. We stopped at the lumber camp…ate lunch…[and talked about Rondeau]. Things like how he lived for more than thirty-three years minding his own business back in a remote spot at Cold River Flow.

The lumber camp wasn't that far from the cabins. We walked the short distance. At that time I hadn't heard…[as much about Noah's life]…as Monty and Eleanor Webb did… I told the Webbs I considered Noah John to be the most authentic hermit we had in the mountains…

When the investigating team reached Cold River Hill they nosed about the place. Over the years, Harvey pointed out, the "contents were pretty well picked by the hunters…"

"We sat inside Rondeau's cabin for a while and I told them how he once tried to store his potatoes by putting them in a burlap sack and dropping some rocks inside the bag. Then he chopped a hole in the Flow ice and sank them to the bottom so they wouldn't freeze, but the beaver ate them. He did the same thing with his canned goods."

Harvey shared, "Well, quite a few, thought it was a stupid idea to think of putting an old dilapidated thing in a museum…you know 'let it [the cabins] rot all down' and all that… They wouldn't…have lasted another five years."

The Cold River Hermit's display at the Adirondack Museum. 1973.
Postcard image provided by Stephen Klein, Jr.

While some less historical-minded people had scoffed at Harvey's wish, Monty and Eleanor understood his interest. When they saw Rondeau's camp it was as if they had inspected it under a microscope. It was clear to Harvey the Webbs planned to do what they could to advance his idea.

Monty said they'd talk to Dr. Inverarity. "It wasn't long after Monty, Eleanor, Mary and I had…returned home from Cold River…that we were sitting right here…[He pointed to the kitchen chairs we were sitting on] eating supper and right along I got a telephone call from the operator saying this was a person-to-person call from Dr. Inverarity in New York City…He had heard from Ralph and the Webbs…I was really enthused. He said, 'I hear there is a possibility that we could get Noah John Rondeau's camp.' He knew about Rondeau back in there. 'Course that was his job as curator to know those kinds of things. 'By all means we'd like it if you can get it out.'"

"I told him, 'Yes, well if you'd like it I can get it out for ya.'

"He said, 'You got any idea what the expense would be?'

"I said, 'No expense. If you want it, I'll bring it out and give it to you.'

"He said, 'We [the museum] want to help all we can.'

"He even talked of sending a helicopter crew up there with some carpenters who could build a framework around it and airlift it from there to the museum…Knowing the camp's condition and the woods and so on, I knew what *I* wanted to do…you know they were even going to send a television crew and all that stuff and it was going to be getting late [in the season]…and I knew I'd have to get [it] out of there [before the spring thaws began]…'course the helicopter could have gone in there after the snow…had melted.

"I said, 'No. I don't think Noah John would care too much about that…idea…' Of course, Noah John had no legal hold on anything back there anyway but morally it was still his camp. 'No, if you want it, we'll bring it out,' I said. 'What I'll do is take it apart piece by piece. I'll number every part and put it back together exactly the way it was and it will be about the same camp…I don't go in for big deals anyhow. But Mr. Inverarity,' I said, just as calm as you please, 'There's just one thing about that camp…I'm giving it to you forever, but if something happens and you don't want it after all, I want it back…'

"I know when I mentioned it to Dr. Inverarity, he sounded excited, just like a kid after you offered 'em some candy…He was tickled to death…

"…Of course it's all inside [now] under temperature control and its good…I suppose at least for 150 years."

"Why did you choose to bring out the Hall of Records, Harvey, instead of the Town Hall?" I asked. His answer was simple. "It was in better shape…I took the glass out the Town Hall and everything…and kept it [as] authentic as I could…"

"I did every bit of it myself. I'd been a lumberjack, not a carpenter, but I knew I was going to do it my way.…anyway, I brought it out and what I had to do was borrow one of Croft's bulldozers—and break a road down to [Rondeau's] camp. I don't remember how deep it was, I do know the snow, we had four feet of it in the winter…

"…we were logging about a half—err quarter—of a mile away, so what I did was just push the snow…[to make a roadway]…and I took Crofut's Army personal truck because I couldn't get in with my little Chev pick up. I cut hemlock logs for a day to pay him for the use of the tractor and truck…I did it all myself…So I brought it out…along with an old iron stove, some cookin' kettles, a coffee pot as well as a hollow stump Noah John had used as a 'wet sink'…and the only thing I replaced were the bottom logs…"

Harvey Carr was a true-blue yarn-spinner, but his story of how he single-handedly saved an important part of Noah's historic legacy was no tall tale.

As for Noah, nothing ever overwhelmed him as completely or humbled him as sincerely as being honored by the Adirondack Museum's Cold River hermit exhibit. That seems clear in this letter to C.V. Latimer:

"Yes,-my Cold River City, is a Shrine at Adirondack Museum at Blue Mt;- and I am more proud of it- Than I would be of all the Shrines of Traitorous H.S.T. and Dexter White on top of it."

Noah's Secret Code.

⊖⊹|ρ⊖∘| ´∘⊖ ×ʔ|⊹ ⟋⟍ |⊖ᵟ⊖∘⊖□ ⊖´∘×T |⊹´×⊖| ʔ†
|ʔ⊖ ᵟ×⊖ ⊖´∘×T ⊹| ⚷ᵟρ ⊹⊖|⊖∘´××T ⊖´∘×T ⚶⊖ʔᵟ
⟍∘⊹|⊹| |ʔ⊖ ρʔ |ρ´T ⟍|ρ⊹× ×´ρ⊖∘ ⚶∘∘⊹×ᵚ ⟋⟍ †ʔ∘´
†⊖⊖ ×ʔ|ρ⊹| ⊹ρ ∘⊖´⟋⊹⊖| ´ ⟍⊖∘ρ⊹ ʔ† †ʔ∘∘ †⊖⊖ρᵚ ⟋⟍
⊹| ρ⊹⊖ ⊖ᵟρ∘⊖×⊖ᵚ †⊹ᵟ⊖ †⊖⊖ρ□

Winters are long and severe. Early shakes of snow come early in Oct. generally early Nov. brings snow to stay until late April, and for a few months it reaches a depth of four feet, and in the extreme, five feet. —NJR to Hubert Toomey, Keeseville

Chapter 21

Oscar Burguiere's
Cold River Express

As a teenager growing up in Bayonne, New Jersey, Oscar Burguiere was drawn to the Adirondack wilds. Working as cook, bottle-washer and all-around gopher for the transient High Bank Gang,[4] he embraced a woodsman lifestyle, though avoiding the pitfalls of members of the clique he was employed by. When Noah took him under his wing, he devoted himself to emulating his new-found hero. Richard Smith, who first met Oscar around 1938, said wanna-be-woodsman Oscar's common sense took a backseat to earning a sustainable living during the months he took off to stay with Noah each year. Later, working in the shipyards in New Jersey, Oscar concluded he needed a more practical balance. He knew he had to work to support his day-to-day survival, but he still held a passion for Cold River living.

Like Jay and CV,[5] Oscar and Richard were aware of Noah's needs. Jay and CV helped their low-income neighbor with provisions and monetary assistance which Noah recorded as guide fees:

> *November 4, 1941 Tuesday. Big Dam to Latimer's.*
> *Hunted 3 Legged swamp to Latimer's. Met Dr. and [son] Greer.*
> *55 dollars for guide.*

Richard's and Oscar's contributions, on the other hand, frequently took the form of physical labor, such as the day they salvaged many useful items, including a cache of galvanized trash cans and some steel 50-gallon drums, from the dump at the former CCC Cold River side camp where Gay Prue[6] had served.

Doc Jr. called the incident The Cold River Express. The truth is, it wasn't anything more than business as usual for Noah, Oscar and Richard back in in the day. They were always finding ways to make use of what was left in lumber camp debris. This particular rescue and reuse wasn't any different, and yet in some ways it was, because it is another example of the hermit's creative talent and the time the boys spent with a guy everyone loved.

According to an October 24 notation in Camp Seward's 1943 journal, Burguiere related the "Cold River Express" event during an evening chit-chat following a "quite cloudy and pissy [day of] snow" yet a day of celebration following Jay's defeat of a four-pointer.

CV Jr. said when he would "trot upriver," he always recalled Oscar's telling about the Cold River Express.

> *Looking upstream, I traced the path the 55-gallon drums took after the boys rolled them over the high slope where the CCC camp had once been. I pictured the day and thought of Rondeau reaping benefits from the former government encampment.*

This is CV's telling.

> *Over the years Noah had several oil drum stoves in the Town Hall before Oscar carried in the cast-iron woodstoves. Smith and Oscar were instrumental in furnishing him the makings of at least one, if not several, of those barrel stoves.*
>
> *By the time Smith had built his [outlaw] camp on the upper Chubb River in '39, the CCC had long pulled out the side camp that stood at the upper reaches of Cold River. After the Corps had completed their work, it was vacated and a new camp was established at Shattuck Clearing.*
>
> *Of course a lot of useful things were left up there in the clearing, including boards from the tent platforms, nails, sheets of galvanized tin and perhaps a dozen 55-gallon oil drums. A root cellar*

THE HERMIT AND US

Oscar Burguiere said he longed for each Cold River vacation. It gave him a feeling of remoteness and calm and timelessness that made the scramble of everyday life seem like a half-forgotten and entirely aimless dream. *Courtesy of Dr. CV Latimer, Jr.*

dug into a bank was also left intact—door and all, which one of Richard Smith's older brothers and a friend used as a hunting camp in 1937.

In the latter part of '39, as Oscar and Richard passed the oil drums they thought of Noah and asked if he could stand an update in his stove, which by then was showing many pin holes due to age and the ravages of rust.

Noah said, yes, he would like a new wood stove but a six-mile trip rolling one over the Northville-Placid foot trail put a damper on the idea.

Then someone mentioned the Cold River Express. The river itself could transport all the drums the same way logs were once floated to Big Dam. The thinking was if enough of the drums were cast upon the waters, sooner or later one of them would arrive at Big Dam, and if Noah was vigilant enough, he would be on hand to sign the claim check and receive the merchandise.

Noah agreed the plan could work. He suggested rather than dropping all the drums into the river at once, they should send a couple of them each time they passed by the old site, and only when the water was high enough to float them down past the rocky-mile-or so Black Hole section until the river reaches a more level bed. That section by the lean-tos and canyon is so infested with rocks, it would be something of a miracle if a barrel could get past. Fishing the river at that point, I found where the lumbermen had blasted the tops off many of the rocks and had chained logs to many of them to keep the rest of the driven logs from jamming. As these guide logs were as much as twelve feet above the river bed, I could readily see why several dams were needed to create enough water to raise each drive of logs over some of these giant boulders.

At one place on the river two huge boulders all but blocked the passage. Here a log wall had been constructed, and guide logs were placed, chained to large eyebolts fastened to the rocks, which sent the logs onto the shore in a dug sluice way, and after a hundred yards back again into the river. Of course, the log work had long disappeared when I saw it, but the ring bolts drilled and plugged into the rocks were still there, and over the roar of the river I could almost hear the cussing of the lumberjacks working to keep the logs moving.

Somehow or other during the succeeding months, out of the eight barrels that were dumped into the river, Noah managed to rescue three of them at Big Dam. How many got by during the nights will forever be a mystery. Noah told me he found one a long time later at the Big Eddy, but it was half buried in the backwash and had begun to rust away. Oscar rescued one a short distance below the dam in a large pool, but it never got any farther than the side of the river.

With a couple of barrels in reserve, Noah decided to sacrifice one to construct a fireplace. In theory it should have worked. Oscar had done an excellent job of cutting a stovepipe hole at the back of the top end, but he over-cut the metal, making it seven inches in diameter instead of six. Six-inch stove pipe was all Noah had. Not to be beaten, Noah solved this problem by cutting the bottom from a two-gallon coffee pot which had a seven-inch bottom and a six-inch top. Cutting a hole at the bottom, he was ready for the trial run. Noah's idea was to eliminate wood-cutting completely. Instead, he planned to push long logs into the fire pot through the door as they burned. He would use a stool made just the right height to support the log on the outside.

Well, the small starter fire worked fairly well, with just enough smoke escaping from the converted coffee pot spout to give the illusion of a boiling pot of coffee. When Noah pushed the long logs into the drum stove, however, the fire crept back on the logs too close to the opening for safety and, of course, it burned so badly it drove Noah out of the cabin with smoke. The smoke was so thick at times that it billowed out the cabin door and all the while Noah cussed in French. Oscar claimed he was able translate the gist of it as being "You American S.O.B. You never were any good. You came to Cold River City just to torment a poor old hermit!"

After a few minutes of listening to Old Whiskers yell in irritation, Oscar and Richard were pounding each other with delight and laughing out loud. They didn't dare make any comments about the failed invention. It was obvious all the time put into it was for nothing. They just let Noah carry on, venting his aggravation and wondering if some of Noah's free verse might have included something about their amusement in his irritation.

When Noah calmed down and re-entered the once smoke-filled cabin, he tossed a bucket of water into the firepot and began pulling out the smoldering logs. When the unworkable oil drum fireplace invention had cooled, it was removed from the Town Hall. Noah immediately kicked it over the bank. It rolled down the slope face we called The Can Dump, because it was becoming littered with metal and tin cans in various stages of rusted decay. The drum dropped into the water, bobbing and banging against the rocks. A final French exasperation was spoken, and Noah settled.

"You want us to go down there and bring it back? We could try setting it back up and make some adjustments," Oscar said.

Noah looked funny-like at him and just started to laugh, saying it was all his fault for using the wrong plan. "I should have turned it into one of those washing machines rather than a fireplace."

CV also filled me in on the details of a heavy galvanized tank Noah and the boys had earlier lugged from the CCC dump site to the Dam camp to make into a cooking stove:

Oscar looked forward to fall hunting at Camp Seward. Instead of vilifying the cold temperatures he loved being in the woods during the time of year when the deer hunters gathered at Noah's for a bowl of piping hot Everlasting Stew and hot corn muffins. *Courtesy of Dr. CV Latimer, Jr.*

By placing the tank horizontally on a raised platform and cutting the top off, they converted the useless tank into a useful stove with a thirty-inch cooking surface. A hinged door was placed in one end; they fashioned a smokestack, and added a flat iron cooking surface. When it was completed, Noah could place a fry pan, coffee pot and pancake griddle side by side with no crowding. It was necessary to fiddle around with a damper and draft control until he was able to keep a space about the size of a coffee pot's base red hot. This produced perked coffee in very short order.

There were enough extra drums to keep a future potential stove always on hand. And besides, Oscar felt responsible enough that he promised that in a short time he would bring in to Cold River a real stove worthy of a man who was called Mayor of Cold River City.

I suppose this story proves even the best-laid plans don't always work, although The Cold River Express plan of transporting the drums did work out well.

Sitting by the river today, listening to the river flow, I imagine I can hear the clanging of the metal drums as they came tumbling downstream.

Noah hoped Cold River would always run wild—and it has.

In each splish-splash-gush of coursing water, every drop is imperceptibly eroding rock and river bank; misty sprays of prisms shine in the sunlight. The flow of water is a noisy kind of wild silence. It's timeless in certain ways, even though you can tell the landscape has changed. Big Dam is gone, the Hermitage vanished. And yet I always hear voices in this intimate spot.

Cold River Hill is still a notable hermit hot spot. The thoughts and feelings of those who pass by churn up its memories. It hasn't lost its essence. The face of the former Cold River country will forever live on because of the many stories Jay, Doc and friends of Noah's loved to tell.

Chapter 22

A Visit to
Singing Pines Camp

One summer morning in 1965, Chester Rock, Noah's nephew, and Chester's friend Jeff Pescia were out investigating garage sales when Chet decided they should stop in at Singing Pines to visit Chester's Uncle Noah. Noah was in his garden tending his tomato plants, and Jeff was immediately taken with the idea that he was going to actually meet the legendary hermit.

Jeff was interested in fishing. He knew of Noah's skill and reputation from numerous local newspaper articles about the former hermit's experience in the mountains. While Noah no longer had so much energy that he wouldn't let streams that were still high from meltwater and rain deter him from wetting a line, his mental interest still was strong. The old woodsman was happy as a spring lark to talk of the many June fishing get-togethers he had enjoyed with fellow angling friends, a hungry season for trout. Talk in the warming sunshine as robins scratched in the fresh-turned garden soil made him itch to be at his hermitage once again.

The experience so impressed Jeff that he soon began what he called his "Memoirs of Noah."

> *The summer day began like many days in 1965. Chester and I were (and still are) close friends. At the time we were in the Wilmington area, looking for antiques or good used furniture for our used furniture and antique shop. As we approached the four corners going west on Route 86 from the little village of Jay, Chester mentioned that if we were to take a right turn we could go and see his Uncle Noah John, who was residing in the woods.*

He further stated, "My uncle was a hermit." I remember I looked at Chet in disbelief and told him he was crazy. But as things would go, I made a right hand turn and traveled approximately three to four miles, whereupon Chet told me to pull over to the side of the road. I did so upon his request; we emerged from the vehicle and with Chet in the lead we walked along a very narrow path. To the best that I can recall, it was about 200 or 250 yards when I observed an opening.

In looking around to the left I noticed a huge boulder, inscribed with what I believed to be paint was the name Noah. The penmanship, well really brushmanship, was just phenomenal. (Over the years many times I thought about his penmanship.)

Throughout the opening I noticed many wooden wigwams which reminded me of Indian teepees, a small building I believe to the right of us. I observed the words "Singing Pines" written somewhere on the building. The color of this building was greenish. Years later Chet and I learned that this building once housed chickens.

I then noticed a very frail-looking elderly gentleman with a long grayish beard. He wore wire-rimmed glasses. He was of thin build and stood about five feet six inches. I estimated his age to be in his late seventies or early eighties. His shoulders stooped forward slightly.

I thought for his age he appeared to have most of his hair. I also thought to myself when I saw Noah that there was a strong physical resemblance to Chet. His clothing consisted of a bluish shirt and I think old baggy jeans with suspenders to hold them up. Upon Chet introducing us, I recall in shaking his hand that it was a weak grip and I, of course, attributed that to his age. I had further observed outside in front of his cabin a cooking area with a frying pan in the middle of it. Noah John spoke very softly and sometimes his terminology was a little different than ours.

Also, I had noticed a homemade rocking chair in the front of his cabin. Noah had invited us inside his bungalow, or cabin; I

Noah's cooking at Cold River and at Singing Pines was very undistinguished in character. His idea about stretching a sparse amount of food over several meals involved making chowder. Whether it was deer or bear meat, muskrat or beaver, fish or vegetables he'd say "I'll make nice chowder." *Courtesy of Bill Frenette*

noticed what appeared to be a bench wide enough to be his bed
with blankets at the end and a small table with cans on top. I
should mention that this day was bright, sunny and warm.
There was a small box-type stove inside. I remember Noah saying
"perfect sunshine." I remember that because I never heard that
expression before or after.

Noah and I talked about fishing. He stated that he caught
mainly trout in the brooks, some Rainbow and Brown, stating
they were good eating. We talked about deer and bear hunting.
He stated that he killed many and lived off the land and "never
wasted anything." He made use of all that he killed for clothing
and eating and heat. Also I recall him saying that he had to get to
the berries before the animals did. He said he kept a good amount
of his canned food in the river where it was cool, and non-perishables
in caches of discarded galvanized CCC [Civilian Conservation
Corps] cans which prompted the remark, 'If a mountain climber
ever got low on their own food, I'd tell them to stop by the Town
Hall and Rondeau and he'll give you something good to eat out of
the garbage can.'

Possibly a few weeks passed, and Chet and I once again went to
visit Noah. Noah was about to have tomatoes and stated to us that
"tomatoes belong to the 3-R family," which was Red, Ripe and
Ready. We didn't stay very long and I recall the conversation was
"How have you been?" and "Are things going OK?"

I found Noah to be humorous, witty and a joy to talk with. I
further found him to be very intelligent, with a vast knowledge of
the wilderness. He had survived deep in the mountains of the
Adirondacks for years by himself and must be commended. His
everyday experience helped him through the life he chose and loved.

I went to visit the Adirondack Museum at Blue Mountain
Lake many years later. How surprised I was to see in the Woods
and Water exhibition the many items Noah had donated. Along
with the hermit's articles stood a life-size realistic figure I learned
Bob Longhurst carved from a single block of laminated white

pine. Longhurst's carving is incredibly lifelike. He even captured the folds and creases of Rondeau's clothes. It certainly brought back many good memories for me. I will never forget Noah John, his rocking chair or his penmanship.

Years ago I was in Tupper Lake, New York, and in a store there I came across a large framed black-and-white photo of Noah John hanging on the wall. The shop owner and I got into a conversation about Noah John. I mentioned he was my friend's uncle. He'd heard the reason Rondeau became a hermit was because he had once been engaged to a girl and that she stood him up. Chet stated there had been three general areas of speculation about why his uncle had sought out the company of the mountains. One had him driven crazy with a broken heart due to a failed romance. Another branded him a draft dodger. The last accusation had him evading the law.

Singing Pines Camp, Wilmington, NY. *Courtesy of William J. O'Hern*

None of the rumors were true. In fact, he became a hermit because of being an abused teenager. Noah never forgave his father. He kept an unrepentant hatred toward him for the way he claimed he was treated. He even considered his Aunt Maggie Miner more affectionate toward him than his own mother. Noah had a light side and a dark side and he didn't try to hide either. Both were glaringly evident. Chet said he had received this information from his mother, who was Noah's sister.

Jeff almost certainly would have been entertained by Noah's standard reply to a *Knickerbocker News* reporter's question about his flight to the woods because of a disappointment in love.

There was "never...a woman in my life. You know they talk only once a day—from morning 'til night. Besides, they want to boss a man around. Then they sometimes want to bring their mother to live with you. No sir, no women for this [rooster]."

Jeff wishes he now could remember more specific conversations, but feels he and the old man were of the same mind in many ways. "My interest was in his former lifestyle," he says. To live in the wilds, be responsible for your own survival, to be totally pleased with your own company and thoughts, to withstand the frigid cold and be almost twenty miles by foot from the closest human. That's something I might dream about, but Noah John lived the life.

"I was fascinated with what his daily activities had been like, how he carried out alone the hard tasks of felling trees and lugging them into camp, and the constant string of nature's events that kept him company."

Jeff's curiosity was not unlike that of so many others who enjoyed the company of the former hermit over the decades.

"Noah was witty in the words he used and he was comical in nature. I found his choice of words worthy of note: He would describe a hike in an unorthodox style: 'I take a five mile walk over hills and valleys, woodsy nooks, mossy swamps and ripply brooks.' He was a bit unusual—not like your typical grandparent. He liked to kid and laughed a lot," said Jeff when

Jeff was all ears to learn about Noah's fishing Cold River experiences. 1940s.
Courtesy of Burton Rondeau

THE HERMIT AND US

asked what most tugged at his heart about the lone individual living at Singing Pines.

"I had an itch to talk longer, but Chet and I needed to leave," he said. "We had more garage sales to investigate. "I looked around his yard a final time and thought his teepee woodpiles were a practical, timesaving but very old-fashioned way of drying wood. He was so friendly, very easy to talk to, and ready to continue conversing."

Noah, shading his eyes, looked toward Whiteface Mountain in the distance. Jeff thought, *You had some wonderful times, Noah. The mountains are so beautiful.* Jeff had recently seen large snowfields remaining on the shady sides of the higher peaks in the Lake Placid region. Those ancient giants were some of the towers of strength and grace Noah's eyes had fixed on from the top of Cold River Hill. Certainly they were bittersweet sights—rock monuments to the natural powers that created them, primeval reminders of the wilderness that had presented him with numerous challenges and yet had yielded the means for him to live as he chose.

Before Jeff left, Noah encouraged him to backpack into Cold River to try his hand at the trouty Black Hole a few miles above the site of his former digs. Fishing the river one last time might have been an unattainable dream for Noah, but the thought of Jeff doing so must have pleased him. Little could Jeff and Chester have known that Noah's remarks about other people's interest in his hermit way of life would prove prophetic in later years, as Uncle Noah rose to be a folk figure in Adirondack history.

Noah's Secret Code.

⊕ ⨯⊦⨯θ ´⨯⨯ ℘⊦θ |θ´|℘|| ⟍ᵇ℘ ⊕ ⊣ᵇθ|| ⊕ ⨯⊦⨯θ
ℚ⟋∘∘⊣|⊦ ⟍θ|℘ ℟⊦ ´⨯⨯▫ ⊕℘| ℘⊦θ ℘⊦⨯θ ℟⊦ ⨯⊦⊦θ
℘⊦θ ⨯℘|℘ ⊦|⟋∘⊦∘⊦|⊦▫ ♂⊦θ ⟍⊦∘⟍ ↗|⨯θ ⟍´⟋⨯ ↗↖
⊣θ℘ ⟍ᵇ|℡ ⟍ᵇ⊦⨯ˋ⊦|⊦ ℘⊦θ⊦∘ |θ|℘ᵒ ∘∘θ∘´∘⊦|⊦
℟℣∘ ℘⊦θ⊦∘ ℙ℟ᵇ|⊦▫

"I Like all the seasons but I guess I like Spring the best of all. It's the time of life the most inspirin'. The birds come back and get busy buildin' their nests, preparin' for their young." —*NJR response to what season he favored most.*

Section III
Cold River Stalwarts

Jay L. Gregory, an attorney from Binghamton, New York, and Clarence Vinette "CV" Latimer Sr., a family physician who practiced in Deposit, New York, were two Southern Tier sportsmen who called Cold River home following their first deer hunting trip in the fall of 1913. The professional friends agreed that it would be ideal to have a fishing and hunting camp in the Adirondacks. As they discussed it, they built up a cozy little picture of a backwoods shanty a few miles beyond Shattuck Clearing.

Following several exploratory trips when they used uninhabited huts and shanties, they settled on a cabin site within an easy walk of the falling-in lumber camp complex high on the southern flank of the Seward Range, within hearing distance of a brook that drained the mountainside.

Over time their wilderness paths crossed with Noah John Rondeau. While their lives were filled with job pressures and personal commitments, they respected Rondeau's philosophy that life is too short to get mixed up in the rat race.

"Noah would tell us his observation," commented CV, "about how society's scramble dealt with people placing too much emphasis on the almighty dollar and not enough emphasis on the real treasures of life such as friendship, nature and leisure. He joked that if he worked long and hard and invented the perfect mouse trap, he'd be too old to enjoy the fruits of his labor."

During each two-week spring fishing and fall hunting trip, Noah became the men's honored guest at their supper table, as were they at his hermitage. Noah was also the official caretaker of the men's Camp Seward.

"His partiality for all kinds of home-made hermit chowder meant it was often the main meal he served," Gregory said.

Lt. to Rt. Dr. C.V. Latimer Sr. and Jay L. Gregory by abandoned Boulder Brook lumber camp complex a short hike from their Camp Seward. *Courtesy of Dr. CV Latimer, Jr.*

Throughout the years the men were glad to have been on the trail with Noah. They enjoyed "laughing good times," crisp comfortable temperatures, and well-learned lessons taught by the grandmaster of woodsmen.

CV remembered, "Following a fine supper of bear steaks and onions, garden-fresh potatoes and carrots, we spread ourselves around the yard to rest. Constant conversation was not necessary, nor did it occur. We respected each other's space and privacy. I believed then, and still do, that if friends could comfortably share long periods of silence side by side, their friendship would not only strengthen, but last forever." They were like brothers in friendship.

As Rondeau grew older, Gregory and Latimer looked out for Noah's well-being, both financially and medically, never loosening their clasp of friendship.

The complete story of Jay and CV's life and times with Noah can be found in *Adirondack Pastimes: Family Camping and Sporting Adventures in the Cold River Country with Noah John Rondeau (1913–1950).*[7]

What follows are some examples of the kinds of correspondence that passed between the men. 🐾

Noah's Secret Code.

⟨coded symbols⟩

"Some of these kids nowadays who want to quit school make me sick. I've been on my own since I was a little shaver. Practically everything I know I picked up myself. I never could make money enough to get to college, but I'd like to have made it." —NJR *in a conversation about lost opportunities.*

Chapter 23

Letters to Jay L. Gregory

Jan. 1st 1940
Coreys N.Y.

Mr. and Mrs. Jay L. Gregory
36 Beethoven St.
Binghamton, N.Y.

Dear GrandPa and GrandMa

The Mayor of The Wigwam of Cold River congradulate you because you are Grandparents—because 1939 brought you a splendid Grand child.

Good Luck to you and young Ann.

I came out from Cold River – Dec 21st and I got your letter. The package referred to did not arrive yet but I'm not worried. – Christmas mails are heavy; and even here at Bartlett's we don't go to the P.O. every day.

Will Oscar Burgiere and his nephew (Robert Henry of Thomasville Conn) were with me from Oct 21st to Dec 2nd. Oscar got a seven point buck and Robt. Got a ten. I got a buck that was just as little the biggest of the three and no doubt he was an eight pointer, but some how he had broken off one of his antlers and so he only had six points left to count. There was not much difference in the size of bucks; Robert's had the best head; we were glad of it. Robt. Is only 17 and it was his first Deer Hunt.

They had a very good time and went home happy. I just got a letter from each and all is well.

Dr. Chrisiernin wrote me about the time you wrote, and he made mention of "The Pictures" you left with him. He said "The shots at the town hall made me- Home sick." I got a letter also from Dr. Fellows; both Doctors promise to come fishing next May.

My Christmas started as soon as I got out of the woods and will last well along in January.

Christmas we had the usual "Tree" at Roy Hathaway's.

Christmas day, six of us tried to eat a 16 pound turkey. We made a splendid start; but it took all the next day to finish.

I got a load of useful presents and an armful of Christmas Cards and splendid letters.

Last Friday, a friend of mine (W.H. Burger of West Port) came to Bartlett Club and got me with his Gass Buggy and he took me to his home, South of West Port Village, on the shore of Lake Champlain for a visit. I had a nice time.

The drive is most beautiful. The mountains and hills are anything from 5000 ft. high, down to the size and symmetry of a Hay Stack. The snow is a foot deep at Bartlett's and only 1" deep at West Port.

Along the road: all you can imagine for kaleidoscope; that can be made with Mountains, Valleys and Hills.

A solid wilderness that borders a narrow road; little trees that brush the car window with their green finger-tips through their mittens of snow.

Then open farm fields: tall elm trees and distant scenes of "Mountains that skip like Rams and little hills like Lambs," as far as natural vision can see. And in the 62 miles, five villages, many brooks, rivers, rustic bridges, historical John Brown's grave and all the rest of the variety—-all plastered with snow. Or, perhaps, not "plastered" but every rail and stump and stone and shrine, carefully sprinkled with a snowflake at a time.

I notice it would be too lengthy to give you my report of Mr. Burger's Camp; the evening program, etc...

Jan 2nd

Today: I went to Tupper Lake; got a tooth pulled and bought a hunting and fishing license. And on the way I got The Package at Coreys P.O.

Now I thank you, and all The Gregory's involved in sending me such a wonderful package of splendid and most useful items.

I must write Dr. Bill a chunk of my mind too and tell him what I think of his Bum Fishing and Little Ann, etc...

Jan 3rd

Today: Its cold and crispy; Roy Hathaway and hired man (Geo. Breen) are sawing wood with engine and drag-saw.

Mrs. Hathaway is pealing apples; Joan Hathaway (16) is in high school at Saranac Lake.

AnnaBelle Hathaway (19) is reading a newspaper, just now.

The Mayor from Cold River-Town Hall corner of Seward Brook St.- and Thistle Ave., just had a little "Hermit-Sling" and now he's scribbling with a stub pen that don't write too good.

Lt. to Rt. Jay L. Gregory, Maude Gregory, Ruth Gregory, Noah. 1938.
Photograph by Bill Gregory. Courtesy of Dr. CV Latimer, Jr.

And now: Closing!
Good luck to you Grampa and GrandMa Gregory.
And I hope to see you ....at Seward Pond in June.

> *Very Truly*
> *N.J. Rondeau*

June 2nd 1947
Noah John Rondeau
Mayor of Cold River
Coreys, NY

Mr. Jay L. Gregory
36 Beethoven Street
Binghamton, NY

Dear Friend Gregory:

Since I saw you at the Replica of my "Town Hall" at Grand Central Palace, Feb. 19th, I often thought of you and wanted to write; but the best I could do was a brief line on a card.

I have been more busy than the "renowned cat" on the metal roof.

Since Feb 12th, when I came out from Cold River by helicopter, many things have happened to me that would seem unusual for a Hermit Rondeau.

Your publicity of me, 10 years ago, seem quite forgivable now. In fact, the last 3 months, I collected clippings enough of personal ballyhoo to fill a large scrapbook.

I had 38 full days at 5 Sportsmen's Shows and as many days between shows when I was kept very busy speaking at schools, hospitals, clubs and radios.

I was called the 2nd time by "We the People Program" which is quite unusual; I find directly from the management that not more than one is ever called the 2nd time of 300 participants.

While in New York (Early May) I took in the Hayden Planetarium; I watched Solar System Parade for an hour; and then the Sky Show in the dome and I listen to 40 minutes talks: The speaker made a slight mistake on "Transit of Venus" and I caught him at it, so, just between Gregory and me, I flattered myself, that is, they put anything over, they will have to stretch their radius beyond the elementary yard stick.

And next day I called at Dr. Fellows office and he called ½ a dozen of my old friends, within the block and we had a reunion in Dr. Fellows office. It was a pleasant occasion.

Now I'm back to Cold River, I suppose for months.

I could have stayed out, in fact, I turned down two shows and chance to address several clubs in order to return to C. River.

We've had a late spring; but now, grass is green, flowers are blooming and a Robin is nesting in my Wigwam.

Until further orders—

Address
N.J. Rondeau
Long Lake, NY
C/O Mr. Lucius Russell

I hope it's well with you and yours and that you are enjoying this Vernal Season.

N.J. Rondeau

Noah's Secret Code.

"Never did find out who holds a title to it. It isn't state land, anyway. I'm never bothered with the assessors or the tax collector, anyways." —*NJR's follow-up when questioned about the ownership of the gore, his little strip of land he called "my woods."*

Chapter 24

Dr. Clarence Vinette
"CV" Latimer Sr.'s Camp Notes

From Camp Seward Journal

Mon. Oct. 25, 1948: *Rested my old feet today. Did not leave camp. Prepared quite a lot of wood for next summer. C.V. hunted Cobblestone. Mild. Noah came down today for his annual visit. He is very fat and has a belly like Santy Claus. He is full of plans for this winter [sportsmen] shows. Chicken & biscuit and good fellowship. Early to bed. Mild about 20 degrees*

Tues. Oct. 26, 1948: *C.V. reading. Noah writing to Mrs. La May. Cabin is nice and warm. All relaxed after a boiled dinner with lemon pie. C.V. & I hunted north of cabin and Noah Burnt Mountain. No deer or signs of deer. Continued fair & mild. Erected the new ice box today. Tonight 20 degrees.*

Wed. Oct. 27, 1948: *Hunted north of Miller Falls. Some deer signs. Found a nice stove at Tusck's cache! Door and swinging top were gone. Woods are very dry and noisy. No rain or snow for a long time. Noah walked to Big Horn Camp. Said he planned to paint 24 covers, cans and jars. Wonder what for? Mild, about 50 degrees in day and 24 degrees at night. 4 cans of evaporated milk for two men and a guest for 7 days.*

Thurs. Oct. 28, 1948: *Fair and clear after sun came through the morning mist. Noah returned. Reported four Staten Island hunters stopped at Shattucks. They are staying at Plumley's. C.V. hunted the Broken Bridge swamp… I fixed a new prop in cabin and leveled the table. Camp is in fine condition* now for the winter. A new brace in corner back of stove and two new ones in front of stove as well as one near the foot of bed. Replaced wooden frame at base of stove and new shelves near door (orange crates). We also banked the east side of camp so that it is wind proof.

Fri. Oct. 29, 1948: *Noah left for home today after spending 2 hours hunting for a stove door part and top plate that he hid 13 years ago. No luck so we have to get new parts if we are ever to use the stove next year. Noah came down last Mon. and made us a good long visit. He visited Russell Wed. and returned here Thurs. He is very fat and lazy. He did a small amount of hunting for us. Clear & mild.*

Sat. Oct. 30, 1948: *Worked about camp today. Finished our wood pile for next year, packed corn meal, white flour, sugar, etc. in jars; wax paper, bourbon—to be left in the cache for '49, and practiced with the pistol. A nice quiet family day. C.V. washed dishes all the time.*

Doc Latimer (middle). Camp Seward. 1941. *Courtesy of Dr. CV Latimer, Jr.*

THE HERMIT AND US
Our Adirondack Adventures with Noah John Rondeau

Section IV

Hermit
Stories

"Noah sure was a magnet," Richard Smith underscored.

> *He attracted people from all walks of life to Cold River. I often thought, when he was feeling a mite lonesome following months of having no human contact, that he would step up the power [of the "magnet"] and before long someone would show up, whether it be a hunter, a fisherman or just a hiker or mountain climber stopping by to say hello.*
>
> *I know how often I would get an overpowering urge to visit him, and as I neared the City my often-dragging feet would have more spring the last few miles, anticipating the joy I would soon feel in the presence of my most unforgettable character. Wishes were fulfilled here.*

The following are two of Smith's stories based on events from Smith's real-life experiences in the Cold River country, his memories—individual and outdoorsy—and his life with Noah John Rondeau. These stories paint a vivid picture of just what it was that made Cold River life an amazing experience.

By living a hermit's life, "Old Whiskers" realized a degree of freedom many of us only dream about. *Courtesy of Richard J. Smith from Noah's photo album*

Smith's stories started when he graduated from high school in 1939 and put down roots in the mountains, first in a cobbled-together camp in the headwaters of the Chubb River and later in a cabin near Duck Hole, headwaters of Cold River. From it, Smith had almost constant access to his mentor, Noah Rondeau. The diverse tales are sometimes related in high spirits, sometimes in a matter-of-fact tone, and occasionally in a reflective way. The real life stories explore Smith's life with Noah in the days of the old-time woodsmen.

A particular fond memory Smith always carried was of a special bottle of spirits the hermit kept at the Hermitage. Smith's remembrance of the booze jug and its hidden location at the Mammoth Graveyard—Rondeau's secret place where he stashed valuables in Ouluska Pass—set me on several unsuccessful bushwhack to find the hidden collection of galvanized garbage cans. Noah collected them from former Cold River side camps when the CCC pulled out, and found them perfect for storage of many items.

Smith related that to mark special occasions, Noah would bestow a dollop of scotch from his Trophy Bottle upon any deer hunter companion who bagged a buck, then record the event in his hieroglyphic code on a piece of white adhesive tape affixed to the side of the long-necked whiskey bottle.

Noah's Secret Code.

When I hear of men holding a banquet to speed "Wild Life Welfare," I conclude for myself, "If a Cold River Deer could attend, and hear and comprehend the keynoter and spell binders, he would kill himself laughing before he'd starve on Hemlock boughs. —NJR in reply to Ranger Toomey telling Noah about efforts of sportsmen's clubs feeding deer.

Chapter 25

Willie, My Pet Weasel

In my wilderness travels I once chanced upon a would-be trapper. He established his headquarters in an abandoned blacksmith shop, the only remaining structure of a former lumber camp located between Moose Pond and the dam on Moose Creek outlet. He seemed rather proud of his novice accomplishments and invited me to join him for a meal. I wasn't set on arriving at my Duck Hole camp at any particular time, so I decided to accept his invitation. Curiosity rather than hunger was my motivation.

His lack of woodsmanship was immediately apparent. I was truly amazed at how inexperienced and naive he was when he proudly pulled from a wooden shelf a container of rice. It was one of a few dry goods left behind, no doubt, by hunters the previous season. The leftover groceries played well with his notion that a woodsman must be able to live off the land. Apparently it didn't matter what the source of the food was. Without questioning the palatability, he had been eating the rice. He pointed out that this package must have originally been incorrectly filled, because it contained a lot of black, unprocessed rice mixed with the white kernels. (This was a fairly common status for poorly-stored rice in the woods.) No matter, though. He had eaten over half the contents and hadn't suffered any ill effects. I didn't have the heart to tell him rice was not naturally black. I did, however, strongly hint that he should keep all his food in confining containers. Shortly after, an inner voice told me to cut short my visit and continue on to camp.

In contrast to the greenhorn's cabin, my snug cabin, I'm proud to say, was free of any signs of 'Knaw-it-run-abouts'. This was due to a woods lore

Richard Smith, 1992. As Richard paddled with the author he told story after story.
Courtesy of William J. O'Hern

lesson learned early in my career. When I started trapping, I noticed weasels regularly visited the interior of my wilderness abode. Setting a trap inside the camp seemed an easy way to make a few extra shekels. I caught several weasels with a yellowish tint and a large pure white one during my first season at the Hole. To my surprise, when I received my check from the fur house, the yellow tints brought in only $1.50 to $2.00; whereas the ermine pelt rewarded me with $15.00. A written offer was attached to my payment, noting the fur house would take all the pure white weasels I sent in. The financial reward was music to my ears, but I never trapped another weasel after that first season.

I had observed that when there were weasel signs about the camp, mice were nonexistent. I concluded it was more important not to kill the goose that was laying the golden eggs.

Shortly after hunting season had closed during the second winter I stayed at the Duck Hole, I discovered a large white weasel had made a nest on a shelf in a remote corner of the cabin. I was happy he had come to live with me, but I must admit I felt a bit leery going to sleep once I had learned of his presence. That first evening of the discovery, I rationalized that this vicious killer had probably remained undetected for quite a spell and had been sharing my bunkroom all along. If indeed he had, then he was 'friendly.' Respecting his skill as a great mouser, I wanted him to remain. But the first week I slept like a crow with one eye open for safe measure.

One morning I awoke to find him curled up at the foot of my bed. From all outward signs he appeared to be fast asleep, but as my eyes lost their sleepiness, I noticed he too slept with one eye open and was looking right at ME! In the ensuing weeks I coaxed him with bits of food, attempting to develop in him a sense of trust that I meant no harm. Eventually I could actually hand feed him as he stood on his hind legs. His squeaks were friendly sounds. Not only was he good company, but his presence kept me from talking to myself as much as I might have.

He remained through the end of February, sharing the warmth and protection of the cabin during the frigid depths of the winter. Whenever the temperature warmed to zero he would disappear for a day or so, and I would actually miss him.

I recall a conversation I once had with my good friend Noah Rondeau regarding pets and isolation. He too was often alone for months at a time, holed up in his tiny cabin back at Cold River. I had spent enough time with him during the winter to realize that one activity he engaged in to idle the long hours away was to devise different ways to catch mice. He even recorded their capture in his journals, as illustrated in the following entries for February, 1940.

A mouse tried my Victor trap Richard brought me.

And the following day he had added:

The mouse that got killed in the trap yesterday is still dead.

Of Rondeau I had inquired: Wouldn't a pet both remove some of the isolation and serve a useful purpose?

"Richard," came his response, "a dog has to have something to chase and if not chipmunks and squirrels it would be the deer that come to my garden and camp yard as friendly as can be. Deer would not jump on me with muddy paws or unnecessarily bark at three o'clock in the morning. Or for that matter bark twenty-four hours a day scaring all the animals off for miles around. No, they're helpless fools."

"As for a cat, they're too stuck up," he continued. "I used to have one during my barbering years when I lived on Greenwood Street in Lake Placid. That cat kept making a mess on the floor. I should have wrung its neck but I tried to cure it from this bad habit. I'd vigorously rub its nose in the mess and toss it out the window. After a week of that the cat learned what I was trying to teach him too well. If he had to go to the bathroom, even if he was way out in the field, he would run to the house, make a mess on the floor, rub his nose in it and jump out the window. Cats are intelligent, as you can see. They can learn and might make good pets if only they wouldn't get it all wrong."

He had a twinkle in his eye, knowing he had caught me with that one, but I continued to press the issue after we both enjoyed a laughing good time.

"But couldn't they keep down the rodent population?"

"They're just too stuck up, Richard. They never kill every mouse or rat because they feel they must save a few for a rainy day. And it only takes one mouse to add 'black rice' to white. Besides a cat tires of mice and would soon be after my birds. I'd much rather hear a bird sing than a cat's yowling. And if it killed one of my birds, I'd have to condemn it to death. No I don't need pets. I have enough wild ones to enjoy, and I don't have to feed them when there is hardly enough food around in winter for an old hermit."

Regardless of Noah's attitude toward keeping pets, my weasel was a real pal; he truly shaved the edge from my winter lonesomeness. When he left in the spring it was the last time I was to see him. The next winter two younger weasels came by the cabin on a mouse hunt, and as they were both white, I like to think they were the offspring of the pal I had affectionately named Willie.

Handsome Hill. Richard Smith's River Road cabin outside of Lake Placid, NY. "Maybe there are always changes in everyone's life—it's just the nature of things. Changes can be opportunities, not problems. My thinking is that Richard made those opportunities by inviting me into his life. I will be forever grateful."
—The author. *Courtesy of William J. O'Hern*

Chapter 26

A Badge's Authority

The company at the Dittmars' Silver Lake camp was a friendly, short gentleman—a true woodsman. He stood about five feet tall without the felt hat he wore, which had been painted with many coats of green paint. He said it kept the hat water-tight and stiff. Where he usually wore a leather jacket, sort of a vest, wide baggy trousers supported with suspenders and L.L. Bean boots, today he was dressed in his Sunday best outfit, a lightweight black suit and tie. His combed long white beard made him look perpetually happy and contented; his charisma went with his face.

He looked Ditt, Mary, Bill and Helen over thoroughly and skeptically. They were dressed in swimsuits, and they were familiar with the old man. By nature and habit, he was not a man who enjoyed suiting up, although he was sitting poolside.

"Ain't no reason for you kids to get any water on a tired old hermit," he said cheerfully. "I'm fixing to tell you a story anyway."

The group knew what that meant, and they would much rather listen to Noah's stories than swim. They could always swim when he wasn't there to entertain them. They gathered around to listen.

> *This is the kind of time-honored story Noah told over and over. The Dittmars heard a version of it. Without a doubt it is an old guide's tale I call "A Badge's Authority." This is how Burton Rondeau recalled Noah telling it.*
>
> *Well ya know a game warden, out on his patrol, stopped at my trapline jungle camp back in the '20s over by Peek-a-Boo*

The Cold River teller of true and tall tales. *Courtesy of Richard J. Smith from Noah's photo album*

*mountain to talk a while in the name of nosyin' about. He
says to me, "Noah, I need to inspect your wigwams for illegally
obtained furs."*

*I says to him, "Go ahead. You ain't gonna find none but don't
go in the furthest one over there by the garden," and I pointed it
out so's he'd know fer sure the one I was talkin' about.*

*About then the durn sonofafox bureaucrat verbally explodes
in words as he reached for his coat lapel exclaiming, "Mister, I got
the authority of the Conservation Commission with me," as he
flashed his shiny badge and pompously pushed it into my whiskers.
"You see this here badge? This badge means I am allowed to go
wherever I want on anyone's land. Into anyone's place. NO
questions asked and NO answers given. Have I made myself clear?
Do you understand?"*

**Caption: Edward A. Harmes and Noah resting and talking during a hike to
Couchsachraga peak. 1946.** *Courtesy of John M. Harmes*

So I see what this officer was all about. Darned if I was gonna listen to him bark any orders at me, so I nods politely, "Suit yerself." 'Twas clear he didn't want to hear nothin' from me so I gone on about my woodchippin.'

I 'member it weren't long I hears a loud scream and sees the stuffed shirt runnin,' leapin' for his life and yellin' beaRRRRR as he flapped and flailed his arms like a crazy goose. That black bear hadn't been fed no supper yet and saw him as the dinner bell.

With every lop that bear was gainin' ground on the officer, and it seems likely that his hide would surely get ripped to shreds before he'd reach something safe. The fool was plainly terrified.

I was 'bout as excited over this in a good way, as he was nervous.

After what seemed like a few long minutes, I throws down my axe, ran to the edge of the clearing and yelled at the top of my lungs.....

"Your badge. Show him your BADGE !"

Noah's Secret Code.

ᑫᔨᕽᘛᕒᕲᕽᕽᘛᖲ ᕹᕒᕲ ᐧ ᕬᕒᐤᕽ ᕽᕽᕹᘛᖯ ᕽᕲ ᕹᘛᕒ ᕽᕒᐧᕹᕲᕹ ᕬᕍ ᕽᘛᘛᕽ ᕒᕽᘛ ᕲᕽᕽᕽ ᕽᕽᕽᘛ ᕬᕝᕲᕝᕽ ᘛᕽᕲᘛᖯ ᕽᕲ ᕹᕾᘛᕅ ᕒᕽᕽᕅ ᕽᕽᕽᘛ ᘛᕨᕾᕽᕍᕒ ᕾ ᕅᕨ ᕽᕾᕾ ᕽᕨᕒ ᕾᘛᕨᕾᕽᘛᖯ ᑫᕾᕒ ᕒᕽᘛ ᕀᘛᕍᕾᕲᕅ ᕾᕽ ᕍᕒᕾᕾᘛ ᕬᕍ ᕽᕽᕽᘛ ᘛᘛᕾᘛ ᕽᘛᕾᘛ ᕽᕾᕽᕽ ᕀᘛ ᕽᕾᕾᘛ ᕽᕾᕽᕍ ᕽᕽᕽᘛ ᕍᕒ ᕒᕽᕾᘛᕍᛁ ᕬᕍ ᕒᕽᕒᕒ ᕍᕾᕾᘛᕍᕽᕒ ᕒᕾ ᕽᘛ ᕽᕾᕾᘛ ᕒᕽᕍ ᕒᕽᘛ ᕾᕽᕒᕽᘛᕒ ᕾᕽ ᕒᕽᘛ ᘛᕾᕾᕽᕽᖯ

"Sometimes it's a hard life. I get hungry and feel the cold like anybody else. I guess this life wouldn't do for most people. But the beauty of nature and life itself were here long before human life was coined, and that appeals to me more than the riches of the world." —*NJR in response to people who ask if he is happy living among the mountains.*

Chapter 27

How to Trap a Bear

This telling has been adapted from a tape-recorded oral version.[8]

"So you want a story about how to catch a Cold River bear do you?" Noah questioned the small gathering of old friends who once were regulars at his Cold River diggings.

According to his daily journal, Thursday, August 8, 1963 had been "hot, a mixture of sun and clouds." He watered his bachelor buttons and cucumber plants and noted the "Rabbits trim Carrot Tops" the previous

Lt. to Rt. "Ditt," Noah, Mary Dittmar. At the Dittmar's Silver Lake camp.
Courtesy of Helen C. Menz

evening. Of personal interest, he recorded the event that eventually lead him to choose the "lesser traveled" life path—a solitary woods life rather than living a predictable one (job, marriage, home and children). He penned: "65 years ago I left Jackson Hill. Ran away from home. Left Peter Rondeau and His Stick, His Abuse, His Religion and His Fool God."

The camp crowd, former mountain climbers, their children and grandchildren turned to their honored guest. The audience wore bathing suits. Noah was attired in his Sunday best (and only) worn black suit, vest, tie and rounded crown bowler-like hat. Helen Menz said he sat in a red Adirondack-style lawn chair near the water's edge and never once complained about being overdressed in the summer's heat. Noah blended well at the annual family gathering. He enjoyed the children, relishing all the attention bestowed on him.

Aldoph "Ditt" Dittmar turned the lever to record and the reel-to-reel tape recorder began to capture Noah's telling about a bear hunt he had.

"So a story about Cold River life and so forth is what you want. Well I'll give you one that will make your head swim," he went on. "Anyone who has been up to Cold River knows something of the area but has only seen, maybe, half of my tricks. Some of them tricks I've played on bears. In fact your friend Mr. Clements, here, came up to my country and he got to talking to me about fishing and fishes until I was pretty near sea sick!

"Well, you've been up there and you've seen some of those mountainsides where I've skinned bear and taken the hearts out of them when they are warm and so forth and so on." Noah was referring to his run-of-the-mill bear trap circuit that began at the Great Anvil lumber camp. There he placed his Audel trap. Each bear trap had a different name. Audel, the meaning has been lost to history, was placed on the outskirts of the shanty clearing. It was his most active trap. Each of his large, heavy traps were never carried back to the hermitage when he picked them up from their cubbies. As an alternative they were hung beneath nearby evergreen trees, to remain protected from the weather until trapping season came around again. From the lumber camp clearing the route passed Mammoth Grave-yard and then split. One fork went southwest to Ouluska Pass Brook and his trout pond beyond. The other continued more westward to the clear-ing of the old Santa Clara High Lumber camp below Mount Emmons. A connecting route followed upstream past the Devil's Cauldron. The entire route was no longer than a solid two miles — short enough to tote the dead weight of a bear out of the woods.

"Well sir I went out for a bear one day and well, errr, I climbed high — went way up the mountain. Made quite a circle. I had a hatchet, and my bag, and I had a lunch, and I had some other things. I went way up the mountain — made quite a circle covering by a long walk much ground." Noah, skilled in looking for signs of bear, was also a master at embellish-ment. He knew black bears are generally timid and avoid people. As a result he "looked under leaves and peeked behind bushes." The bears he hunted were wild, unlike many bears in the mountains today that have been allowed to become tame by finding food near bird feeders, garbage can, dumpsters, barbecue grills, tent sites, unattended vehicles, outbuild-ings and houses."

Noah continued to bring his hunt to life.

"On my circle back home I stopped near a brook to have my lunch. I used my hatchet to cut some wood, and I made a little fire to boil a cup of tea." The small stream that ran down the mountain far below the sum-mit was so small a stream that a bored-to-death hermit could move as much water in three butter pails than what ran downhill in what would more properly be called a briblet. As he sat he surveyed the surrounding area, careful to register any clues of bear whereabouts, knowing bears will take advantage of almost any readily available food source. Due to the ex-tremely dry conditions in the mountains that spring and summer, the bears' natural food was much more difficult to come across.

"I had my lunch, I didn't put out the fire. I just up and walked away. When I arrived at the Town Hall I noticed my hatchet was missing from the leathered scabbard on my belt. I forgot it, you see, where I had eaten my lunch. So, all right, I went along without the hatchet for a few days. Then, I determined I didn't get a bear that first day, you see, because I had lost my hatchet. It was a case of bad luck. So I concluded I was going back up the mountain, find my lost hatchet and get a bear.

"Well then, I left my Handsome Hill on Cold River and figured I had about three miles to go up to that little brook and back. Well, I went about a mile and looked pretty gingerly about every tree top and peeked behind every boulder, you know where there might be a bear, and you know, I didn't see a bear. So I went another mile and, you know, I still didn't see a bear. Well, I went the last mile and got pretty near back the camp, close as a 100 feet so as I could see the wigwams and I looked back and around and I couldn't see a bear atall. So I put my gun up in camp and I reached the conclusion I wasn't going to get a bear that day either. Can you beat that?"

Several days of solitude passed at camp. He liked the quiet. Then during breakfast he realized he was tired of gabbing to himself. Consequently he told himself to load up some gear in a pack basket and get going. He didn't want himself under foot any more. And he did. "Well, a few days later I wanted to go back into the woods and get a bear so I filled my pipe with tobacco. When I opened my wooden matchbox I noticed I only had one match. I don't like to go hunting with only one match because I never knew if the match would be any good or not, so I scratched it on the strike plate and it was good. So, I went hunting. Looking right and left and ahead and backwards I searched the woods for signs of bears. I also figured on looking for my hatchet when I went off because I had forgotten it the last time I went out a few days before."

When a bear hunter walked into Ouluska Pass real labor and brainwork was involved. Noah didn't need God as his copilot. He was an experienced trapper-hunter. He walked the pathway without map or guidebook. He just walked by instinct. For that inborn ability to flawlessly guide himself he earned the admiration of the mountain climbers. He had the human equivalent of that of the mobile bears he hunted: excellent olfactory senses and a homing ability.

Upon reaching the tiny water course he called Paper Bag brook, Noah jumped the wash then continued to follow it upstream to the lunch site of a few days ago. "The fire I left there had burned quite a little circle around. It had burned up the leaves, and the little sticks, and the big sticks and

Noah hunted bears as well as he enthusiastically told bear stories. Circa early 1930s.
Courtesy of Richard J. Smith from Noah's photo album

even more. It burned up the ax head, but I found the wooden handle! I turned up all them ashes and I couldn't find that iron head at-all—only the ashes, but by golly I got the handle. Ohhh that was a great rescue so I came back to camp.

"Well I didn't get a bear that day either so I went back into the woods and I set a trap for a bear, and while I was at it I killed a couple of rabbits and a woodchuck and then beat it good back to camp and waited a couple of days." The neighborhood bears in Noah's neck-of-the-woods did not usually put him through the tireless job of fending them off. Keeping the hermitage free from raiding bears in big fur coats did not, however, prevent boredom. While he didn't fear bears he did consider them to be a nuisance and dangerous. Keeping the home place clean avoided the complicating factor of bears raiding camp and destroying property.

As an aside, Noah's only close call was with a bear that had lost some toes on a front paw, the appendages torn out while escaping the hold of a 415X high-grip Triumph bear trap set. As a result, it's assumed, it avenged its physical loss on "Old Whiskers." Noah's friend, Richard Smith, humorously retold the tale in a three-paged recollection titled "The Bear That Tried to Polish Noah Off," which I have reduced to bare bones. Apparently the bear knew how to add. One man in the woods + being injured in a trap = trappers are trouble. When Mr. No-Toes spotted Noah lounging against a tree, puffing on his pipe, the bear gave two "woofs" in between a clicking of its teeth as he approached. Startled, Noah jumped to his feet, immediately saw the angry bear coming at him and lighted out. He wasted no time shinning up a tree.

From his treed position Noah did the equivalent of putting salt on a wound. He jabbed at the bear with lethal words. "Ohhhh Mister Bear. So you think you want to tickle my feet." That comment only added insult to the bear's earlier injury and a chase ensued after the bear shook Noah clear from his tree perch. The pursuit eventually ended at his Cold River metropolis when the bear dropped dead in front of the Town Hall cabin.

With all the mild weather Noah wasn't surprised he hadn't seen any bear tracks. Because there was very little food to forage, he assumed the large animals might be denning early. If so they wouldn't venture out until late spring greenery appeared. Regardless of how the state of affairs was stacking up, Noah was bound and determined to have an argument with a black bear. "So I went back to see my trap and it was gone." His fortune had taken a lucky turn. "The forest floor and trees was all clawed up and ribbons of shredded bark hung to the ground from big balsams. I sat down, smoked a bowl of tobacco on the situation. I surmised a big bear had stepped into the trap, pressed the pan down against the frame, and held it, you know"

That bear needed to improve on his manners. You don't accept the mayor of Cold River city's invitation and then run away with his door prize before exchanging at least a few words.

"'Where did he take off to with my bracelet?' I thought. I looked about. Checked every tree to make sure he wasn't hiding behind one. And then, I spotted the rascal's trail. Sure enough, he'd gone off with the trap. So, I followed along and pretty soon I came up to the bear." The bear was in no mood to offer the mayor a customary Cold River handshake. The drag chain had wrapped around a tree, preventing any further advance. With his escape foiled he snarled, kicked up a fuss, threw dirt Noah's way and reached out with his claws, maddened more with each swipe that missed its intended human target. That's a bear's only revenge, you know, what with his ancestors routinely taken in leg-gripping traps with teeth in the jaws.

"Well, he was an awfully big bear and he was awful mad. He had circles around his eyes and froth dripped off of his chin and his tongue run out a foot and he looked at me and then he'd look the other way then he'd growl and so forth..."

The old hunt became clearer as he continued describing it and recalled more details. His expressions were sometimes zany, yet they conveyed the particulars of how he thought and acted. To his listeners this beautiful little story line came welling out of him. "Yes sir, you know—as I was telling you, the bear growled. Well, of coarse that made my hair stand right up— pretty near to the moon and ummmm, well, he was a big bear, and of coarse I didn't want to go and curl his mustache. I ain't much afraid of bear but then I don't like them to take a hold of me. Ahhh, did you ever have a bear take a hold of you, doctor?" Ditt replied little more than "'No, I haven't.'" It was obvious the hermit was in command of his audience, and

Ditt was wondering just as much as everyone else what happened to Noah. This was obviously not the time to ask questions. Everyone wanted their curiosity to be satisfied.

"Well they take a hold right around, you know, and stick their claws in. Well, that ain't so bad but what gets me is when they let go, they let go quick and that makes me awful nervous.

"Well, I shot that bear anyway, you know, and I killed him. I went up to him and he looked pretty dead. But you know what I do in a case like that? I don't take a chance. I sit down and watch him for five minutes… ahhh to see if there's a breath in him you see. And if he can hold it for five minutes, I think he's a good bluffer or else he's dead.

"Then I go up and give him a kick in the backside, you know, and he shakes all over. Well then, I get a hold of trees and I get right up on the bear and I walk on his hips and then on his flanks, and then when I step on his ribs he says, " Aaahhhhhh!" He's dead but I squeezed the wind out of him, you know, and it makes him growl, I tell ya. Well that kind of starts me again, but I know he's dead so I take him by the ears and turn his head up to look at him, you know, and there's a pool of blood, a clot on the ground.

"Well that's the way I killed that bear and that must have been fifteen years ago, and he's been dead ever since. But mister, I'm telling you when they get a hold of you it's bad enough, but when they let go quick that starts me and I can't get over it for five minutes — that's the trouble. I don't mind them taking a hold of me but I hate to have them let go the way they do. It's a bear hold, you know, and if the bear lets go, and you can't understand it until you get it and it don't set good with me 'tat all. Of coarse, maybe it's better you should let go than to hang on. But that's what gets me. Well, of coarse I had the bear and there was a big trap on him. I talked to him, and in fact before I shot him I said, 'Where'd you get that trap?' The bear replied, *Grooooow!*. So I declared, 'Don't you know it's against the law to catch a bear in a trap?' He said, *Rrrroooll!*, so I shot him and he didn't get a bear in a trap after that. That was the last of him.

"That's the way to get a bear. So, I took a knife and rolled him on his back and cut off his foot and threw it aside, and I rinsed him, you know, from one end to the other. Well, the bear was on his back and I just went at him with the knife as usual and I dressed the skin on his legs and cut off those big fingers, you know, called the flangees, and left the toenails in the hide and I just ripped it down to his knees. I went at his hind legs in the same way and I pulled the cords out and I went and got a stick, put it through his hind legs and tried to lift him but I couldn't. I got about half of him off the ground and dropped him on a big crotch of a big birch tree. Well, when I pulled the hide off of him I was curious. I opened him up and I thought I was quite a doctor. I thought I knew what was the kidneys and the liver and what was the blood and so forth. I held an examination of my own there and his kidneys was all in little lumps. I looked it over real good — spent about two hours with him examining carefully, you know. In case I ever find a sick bear I might want to operate on him, you know, and I'd know just what to do.

"Well, I left him hanging there and his fore quarter was on the ground a good deal, so I put a few spruce boughs under him so he wouldn't catch too much topsoil and rotten leaves and so forth and so on. And I took a chunk of liver and the hide and I started off to Big Dam. Well, pretty near to camp I stowed the skin in the woods, stretched it on a pole that I had up between two trees and I went on the rest of the way to camp. There I had a feed of liver.

"You know if you had come along you could have help me bring the meat in, doctor. It took me two or three days later before I had all the meat toted back home. Ohhhh, why it tasted better than chicken, don't ya know? I eat bear until bear grease runs down my chin.

"Well, that's pretty much all there was to it. You know a big bear lasts a long time and between time I like to go get other kinds of meat. There's a lot of variety at Cold River. Of coarse you don't have any automobiles or gas stations, or you haven't got a Forty-Second Street or Times Square but there's a little river a hundred feet from the camp and that's where I get my trout you know and so forth and so on. And there's where I go down with a cake of soap and wash my hands and sometimes I make a little fire right down on the bank and roast my meat right there."

Having related his story, the old man in a zone of remembrance said without thinking, "I want you to come to Cold River next season, Doctor, and have a bear hunt with me."

Ditt replied, "I'd like to."

"Ohh it would be fine," Noah returned happily. "Well, have to make sure, ahhh double sure, we'll set a trap like the one I told you about. And then when we overtake the bear we'll be BOSS. We'll teach that bear how WE hunt bear."

Noah had transported himself, and everyone else, back in time. There was nothing like lounging around and listening to former hermit retell tales. His rich experiences, his fluid, sometimes quirky vocabulary and colorful descriptions helped make him an enthusiastic storyteller.

Noah's Secret Code.

"No, of course everyone has a lonely experience, and no two [are] alike. I've been more lonesome waiting two hours in a railroad station than in a whole cold winter alone in the mountains. Lonesomeness isn't jest when you're alone; it's when you're destitute, and lost." —NJR's answer when quizzed if he was ever lonely.

Noah at the edge of Boiling Pond (a.k.a. Seward) 1944. *Courtesy of Dr. Adolph G. Dittmar, Jr.*

Section V

Rondeau Family Memories

Rondeau Family Memories celebrates both the blessings that come to those who are related to a celebrated figure and the gentleness, humor, and love family members can share of a unique connection.

The following pages tell Noah John's story through the eyes of family members, so striking on its own and so bound up in the history of Adirondack lore.

Chapter 28

Uncle Noah: Rondeau Family Stories Hold Fond Memories

By the late 1980s, Rondeau's biographer Maitland DeSormo was still going reasonably strong. In his eightieth decade of life, DeSormo, along with Fran Yardley and Joe Bruchac, was regaling audiences statewide with tall tales and local legends. According to DeSormo's advertising flyer, one unidentified eighth grader from Lake George Central School declared, "I could listen all day to that guy (DeSormo)!"

As young people, Jenny and Daniel Rondeau didn't agree. Jenny remembers she and her brother tried to distance themselves from the spotlight of their regionally-famous uncle.[9]

> *I can tell you, growing up in Lake Placid and going to school at Lake Placid High, my brother and I were the only two Rondeaus. Iit was either 1986 or '87 and all the students were called to the auditorium for a show of some sort. When we got there, it was all about my Great-Grandmother Delia Rondeau Rock's brother, Noah John Rondeau. She was Noah's youngest sister! I was about fifteen years old at the time, and I can tell you I was quite embarrassed. I think what was most uncomfortable was I thought the kids considered Uncle Noah an old man who was homeless in the woods, who had nothing, rather than being a person who was doing just what he wanted. He did what he enjoyed and he was there because he wanted to be and not because he had to be. All my friends knew about hermits was that a hermit lived in the woods. I*

sank down in my seat. Later that day, when Daniel and I attempted to tell our friends that he was our Uncle Noah and tried to explain his situation, no one believed us. 'No way,' they said. As I grew older, I realized I was the type of person he was—a very independent person. I am proud to call Noah my uncle.

"He certainly was a courageous person. Some people have tried to portray Uncle Noah in a less than favorable light. They even have claimed he never was a true hermit. I know some family members were upset over that. Uncle Noah was a true hermit in our eyes. He walked everywhere, he lived off the land to a great degree, and took pleasure in his extended family even though no one saw him very often."[10]

Some of Jenny's extended family members who did visit Noah were relatives of her mother.

She says, "My mother, Alice Ann Gonyea Rondeau, had two sisters, Viola and Norval Gonyea. They often stopped in to visit Noah" when Noah lived in a little housekeeping cabin along River Road as well as when Noah occupied Richard Smith's Singing Pines camp in Wilmington. "I recall my aunts saying Noah used to put his food up on the table and all

Noah's digs were a popular destination in the late 1940s. *Courtesy of Albert "Bud" Smith*

the animals would come and eat off the table. They also said he used to bury his food in the dirt so the bears would not smell it and eat it."

Jenny isn't sure what the women meant by "bury his food." It could have been their interpretation of Noah's crude root cellar. He did bury garden crops of beets, turnips, potatoes, and carrots. Singing Pines did not have electricity, nor did Noah own a refrigerator or even an icebox.

Burton Rondeau told me he was ten years old when his Uncles Joe and Noah arrived "through snow and fierce wind" at their brother William's home in Black Brook on Wednesday, March 11, 1942. "Uncle Noah dubbed our house a lodge. In many ways it probably seemed that way to him," he said.

"Uncle Joe and Dad were close. They enjoyed doing a lot of things together—hunting, fishing, trapping, outdoor work and so forth. Noah never brought out his fishing poles or rifles on his seasonal getaways from the river. It was never during the legal season. Later on when he deserted the hermitage, he did go out with them on occasion.

Noah pointing out the variety of plants he cultivated in his flower beds.
Courtesy of Bill Frenette

"Uncle Noah was the oldest of nine children born to Peter and Alice Rondeau," Burton told me. He had no memory of "Grandma Alice" (Noah's mother), who died in 1900. "Dad was eight years old when Grandpa died on January 21, 1920. Uncle Noah claimed his father was a disciplinarian, but my father never talked about his father being strict. I didn't know Grandpa [Peter Rondeau] well." Life was challenging for the family after Peter's wife passed away.

"Back then it was typical for Grandpa to work two to three different jobs. I recall he worked at the J&J Rogers Pulp Mill and Company. Now, just exactly what he'd done I don't know. At that time he lived in a white house here in Black Brook. He operated a little store and blacksmith shop on the side, from the house. The bringing up of the family was pretty much left up to the children.

"Black Brook was a big, busy place back then. Iron mines made it big. Family members lived all along the main road. Folks used to call it Rondeau Road."

Uncle Joe, Dad, or someone else from the family often picked Noah up at Pine Point Camp. "After Noah went into the woods in 1913, he stayed winters with Al Hathaway on Saranac Lake," Burton remembered of his legendary uncle.

Burton had strong feelings about his uncle.

"Noah enjoyed people back in the woods or out here," he said. He confirmed Noah's personal hygiene "was very good. He was a very neat dresser. Kept his clothes clean. When he lived with us, Mother did his wash. There was no need to do a separate one."

Just thinking of Uncle Noah, Burton smiled. "He got along well with family members. There was a lot going on between the family members who lived nearby. If he wanted to go to Ausable [Forks] he would hire the taxi or people would take him around in their cars. I know he'd go to Wilmington, Plattsburgh and Ausable. What he did I have no idea. Visit people and tell stories I imagine. He'd also visit his sister Delia Rock in Cadyville. He'd actually stay there a few days, maybe a week or even a few weeks—whatever. I don't know about Uncle Charles and Aunt Alice. They went to Canada. Uncle Alex lived between Keene and Keene Valley. He tried to be a hermit but I don't think that went well. I know Noah saw Alex at least once a year, but that was about it. It was not like nowadays, where you jump in the car and travel miles in a day.

"Yes, he was just one of the family. He did try to encourage my father to go back to Cold River with him. Dad didn't want to have anything to do with it. It was almost as if Uncle Noah had a set thing. He was bitter in some ways and gave the impression he didn't care about society. He was a bit of a loner.[11] He had to have his time. When he left he had exhausted his time Outside or he was responding to some kind of emergency."

Burton illustrated what he meant about Noah's family loyalty: "Sometime shortly after Noah's last quarrel with the law he made up his mind he was going to live far away from everyone—back at Cold River. One night a friend of Noah's learned Maggie Rondeau Wilcox, Noah's second-oldest sister, had been critically wounded in an accidental shooting." Recognizing Noah would want to know the gravity of the calamity, "the friend hiked over twenty miles to bring the news to Noah, even though it was dusk by the time he arrived."

"'Where'd they take her?' Uncle Noah asked. With that, pointed to the cabin, told his friend to make himself snug, picked up a kerosene lantern and set off on a nearly twenty-one-mile trudge to the hospital in Lake Placid. At his arrival he found she had died. He made a similar [but shorter] trek to the Sunmount Veterans hospital in Tupper Lake when he learned of his brother Joe's hospitalization."

Burton continued, "He did enjoy people. Those that he met back in the woods or outside. He'd send gifts to family members for special occasions and press coins into little children's hands. Quarters! That was a big deal back then. I remember him sitting in the living room playing the violin. There was no doubt he liked the attention. It didn't take much encouragement to get him to play or tell stories. I clearly remember him sitting at the dining room table. He was never a large eater even when there was a large amount of food on the table. He ate just about anything. He never complained about anything.

"When I was young, I used to think he was Santa Claus. He was an attraction. I just didn't get a chance to see him that much. He paid a lot of

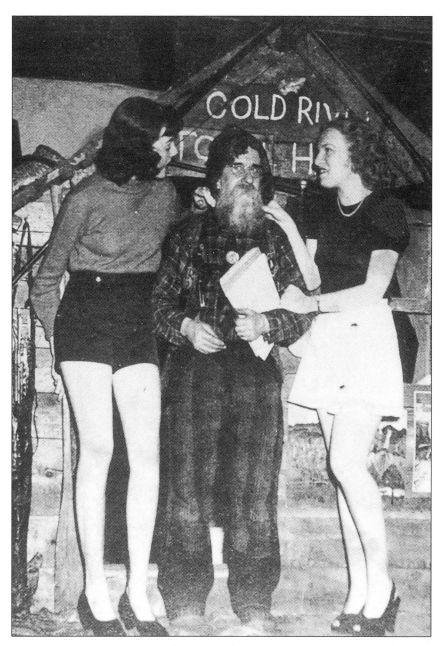

Noah embraced the advertising blitz made of his hermit image. The front cover of the Hotel Belmont Plaza weekly guide read: "Noah Rondeau considers giving up his life as a hermit after this reception of the National Sportsmen's Show, at the Grand Central Place..." February 17–25, 1951. *Courtesy of Richard J. Smith from Noah's Photo album*

Noah and his brothers enjoyed fishing. *Courtesy of Dr. Adolph G. Dittmar, Jr.*

attention to children. He didn't shove us aside. I remember him telling how he killed a bear with his bow and arrows. Shot it several times until it bled out. He'd say, 'I was a little leery because I only had five arrows with me.'

"Well, lucky thing you have a hermit here to teach you how to catch a fox,' he'd tell me with a chuckle." And, like other storytellers, Noah often had a twist to a telling, Burton revealed when he attempted to recreate his uncle's instructions in a voice that is more rustic than Noah's generally more sophisticated one: "You get yourself some boards and nails and a hammer and saw and build a box, a cage you see. Then you attach a door and a trip peg and tie a rope to the door. Lift it into the open position, hold on to the rope and get behind the box. Then you make a noise like a *dead* hen."

Although Burton has told that story many times, he laughs as much now as he did when Uncle Noah first told it. "That's the kind of thing that went on. Stories like that. As kids we were always plugging him to tell us stories and he liked that."

Burton's recollections of Uncle Noah at his grandparents' home held pleasure and contentment. How he loved that home. It wasn't the "have nots" that made this plain house special to him as a little boy; it was the "haves."

"Here's a snapshot of Noah at our wedding reception," said Burton as we reached the end of my interview. "It was an all-day event." He laughed. "I'm sure Noah had a drink or two that day with all the Rondeaus along the road."

Uncle Noah was not a larger-than-life figure to the large Rondeau family. Noah was just the nonconformist who made up his mind he'd take the plunge and live in the mountains alone.

"When it was time for Uncle Noah to return to the river, Dad would drive," Burton recalls. "I remember his full pack basket and long walking stick and the galvanized pail he would carry. He'd pack in staple supplies like flour, sugar, coffee—foodstuff like that. He was short, not a stocky-looking individual, but he was nevertheless athletic. He'd have to be, in order to face both physical and mental hardship. For Uncle Noah to make such a journey in the Adirondack wilds for over thirty years, through mountains and desolate, freezing landscapes, was considered foolhardy by some people whose discussion went on about how he might never return. Add the burden of packing on his back many pounds of supplies to feed himself over the coming months, and you had an assignment bordering on suicide, but time after time Noah proved himself a strong woodsman."

Unfortunately, Burton and the rest of the family must refer mostly to photocopies of select pages of Uncle Noah's collection of yearly journals. To its great credit, the North Elba-Lake Placid Historical Society, unlike many museums, has allowed them, and others, permission to roam through, making the journals available to view on request and putting no restrictions on copying and using the contents.

There will always be loose ends and unexplained phrases related to "Uncle Noah's" writings. Burton has to guess what was meant by his September 13, 1956 entries, journal "I paint Oil Drum for Warren Terry." …9:30 Adlai Stevenson speak from Harrisburg. The 'New Nerve,' is asking public to send contributions for Campaign."

Burton pointed out, "His writing is just one of the things I enjoy looking back on." His feelings are shared by others who enjoy reading Rondeau's journals.

Burton holds fond memories of the times Noah, Burton's father and he reminisced about the old days. Noah apparently recognized the nostalgia in his own storytelling when he exclaimed, "I've killed so many big deer and bear in the living room that I have to walk on livers."

"So Noah often told the kind of stories hunters liked to hear? The kind of tales that kept you awake long after the rest of the house had fallen asleep?" I asked Burton.

"Yes," he replied, adding that Uncle Noah had a God-given knack for spinning a yarn, and his tales were nothing short of spectacular to a boy like him. I added that I suspected this skill was one of the reasons Noah's life has become a classic Adirondack story. Noah didn't fit the typical mold. We both agreed people will probably continue to marvel at the intelligence and resilience of the Cold River hermit.

★ ★ ★

Steve Rock, who comes from a younger generation on a limb of the Rondeau-Rock family tree, wishes he knew more about his Uncle Noah. He

Noah with the newly married couple—Lena and Burton Rondeau. *Courtesy of Burton Rondeau*

and Jenny are examples of the current generation who treasure the memories of Uncle Noah. Said Steve: "The stories told to me were much of the same as in DeSormo's book [*Noah John Rondeau, Adirondack Hermit*], with the realization of Noah being a self-made character. The story of his not worshipping in our churches is true, for he did show up at my Grandfather [Herbert] Rock's funeral in a bearskin robe but chose to stand outside the church door. As my Grandmother Delia exited the church, she stopped to talk with Noah. He offered his condolences, hugged her, then pressed a wad of bills into her hand. My dad said the roll included a hundred-dollar denomination. There possibly was more, as Dad said everything was rolled. That was a lot of money in 1958!! Quite amazing.

"Off and on throughout the 1950s and early '60s I recall Uncle Clifton telling me that when Noah did visit Delia in Cadyville he always brought along a deer head. Clifton always assumed it was stashed with something

Noah fiddling at a family gathering. *Courtesy of Richard J. Smith from Noah's photo album*

important. Money? He didn't know. Uncle Clifton was a storyteller who in the telling made the truth, a lot of times, *sound* better [than it really was].

"Uncle Chester [Rock] might remember more stories [about Noah]. He helped care for my grandparents, being a nurse. He was frequently at their home when Noah visited. Noah stayed in one of the upstairs bedrooms during the later 1950s. Chester lives in my grandparents' house now. It's a two-story building in the rural village of Cadyville, eleven miles west of Plattsburgh on State Route 3. He's the youngest of my dad's brothers."

Surely for the children in the younger generations of the Rondeau family, it must have been an opportunity of a lifetime to meet Uncle Noah. Noah and his brothers and sisters were brought up so differently from later generations that his boyhood stories and even his noteworthy way with words must have been fascinating.

Noah was known for his little gems. "At least *we* [the family] think he had a way with words when expressing common, everyday things," Burton pointed out as he shared a few memorable turns of phrases.

> *"Last night a mouse tried my trap to see if it would work; And, it did."*
> *"Song sparrows are singing and jangling their small change."*
> *"Sweet is the song of honey bees."*

A typical Adirondack March observation that followed a check of the morning weather would go: "To Day. Perfect sunshine. When calendar says 'Spring' among Major Adirondack peaks, -Nights below zero still feel like winter, and hard packed snow is four feet deep."

It had been five weeks since Noah had left Cold River hill when he wrote this entry in his entirely coded diary.

> *January 25, 1943 Monday*
> *Cloudy, Thawing! Black Brook and Ausable Forks. At William*
> *Rondeau at Black Brook. Herbert and Delia Rock from Cadyville*

call to see me. Mrs. Delia Rock is my Sister whom I have not seen in 23 years and 3 days. 3 PM at Ausable Forks. 5 PM at McCasland.

Chester Rock was only four and a half years old in 1943. He doesn't have any memories of Noah on this day that Noah reunited with his baby sister, who was then 46. It's all conjecture why he had not seen Delia since the last days of 1919, and we can only speculate on the exact details of the conversation they had. They had grown up in the same large, disadvantaged family, and during their time apart they had both seen their share of hard times and experienced joyful times as well. They must have had a lot to talk about.

Chester does remember his mother saying that "she hadn't seen Noah in years. Mother never said how she felt about him being a hermit." Her reasons? "She had ten children. That didn't leave much time for traveling and visiting" and reflection on a long-absent brother!

What is known of this meeting is that it was brief. The siblings sat down once again and talked over old times. Then Noah explained his intention to continue living outside the mountains. He had decided to accept his sister Priscilla's and her husband Sherman's offer to stay all or a portion of the remainder of the winter at their home.

Chester Rock has young adulthood memories from get-togethers in the mid- to late-1950s with his Uncle Noah at his parents' Cadyville home and at his Aunt Priscilla and Uncle Sherm's home. Chester also served as family taxi driver, taking his Uncle Noah to Ausable Forks,

Said Chester, "I am the youngest son of Delia Rondeau Rock's ten children. My mother is Noah's youngest sister. He never lived with us—only visited for a few days at a time. The room he occupied here was small—only nine feet by nine feet. The walls were wallpapered. The floors were wide hard pine boards, painted with crocheted rag rugs. The only furnishings were a bed, a small dresser, chair and a chamber pot. We had an outhouse until 1954.

"Uncle Noah lived for a time with his sister, my Aunt Priscilla Rondeau McCasland, Uncle Sherm and their three children Jessie (their son), Jeanette and Sadie at their homestead near Ausable Forks between 1952 and mid-1954 after he was no longer allowed to return to Cold River" following

Family members attested to the fact that Uncle Noah enjoyed a good time.
July 30, 1947. *Courtesy of Richard J. Smith from Noah's photo album*

Chester and Virginia Rock. *Courtesy of Chester G. Rock*

the November 1950 Big Blow. "Once I was old enough to drive I was most often the family's designated driver. I remember well because I owned a 1955 Ford sedan.

"I wish I could remember more about what our conversation was about while I drove him to Aunt Priscilla's, but when I was eighteen and nineteen I was more interested in playing loud music on the car radio like the kids do today.

"Uncle Noah referred to Aunt Priscilla's residence in his journals as Mc-Casland Hill, Hill Top, Hill Top Farm and Hill Top Ranch. The residence was on a hill, but that is about all I remember. I remember going there with Mother. At our arrival, Aunt Priscilla would come to greet us at the car. She'd give each of us a big hug and welcome us inside. It really wasn't a huge farm with acres of grain fields or tens of milkers, by a long shot. It was a small home with some outbuildings. She had a cow, a pig and some chickens Uncle Noah raised when he stayed there in the fifties. I think I remember he also kept either goats or sheep.

"I remember one time when Uncle Noah was staying at my parents' house for a few days I went into his room, opened the diaries, and looked through the large books when he was taking an afternoon nap—his 'beauty rest,' he would call it. Glued on one page was a magazine cutout of a jackass. On the rear end he had written 'Happy Birthday Harry S. Truman.'"

A glance at Uncle Noah's yearbooks gave teenage Chester a new out-look on his out-of-the ordinary uncle.

Chester probably laughed if he read Noah's July 11, 1952, comment about his younger cousins.

> *A hot summer day after rain At Hill Top. I work on Poultry yard. Hoe beans…An American hawk got one of my prize white leghorns…Give Potato Bugs drink of Paris Green. My first spinach from garden. Evening I go to Cadyville with Payro [Sic. Parrow] Family* and Sister Priscilla. The Trip was spoiled by 3 fool kids raising Hell in the back seat.*

[*The "Parrow" family Noah refers to in this entry, according to Shelby Payro Richardson, "must be my sister Mariam and the two foster boys Grandma Priscilla took in. My mother would occasionally bring the boys home. My brothers, Francis, and Lauren and I, were quiet kinds of kids; Uncle Noah must have been referring to those three." Shelby was emphatic: "My brothers and I did *not* get into trouble." She laughed, thinking how long ago the event took place, and yet she did not want any guilt by association.]

The two foster boys Shelby referred to were Kenneth and Clayton Burnah. Judy Sorrell, Kenneth Burnah's widow, credits Priscilla McCasland with always being there for Kenneth and Clayton. It was her hand-up that helped the brothers become survivors in an otherwise hard childhood situation.

"Over the years Ken had related a few stories about Uncle Noah coming down out of the mountains to visit Aunt Ceil, as Ken and Clayton called Priscilla. Ken never forgot Uncle Noah referring to him and Clayton as two brats who were fighting in the back seat of Priscilla's car on a trip back from Plattsburgh to Au Sable Forks. He recalled thinking they felt they could get away with being bad because Aunt Ceil was busy talking with Uncle Noah, whom she didn't get to see very often. Ken was very impressed with Uncle Noah and would mention that he might like to live that life himself, but he remained in society and just thought about being a hermit.

"Unfortunately, Clayton has also passed away. I wish I had snapped some pictures of Uncle Noah, but at the time I was very young and was mostly interested in Ken. Life goes by so fast and now I seem to have time to think back about so much. We have four children who are very interested in the outdoors and reading about Uncle Noah."

Recalling the code Noah used in his diaries, Chester said, "All my brothers and sisters were just as curious about Uncle Noah's secret writing as I was. There wasn't ever much time to snoop in the journals, because if mother caught us there would be trouble! I did think, however, that I would like to have been able to take my time thumbing through all the pages."

Rondeau's entries are often terse and cryptic. On Wednesday, December 7, 1953, the day after Rondeau wrote "I start using heaviest underware," came a telling remark: "Priscilla McCasland sweeps my Bed Room and makes my Bed. First Time in over three months and she has another brainstorm again. I keep her in offensive and follow her up so she don't make a point."

To what might Noah have been alluding?

Chester didn't read that one, but it would have been easy to figure out at a later date when his mother revealed Uncle Noah would be leaving Aunt Priscilla's home. Priscilla had reached the end of her rope. Her seventy-year-old brother had not been keeping up his part of the living arrangement. The family grapevine says Priscilla put up with "worse moments." She did not want to judge Noah harshly because she saw no use arguing—besides, she didn't want the children to her them bickering. Normally she was discreet, but it is a fact she and Noah would occasionally get into a healthy argument-Noah's words, "a brainstorm."

"I clearly remember taking Mother to Ausable to visit her sister Priscilla, and Aunt Priscilla told mother Uncle Noah could no longer live there because he did not have any respect for their parents," says Chester. He was referring to Noah's decision, decades earlier, to run away from home. His brothers and sisters had always felt that he never showed proper respect toward his parents and that he walked out on his family obligations as oldest son following his mother's death.

At seventy years old, it would seem time might have softened his point of view. Yet, he still made a case against the often-unreliable bureaucratic

Conservation Department and political machines on all levels of government as well as maintaining a life-long bitterness toward his father. He'd rather abandon Priscilla's family's kindness than admit he was wrong. In fact, a confrontation, even though it led to a deterioration in their relationship and his loss of a low-cost bed-and-board arrangement, was the route he chose without a single thought toward *What kind of fool am I?*

According to Shelby Payro Richardson, her cousin, Chester, didn't know the entire story of Noah's decision to stop living at the McCaslands' home. Part of it had to do with the two foster children, said seventy-two-year old Shelby as she stirred up old memories. "They were typical boys, if you know what I mean, and Uncle Noah didn't always care for the way they behaved." He maintained the boys required a stricter hand when it came to correcting their sometimes poor behavior." He thought his sister could at least have spoken to them sternly about their tomfoolery, and he held she should have dished out "just punishment." When Kenneth and Clayton really got wound up, "he would tell Grandma they were 'brat kids. The brat kids need 'recommended,'" This was Noah's term for firmer discipline.

The 1955 Ford sedan used to taxi Uncle Noah. Lt. to Rt. Goldie Rock Reid, Marshall McFea, Catherine Rick, Delia Rondeau Rock, Noma Rock Turnage and her daughter, Deborah Turnage. Photo by Chester Rock. Courtesy of Chester G. Rock

Shelby maintains that there were on-again off-again arguments and hard language between Uncle Noah and Grandma Priscilla over the foster boys' upbringing. These, along with Noah's offensive remarks about their mother and father, were of no help in establishing a mutual understanding, even though they did maintain a sister-brother affection toward each other. Noah just grew too furious and intolerant, and as 1954 wound down, he declared he was going to move from Hill Top Farm. Shelby believes the poor behavior of the foster boys was just the last straw.

"New Memory!!!" Chester announced via email. "One day I stopped to see Aunt Delia Rondeau, Uncle Bill's wife, a few years after Uncle Noah had died. She gave me a Bible that Uncle Noah kept. As I thumbed through the pages I noticed Noah had added something to all the pictures. He had covered many of the captions under the pictures by cutting pieces of the glue tab of envelopes and pasting them over the writing. On the tabs he added his own comments. Some were derogatory remarks next to the [original] text. In other cases, he jotted comments. Some of the writing you could make out and in other cases the ink was smeared."

Priscilla McCasland's Hill Top home. West view of house coming up Rolling Mill Hill.
Courtesy of Judy Sorrell Lynch

Lt. to Rt. Clayton, "Aunt Ceil" (Priscilla McCasland) and Kenneth Burnah. 1949.
Courtesy of Judy Sorrell Lynch

Chester was referring to the large Bible Rondeau was given in "about 1925." Noah marked this on the inside cover:

> *"This Bible: I got in the twenties; and smoked it in Cold River Town Hall for over 20 years; And brought it to Saranac lake, Nov. 14,th 1948.*
>
> —N.J. Rondeau"

Discovered in his 1964 journal are three entries admitting his renewed interest in the Bible.

> *October 18, 1964. Sunday. Perfect autumn Sunday at Singing Pines. I read 15 chapters of Revelations [sic] by St. John. First Bible Reading in 27 years.*

> *October 20, 1964. Tuesday. A nice October day at Singing Pines. I read seven chapter—finish book of Revelation.*

> *October 24, 1964. Saturday. Perfect sunshine at Singing Pines. I keep Sabbath. First time in 27 years.*

Billy Burger said he often debated with Noah the question, "Who or what is God?" They agreed that "the question of a God or Gods has puzzled people ever since primitive man tried to account for the good and bad things that happened to him."

Along with his memory about Noah's Bible, Chester recalled a day when he watched his aged uncle, an old man in his vegetable garden, armed with "a pail of water—a can that he was watering the tomato plants

Lt. to Rt. Ken Burnah, age 3; Clayton Burnah, age 5. Taken soon after they moved in with "Aunt Ceil." *Courtesy of Judy Sorrell Lynch*

with." Since he didn't have people drive in on a daily basis, he seemed less preoccupied with the watering and thus spotted the two young men who exited a car at the edge of the road. He raised his hand in the air, whereupon the visitors stopped.

"Uncle Noah, it's Chester. I've got company. This is Jeff—he's a friend of mine."

Noah studied the young men, who were both in their early twenties. "He hadn't seen me in probably five years—not since our last trip in '59 on our drive back to Aunt Priscilla's. It's possible it was 1965. It was my only visit with him at Singing Pines. I never took Mother to Wilmington to see him. I remember that for sure."

Chester had no idea at the time that Singing Pines was a converted chicken coop. He read about that in 2008 "when I borrowed the book *Life With Noah* from my niece, Anna Miller."

Noah looked intently as the young men approached. "Uncle Noah," Chester said again with a smile. His uncle smiled back, recognizing his nephew. "Chester," he said, still a bit surprised, addressing him with a warm hug and handshake as he had as a youngster.

As Chester's reunion story goes, "I introduced my friend, Jeff Pescia, to Uncle. He showed us around his vegetable garden. Besides tomato plants he had planted carrots, beets, and some other crops. They were all small seedlings that had recently sprouted. I'm thinking it was perhaps late June.

"Jeff and Uncle Noah talked about Cold River. Jeff was getting his fishing plans into action. I wasn't interested in fishing. Instead, I remember leaving them to talk as I looked around his camp. He had planted small pine trees about a foot tall all around the place. I also recall as I walked toward the front door a good-size rock with the letters N.J.R. painted on it. Nearby was an old handmade wooden rocking chair. A small old, rusted-out woodstove also sat in front. Several flower pots were set on the griddle lids. I only looked in the door of the camp. I never walked into the building. The room was very small. I recall seeing a table and dirty dishes. There was a jar of honey with many flies on it. The space between the table and bed was barely wide enough for someone to walk between. I called it a bed, but it could have been a wide bench with coats and an old blanket on it.

I do not remember any stoves or chairs, but there must have been. I would not have wanted to eat at that table or sit on his bed!"

Standing in the backyard as a reminder of former days, "Uncle Noah had built a pole wigwam or teepee just like the ones that he constructed back at Cold River." The interior was used for storage.

Chester's last reminiscences were wishes. He wished his mother and father had owned a camera so there would be photos of the family today.

"I remember that after supper one evening Uncle Noah and my father went to Rigsbee's Auction House. Uncle Noah bought my mother a platform rocker. It was old then! I remember it had a foot rest that slid out from under the chair. I wish I had it today. When Mother left the home to me, I brought the rocker to the landfill. It needed too many repairs, but it would have been a nice reminder of him today.

Chester is known to be a dead ringer for his Uncle Noah. "If ever there was a movie to be made about Noah," said Jeff Pescia, "I think Chet could look, play and sound the part very well."

Shelby Payro Richardson, Noah's "Little Pumpkin," remembers Uncle Noah from way back to when she was a little girl. "I was born in Grandma Priscilla's house in 1938. Mother and Father lived there for many years. I was eleven years old when he went to the first sportsmen's show. We were so proud of him. It was a big thing. We had a hermit in the family," she said.

Shelby considers her celebrated uncle an utterly refreshing and engaging caller because, "He told stories." Although she has mostly forgotten the particulars, she does remember he delighted all with the entertaining way he told anecdotes about his childhood, his Cold River experiences, the forest animals, woodland trails and old lumber roads, high mountain ponds and streams, the mountains that surrounded his hermitage and his later years performing at sportsmen's shows. Each reflection was important because his memories covered a long duration of notable years and long-long-ago happenings.

When she was a child, Uncle Noah's tales of the animals about his camp interested Shelby the most. "I would sit on his knee atop his crossed legs as he sang a tune like 'Oh Susanna' as he bounced me, or I'd sit cross-legged on the floor as he played the fiddle," she recalls.

THE HERMIT AND US

Noah claimed he'd live in a pup tent before staying any longer at Hill Top Ranch. "I recall Uncle Noah boarded with Madeline Dodge while Melvin Peck was finishing up an old camp making it livable for him. Uncle Noah moved his belongings into a teepee beside the camp." —Shelby Richardson.

Courtesy of Richard J. Smith from Noah's photo album

Uncle Noah, former Cold River Hermit of Wigwam City, Population 1.
Courtesy of Richard J. Smith, from Noah's photo album

"When I was growing up on Hill Top Farm on Rolling Mill Hill Road two miles from Ausable Forks, Grandma and Grandpa's homestead and farm was like so many others during that time—by and large self-sufficient. Their place was right on top of the hill." The rolling landscape was dotted with large boulders left behind when the last glacier receded thousands of years ago. The land was their salvation, very much like the Morse or Great Gore where her Uncle Noah permanently moved at the end of the 1920s.

"Uncle Noah chose a different way to survive," she reminisced. Nobody in the Rondeau family ever believed he was a blatant game outlaw.

On August 28, 1943, he lamented in his journal the pitfalls of his decision to live in the mountains. "The trouble is: Life is hard, much of it unjustly brought against me by dishonest malignant Conservation Commission of New York. For instance—[they] denied [me the ability to legally] Guide for over 15 years [resulting in an estimated loss of] at least $3,000."

In time Shelby's family moved from Grandma and Grandpa McCasland's to their own place a mile beyond Hill Top Farm. The move was not the end of seeing Uncle Noah. "Oh no. Every time he came he brought me a roll of Necco candy, and although I began to stretch up and lose my round and chubby form he still called me his 'little Pumpkin.'"

Today, sometimes when she looks at the doorway between the kitchen and dining room, she goes back to the day when Noah was showing her father how to hold his bow and draw back the arrow. "As the bowstring was drawn back, Uncle Noah accidentally lost control. His hold on the bowstring slipped. The arrow shot into the archway, making a hole in the plaster wall."

"'It slipped,' he apologized. 'It's my mistake. I'm sorry.'"

Noah John's life continued on at Singing Pines in predictable patterns throughout the 1960s until 1967, which would prove to be his final year. The entire Rondeau clan would like to believe their Uncle Noah spent his last days embraced by an Adirondack breeze rustling through balsam and maples on an August afternoon as he lay in a Lake Placid hospital bed, perhaps dreaming about the good times casting into a cool spring hole at Seward Pond when he was at the top of his game.

All direct and indirect Rondeau family members I spoke to love their North Country roots and they are aware of the need to preserve their heritage because Uncle Noah is *their* relation, and his woods life is now part of regional history. Each appreciates their Adirondack birth, their own upbringing in northern New York, a lifetime of living in the mountains, and their role as living family spokespeople.

The Hermit Hop with Jane Allen, Peru, N.Y. April 18, 1947. Noah recorded in code this was a "day of sunshine" and riches. "I receive a $50. cheque [from] Guideposts magazine." Rondeau had recently shared his views of God's peace in the Adirondack Mountains with Mary Malcolm Creighton, secretary to Dr. Norman Vincent, who wrote for the Christian publication.

Courtesy of Richard J. Smith from Noah's photo album

Epilogue

A Place to Hang a Hat

For thirteen years after Noah Rondeau left Cold River for good, he lived in a variety of settings, moving back and forth from boarding houses to a one-room dinky tourist camp cabin, to friends' homes, as his finances and health dictated. Although Father Time kept ticking away, Noah remained somewhat active in the entertainment business—still selling his "hermit souvenirs" and talking about wilderness life at occasional functions and at the hermit replica sent up at Covert's Seminole Indian Village (Covert's Grove) that stood for years along the Whiteface Mountain Memorial Highway in the village of Wilmington.

Pete Pelkey remembers many a conversation he had with Noah beside the replica: "We had many talks about trapping, bee hunting, making his bow and fashioning arrows, and his rifles. Noah was very unhappy about being forced out of the woods and had ill feelings toward the conservation and government agencies," said Pete. "Oh boy, did he get angry when he talked about Social Services and I believe Social Security." However, the conversation would soften when he talked about his days at Cold River.

He maintained that some June day he would return to his hilltop to fish Cold River one last time, but he surely knew it was only a dream. His legs couldn't carry him that far, and hiking was the only way in.

In 1963 he celebrated a new beginning when Richard Smith announced that he had equipped an old building where Noah could live out his life. "I'm a sentimentalist," Smith said. "I believed in looking out for my old friend."

To bring Noah to a happier setting, I introduced him to my newest investment in July of '63—my land and construction project. I had purchased an old chicken coop from the neighbor across Springhill Road, moved it onto my plot of land and was working on converting the building into a primitive camp I intended to present to Noah as a real home for him to live in for as long as he wanted to stay there. This was a new world for him. My property had a spring, trees, and it offered relative seclusion, yet it was close to the village of Wilmington and to friends he had in the area. It didn't take much to induce him to accept. He looked as if he came to appreciate the quiet natural country setting immediately. Bird sounds and animal sightings in the grove of woods reminded him of the mountain setting in his past life at Cold River. He found so much joy and contentment in natural settings.

August 25, 1948. "There's no easy trail in the wilds," Noah is told as he pretends to be encouraged by Mariam Chadeayne to walk up a forest path. Wilmington offered Old Whiskers good friends and neighbors and a loving community.

Courtesy of Richard J. Smith from Noah's photo album

Smith remembered very clearly Noah's sense of excitement and his new burst of energy when he learned he was going to move into a place he could call home. Noah even did a shuffle dance step when he set foot on the property he dubbed Singing Pines.

They walked around the property together, and Noah was especially excited about planting some fruit trees and growing an annual vegetable garden. "He loved the place," Smith said. "Noah had something to relate to." At Singing Pines, Noah could choose from a whole range of activities. Instead of being a renter, boarder or accepting offers to stay in a friend's spare room, Noah now settled down, knowing his days as a nomad were done.

Smith said that Noah did a lot of remembering the old days "with fondness." He never wanted to do anything more than enjoy his last days—and he did!

Old dear friends came to visit. Curious young folks stopped to meet the "mayor" whose legendary status was well known.

At Singing Pines, he gathered firewood, planted, harvested, and canned vegetables. From time to time he took short trips and enjoyed his social network of nearby neighbors and their invitations to drop by anytime. Richard most often came by in the evening after work. "Our nighttime confabs were a highlight of my day," he remembered. Besides reminiscing about the old days, the two included in their conversations plans for future camp projects and activities.

Noah had a roof over his head. He stayed connected with old friends and still made new acquaintances. His remembrances were gratifying. The amount of correspondence he handled was significant. Life was good. An old Adirondack hermit couldn't wish for more.

Noah's Secret Code.

⊖┼θ∘θ ╲ ℓ┼θ╤ ℓ╱⅄θ ┼θ∘

"**Where'd they take her?**" —NJR's question to a friend who arrived at his cabin at twilight after a 22 mile hike to inform Noah his sister had been accidentally shot. Noah picked up a lantern, told his visitor to "Make yourself at home"—and was off on a 50-mile hike to the Lake Placid hospital.

The Friendly Mouse, Noah's Secret Scratchings

The hermit cipher is the genesis of Noah John Rondeau. Its development began about 1920, and evolved as the years went by, becoming increasingly curious-looking. The puzzling cryptographs have been likened to the tracks of an inebriated chicken that waddled through a tumbled bottle of ink, but in fact Noah had conscientiously developed his code over years of trial and error.

Noah went through several different codes in his search for the perfect disguise for his daily remarks. David Greene, without whom Noah's code might never have been deciphered, has christened the three codes he has studied as the "license-plate" code, the "circles" code, and the "chicken-tracks" code, which was the one Noah finally settled on. Apparently there was an earlier code that Greene might name the "rebus" code, consisting largely of pictures: sun, moon, clouds, fish, bear, deer and anything noteworthy would be sketched, with perhaps some wordplay thrown in—a sketch of a hand might mean "and," or it might indicate part of a place name like "Handsome View." But Noah used that system for the most part before 1939, and his early journals were destroyed by fire in Coreys, NY. A few traces of this early pictorial code can be found in the 1939 and later journals.

For those who may care to match wits with the Mayor of Wigwam City, I have chosen a representative sample of notes written in the "chicken-tracks" code. A careful analysis of Chapter Four, "The Scratchings of an Inebriated Hen" and Chapter Five, "Decoded," found in *Noah John Rondeau's Adirondack Wilderness Days: A Year with the Hermit of Cold River Flow* should reveal to an astute reader the essential pattern of the code. Without any further clues, one should be able to learn how to read and write hermit cipher.

It might take several days to get comfortable working with it. Noah was known to say that "even the experts" wouldn't be able to make sense of his code. A friend of Noah's who considered himself a cryptographic expert spent three months trying to crack the code before giving up in disgust. Without David Greene's curiosity and perseverance, we might still all remain baffled.

The Friendly Mouse—Noah's Secret Scratching. Noah's "friendly mouse" symbol (opposite top) was used to mean "This line is written upside down." He drew it in various ways from a bare-minimum drawing to a fancy representation of a girl in a dress.

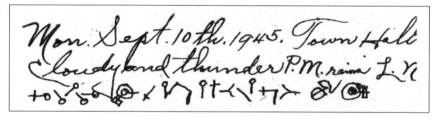

Mon. Sept 10th 1945. Town Hall. Code: I put up 20 laods of <wood>

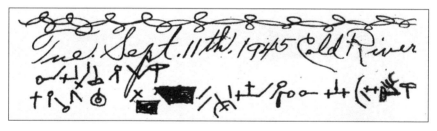

Tue. Sept 11th 1945. Cold River. Code: Rain last night & today. Found I Jackknife at spring (Big Eddy)

Wed. Sept 12th 1945. Hall of Records. Code: Shower last night. Today sun & clouds & cool. I stack 40 loads of <wood>

Thur. Sept 13th 1945. 1945 Pyramids. Code: I stack 36 loads of <wood> cut up 7 loads green <wood>

Fri. Sept 14th 1945. Beauty Parlor. Code: Cloudy & cool. I get bit of wood

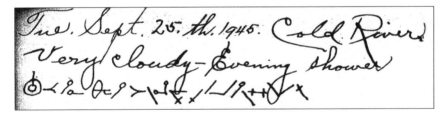

Tue. Sept 25th 1945. Cold River. Code: I <trout> broke law at big dam

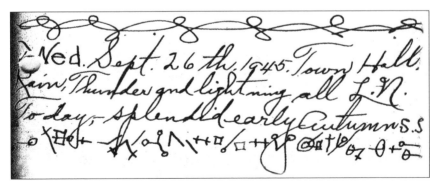

Wed. Sept 26th 1945. Town Hall. Code: PM. I walk around Big V. I got 50 ft. tel. wire

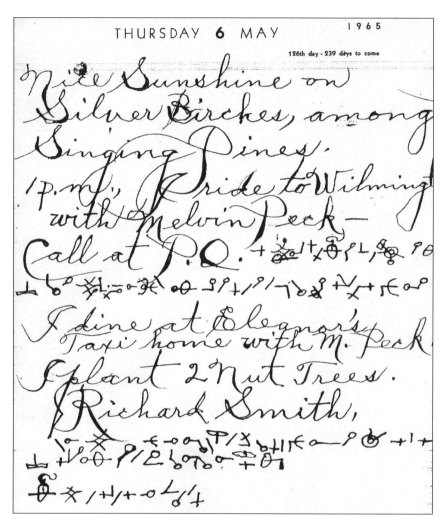

May 6th 1965. First two coded line: Get … [59.40] cents welfare. Nut trees—gladiolus—watch tower–deer repelent. Third and fourth coded lines: Bring 15 trees Shumway and Burpee and Interstate Nursuries. We have picnic

Acknowledgements

My deepest thanks to everyone who assisted with this project. Many hours of conversation, writing and e-mailings, telephone conversations, searching family paper records and photographs came together as I researched the historical background portion of *The Hermit and Us* often with my wife, Bette driving on trips to make this book a special memoir.

This book would not have been written without the interest, support, and full cooperation of many willing contributors. In this respect, I feel especially fortunate for the generous response of the large number of persons listed below who have provided unmediated access to private papers and permission to use detailed information about their lives and early days in and about the Seward Range of the Adirondack High Peaks, and in many instances, have likewise loaned their cherished pictures, most of which were very old and consequently greatly prized by their owners.

Grateful acknowledgment is made to The Adirondack Museum for permission to reproduce from MS 61–7: ALS Noah John Rondeau to Robert Bruce Inverarity, July 20, 1961; Typed Letter Robert Bruce Inverarity to Noah John Rondeau, April 24, 1962; ALS Noah John Rondeau to Robert Bruce Inverarity, April 28, 1962; Typed Letter Robert Bruce Inverarity to Noah John Rondeau, May 7, 1962.

Grateful acknowledgement is made to Peggy Byrne for permission to print Noah John Rondeau's April 28, 1962, letter to Robert Bruce Inverarity.

Grateful acknowledgment is made to Richard Smith for the use of Noah John Rondeau's 1943, 1944, 1949, and 1950 journals, now property of the Adirondack Museum, Blue Mountain Lake, NY; and for permission to print material from Noah John Rondeau's scrapbooks and photo albums, now property of the Adirondack Museum, Blue Mountain Lake, NY.

Grateful acknowledgment is made to the North Elba-Lake Placid Historical Society for access to Noah John Rondeau's diaries.

I am indebted to my friend and editor, Mary L. Thomas for her invaluable support and constructive advice in making this book happen. She has been my invaluable second right hand from the onset of the manuscript's development.

Neal Burdick edited portions of the final draft.

The following businesses and people helped me in ways both great and small. To those who consented to be interviewed for this book, thanks for sharing your memories: *Adirondack Life* magazine; Adirondack Museum at Blue Mountain Lake; Donald "Jack" Anderson; Bob Bates; Lou Berchielli; Robert E. Brindle, vice-president of programming at WGY; Neal S. Burdick; Oscar Burguiere; Peggy and Wayne Byrne; Harvey Carr; Jean Burger Cushman: Maitland C. DeSormo; Adolph Dittmar; Mary Colyer Dittmer; Madeline Dodge; H. P. Donlon; Brad Edmondson; Leslie G. Farmer; Edward J. Fox; Dr. Roger D. Freeman; Bill Frenette; John M. Harmes; John Hasenjager; Grace Hudowalski; John Hickey; Rob Igoe, president of North Country Books, Inc.; Bertha N. Irwin; Nancy and Frank Johnson; Jenna Kerwin; Stephen Klein, Jr.; Ruth King; Miriam Kondroski; Chris E. Latimer; Dr. C.V. Latimer, Jr.; Donald Latimer; Judy Sorrell Lynch; Helen Colyer Menz; Edward Miller; Erwin H. Miller; Bette M. O'Hern; New York State Department of Environmental Conservation archives; Tony Okie; Pete and Alice Pelkey; Jerry Pepper, Director of Adirondack Museum Library; Jeff Pescia; Adam Piersall; Ruth Prince; Gay Prue; Fredric C. Reeves; Edwin A. Reid; Shelby Payro Richardson; Chester G. Rock; Steve Rock, Burton Rondeau, Charlie and Dorothy Russ; Earle F. Russell; Dorian St. George; Jenny Rondeau Kelton Scully; Albert "Bud" Smith; Richard J. Smith; Judy Sorrell; Peter Reeves Sperry; Annie Stoltie; Fred R. Studer; WGY Schenectady Radio; Syracuse University Press; Mary L. Thomas; Eleanor and Monty Webb; Clarence and Stacia Whiteman; Cynthia and Holly C. Wolff; Phil Wolff; and Paul Wollner.

I have made every effort to acknowledge the assistance of everyone who helped; any omission is an unintentional oversight.

—William J. O'Hern

Bibliography

Books

DeSormo, Maitland C. *Noah John Rondeau Adirondack Hermit*, Utica, New York: North Country Books, Inc., 1969.

O'Hern, William J. *Life With Noah: Stories and Adventures of Richard Smith with Noah John Rondeau*, Utica, New York: North Country Books, Inc., 1997.

_____. *Adirondack Wilderness Days of Noah John Rondeau*, Cleveland, New York: Forager Press, 2009.

Engles, Vincent. *Adirondack Fishing in the 1930s, a Lost Paradise*, Syracuse University Press, 1978.

Magazines

Kerwin, Jenna. "Secret Scratchings, the Cryptic Written Language of Noah John Rondeau-Hermit of Cold River." New York State *Conservationist* magazine, February 2011.

Smith, Richard J. "Roaming and Trapping." *Adirondack Life* magazine, April 1995.

Wolff, Phil. "Knowing Noah John." *Adirondack Life* magazine, May/June 2010.

Journals, Manuscripts, Scrapbooks and DVD

Gregory, Jay L. home 1940 Cold River movie, owned by his granddaughter, Nancy Bliss Johnson.

Gregory, Jay L. Log Book Cold River Trips. October 1934 to June 1939, owned by his granddaughter, Nancy Bliss Johnson.

Gregory, Jay L. Letters between Gregory and Noah J. Rondeau (1940–1948), formally owned by Nancy Bliss Johnson. Original letters now property of the Adirondack Museum, Blue Mountain Lake, NY.

Latimer, C.V. Sr. and Jr. Camp Seward Log Books 1931–1948, owned by Christopher Latimer.

Rondeau, Noah John. "Recollections of 60 Years" (unedited and unpublished version), owned by the Adirondack Museum, Blue Mountain Lake, NY.

Wolff, Phil. "Cold River." (2009 original manuscript version).

Newspapers

Burger, William "Billy." "Back with Rondeau." *The Adirondack Record-Elizabethtown Post*, August 7, 1941.

Dittmar, Aldolph. "Cold River Hermit Honored by 46ers." *Troy-Record* newspaper, January 7, 1938.

Mooney, Charles L. " 'Round the Clock with Noah John Rondeau, Hermit of the Adirondack Wilds." Albany, N.Y.: *The Knickerbocker News*, September 11, 1946.

_____. "Noah Rondeau Bulletin." *Essex County Republican*, February 14, 1947.

Rondeau, Noah John. "Air Lift to Fame." February 12, 1947

_____. "Rondeau Arrives in New York for Show." February 15, 1947.

Sillman, Don. "Sportsmen's Show Forced To Jump Gun." New York *Herald Tribune*, February 16, 1947.

_____. "Rondeau Tells of His Experiences at Albany Exposition." *Adirondack Record-Elizabethtown-Post*, March 6, 1947.

_____. "Noah Rondeau Plans Attendance Buffalo Sportsmen's Show." *Essex County Republican*, March 14, 1947.

_____. "The Adirondack Hermit Travels Via Airplane." *Essex County Republican*, April 4, 1947.

_____. *North Creek News*, February 17, 1950

_____. "No Other Hermit." *The Knickerbocker News*, October 6, 1950.

Marathon Independent, February 1, 1951

_____. *The Knickerbocker News*, July 26, _____.

_____. "Famed Hermit of Cold River Flow." *Adirondack Record-Elizabethtown-Post*. August 31,1967.

Correspondence

Anderson, Donald "Jack" to William J. O'Hern

Bates, Bob to William J. O'Hern

Carr, Harvey to William J. O'Hern

Brindle, Robert E. to William J. O'Hern

Burguiere, Oscar to Noah J, Rondeau

Burguiere, Oscar to Richard J. Smith

Burguiere, Oscar to Don Latimer

Cushman, Jean Burger to William J. O'Hern

DeSormo, Maitland C. to William J. O'Hern

Dittmar, Aldoph Dittmar to William J. O'Hern

Dittmar, Mary Colyer to William J. O'Hern

Donlon, H. P. Donlon to William J. O'Hern

Freeman, Dr. Roger D. to William J. O'Hern

Hathaway, Carl to William J. O'Hern

Hasenjager, John to William J. O'Hern

Hickey, John to William J. O'Hern

Irwin, Bertha N. to William J. O'Hern

Latimer, Dr. C.V. Jr. to William J. O'Hern

Latimer, Chris E. to William J. O'Hern

Latimer, Donald to William J. O'Hern

Menz, Helen Colyer to William J. O'Hern

Miller, Edward to William J. O'Hern

Miller, Erwin H. to William J. O'Hern

Okie, Tony to William J. O'Hern

Pelkey, Pete and Alice to William J. O'Hern

Pescia, Jeff to William J. O'Hern

Prince, Ruth to William J. O'Hern

Reeves, Fredric C. to William J. O'Hern

Reid, Edwin A. to William J. O'Hern

Richardson, Shelby Payro to William J. O'Hern

Russ, Charlie to William J. O'Hern

Russell, Earle Russell to William J. O'Hern

St. George, Dorian to William J. O'Hern

Scully, Jenny Rondeau Kelton to William J. O'Hern

Studer, Fred R. to William J. O'Hern

WGY Schenectady Radio to William J. O'Hern

Webb, Eleanor and Monty to William J. O'Hern

Whiteman, Clarence and Stacia to William J. O'Hern

Wollner, Paul Wollner to William J. O'Hern

Wiezel, R.G. Letter to NJR

Interviews

DeSormo, Maitland C. Interview by William J. O'Hern.

Dittmar, Aldoph Dittmar. Interview by William J. O'Hern

Dittmer, Mary Colyer. Interview by William J. O'Hern

Dr. C.V. Latimer. Interview by William J. O'Hern

Nancy Bliss Johnson. Interview by William J. O'Hern

Whiteman, Clarence. Interview by William J. O'Hern

Taped Interviews

Dittmar, Aldoph Dittmar. Interview by William J. O'Hern

Dittmer, Mary Colyer. Interview by William J. O'Hern

Dodge, Madeline. Interview by William J. O'Hern

Delia Rondeau Rock. Interview by Mailtland C. DeSormo.

Wolff, Philip G. Interview by Holly C. Wolff for William J. O'Hern

Preserving Adirondack History One Story at a Time

Ask Adirondack author, William "Jay" O'Hern why he often gives up creature comforts for the demands of real outdoor challenges, and he answers, "the spirit of adventure."

He recollects that he first faced "the unknown" as a young boy. "I was first moved to test the tempting climate of adventure shortly after my sixth birthday, following my parents' move to the country. Undeveloped places were a natural destination for me. I wandered cow paths over rolling pastures, biked back roads to who-knows-where, poled rafts, and built huts. The rural setting provided me with an endless array of possibilities. Every summer vacation took me into the Adirondack Mountains."

Camping, trail hiking, bushwhacking, mountain climbing, paddling and mountain biking honed his self-confidence. His recreational activities and his own natural curiosity led to investigations into the Adirondack' past. Years of personal research and his discovery of undocumented Adirondack history gave him the confidence to commit to learning writing skills.

Since his first successful 1997 book, *Life With Noah: Stories and Adventures of Richard Smith with Noah John Rondeau*, O'Hern has continued to release new Adirondack stories.

Not trained as a writer, O'Hern claims he's motivated by his "imaginative side. I've found my hardest challenge has been the adventure of learning how to take historical information and preserve it in print."

By blending collections of vintage photographs and the personal observations and experiences contained in the diaries, journals and personal remembrances of native folks he has interviewed, he has uncovered the key to writing. "I've found the close relationships helps me to write authentic eyewitness narratives about living in and adventures in the Adirondacks.

"All my writing efforts try to place the reader in the company of woodsmen and women—to be part of the experience (as much as is possible through reading), and to enjoy the messages found in personal accounts of particular occasions.

"If I have succeeded I will have brought before the reader a rich experience from the past. No greater benefit can come from the act of writing."

Learn about Jay's many Adirondack history books and future projects at www.adkwilds.com.

Author William "Jay" O'Hern in Dr. CV Latimer's home preparing to snap copy shots of images used in his books on Adirondack history.

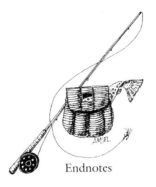

Endnotes

1. Some of Clarence Petty's remarks are taken from the interview conducted by Brad Edmondson on September 13, 2002. Edmondson's transcripts reflect collected oral histories from those who were active in the founding years of the Adirondack Park Agency.

2. Here is how Richard Smith explained Noah's spelling.

"There was no place called *Chattock Clearing.* You have to know Noah quite well to understand sometimes his pronouncing of words due to self-taught education. Noah had a tendency to pronounce and spell some words exactly as his French bearing, i.e., *Shattuck* became *Chattock* though it pertained to the same clearing. Noah had no reason whatsoever to confuse the two words. Another example of his variant spelling was *suffishant.* Noah always wrote it that way when it should have been spelled *sufficient.* You can readily see that his lack of proper education by qualified teachers left a gap in Noah's self-taught education."

Smith footnoted his comment by adding, "But don't get me wrong. I use the examples as a guide to understanding Noah's struggles to get the education he so much desired. I only have great respect for his efforts, and sometimes in its simplicity, I've often wondered maybe he was much better educated (in some ways) than college graduates. There was surely a good solid injection of common sense which always put a garnish of philosophical wisdom on what Noah had to say."

3. This entire event is told in the chapter "Noah's Lickety-Split Ride on Clarence Whiteman's Buck" in the book *Life with Noah.*

4. The High Bank Gang, which Noah labeled "duck asses," were a bunch of toughs from Bayonne, New Jersey, "that had Oscar Burguiere along as an errand boy, cutting wood, cooking, doing camp chores, with his only reward to be able to have a few weeks in the wild, which was a great fascination for him," according to Rondeau. Noah eventually shared with Richard Smith the entire story about the Gang. That information is found in *Adirondack Pastimes, Family Camping and Sporting Adventures in the Cold River Country with Noah John Rondeau (1913–1950),* William J. O'Hern. In the Adirondacks, 2014.

5. Jay and CV refer to Jay L. Gregory, an attorney from Binghamton, New York and Dr. Clarence Vinette "CV" Latimer Sr. from Deposit, New York. The men spent two weeks every spring and fall in the Cold River Country for thirty-seven years. Both were close friends of Noah J. Rondeau.

6. Gay Prue served 18 months in the Civilian Conservation Corps Camp S-63 at Tupper Lake (Cross Clearing), as a squad leader in company 208. In 1935 he worked at the CCC side camp near Mountain Pond. During summer and fall weekends of that year he visited Noah J. Rondeau. Prue's entire interview appears in *Adirondack Pastimes: Family Camping and Sporting Adventures in the Cold River Country with Noah John Rondeau, 1913–1950,* William J. O'Hern. In the Adirondacks, 2014.

7. To be released in 2015.

8. The taking of bears with traps was prohibited in New York State in 1923. However, this did not ban the use of large traps with teeth. In 1929 (or real early in 1930), leg-gripping traps with teeth in the jaws or with jaws larger than six inches were prohibited for trapping fur bearers. Those prohibitions are still very similar today, no leg-gripping trap with teeth or with jaws larger than 7¼ inches in the water for beaver and otter or otherwise larger than 5¾ inches except for the taking of nuisance wildlife and the Environmental Conservation Law still allows nuisance bears (killing or worrying livestock or destroying an apiary) to be taken by shooting or device to entrap. —Lou Berchielli, Black Bear Specialist

9. "Uncle" Noah is used as a general term, because the family connections in this chapter vary. Noah was actually Jenny Rondeau Kelton's great-great uncle. She and other immediate and extended Rondeau family members interviewed for this chapter show great pride in their memories of their relative, who played such an interesting and important role in Adirondack history,

10. Burton was talking in general terms. Certainly he knew Noah didn't always walk everywhere. Burton's father drove his brother places. Other people did too. When Noah was on the Outside, certainly after 1950, but also during winters before then, he frequently got rides; and he didn't really "live off the land" at the Hermitage. There were plane drops of food beginning in 1947; backpackers donated food and supplies friends brought him arrived at Shattuck Clearing and were cached at Latimer's Camp Seward.

11. "Noah enjoyed people" and "Noah was a loner" is a contradiction on its face, but probably representative of a person who was more complex than most people realize.

Index

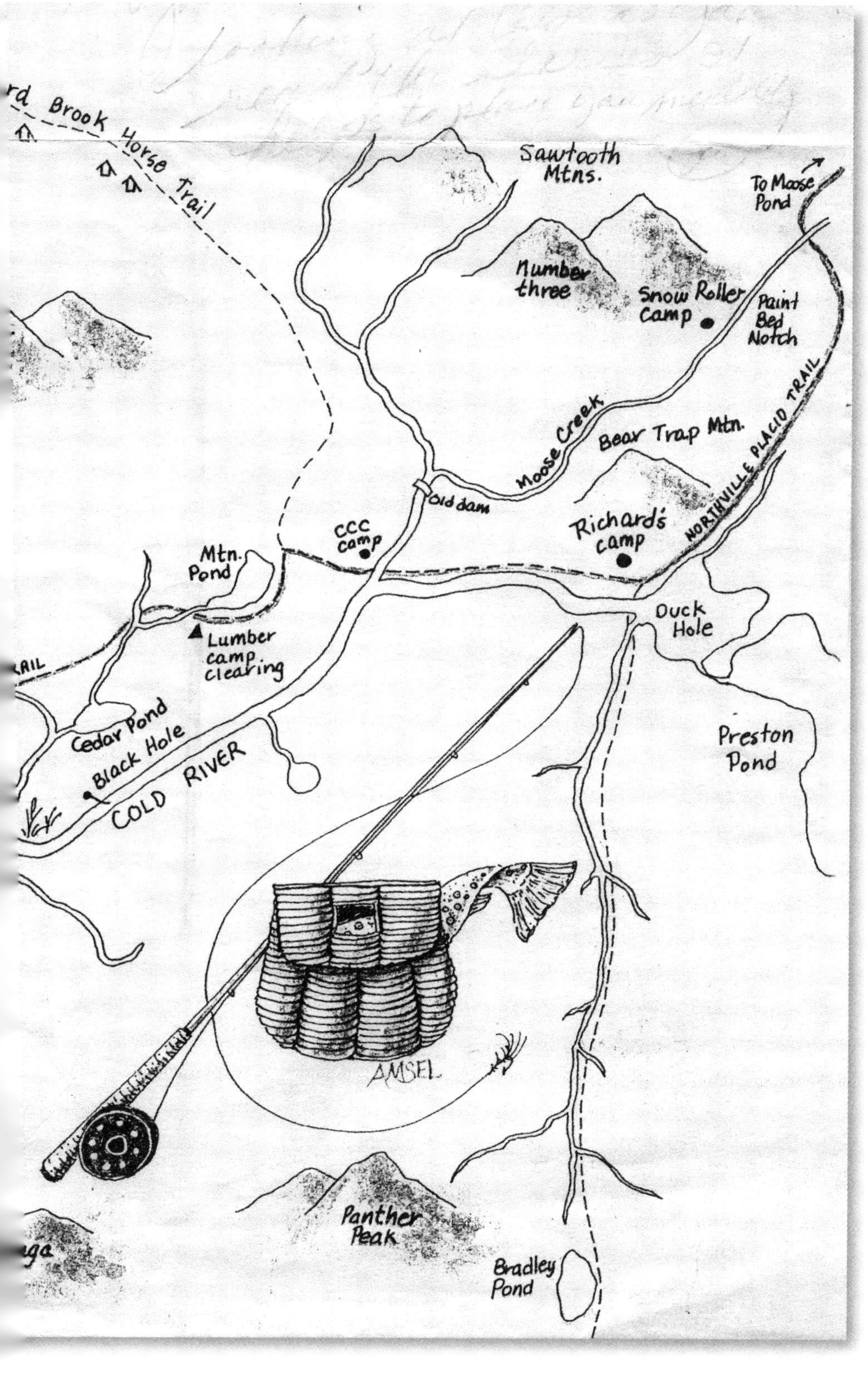
rd Brook Horse Trail
Sawtooth Mtns.
To Moose Pond
Number three
Snow Roller camp
Paint Bed Notch
NORTHVILLE PLACID TRAIL
Moose Creek
Bear Trap Mtn.
Old dam
CCC camp
Richard's camp
Mtn. Pond
Duck Hole
Lumber camp clearing
RAIL
Cedar Pond
Black Hole
COLD RIVER
Preston Pond
AMSEL
Panther Peak
ga
Bradley Pond

CURRENT TITLES
by William J. O'Hern

*Spring Trout and
Strawberry Pancakes:* Quirky Cures,
Borrowed Tales, Camp Recipes
and the Adirondack Characters
Who Cooked Them Up, 2014

*Adirondack Memories
and Campfire Stories*
Edited and with Biographical
and Historical Commentary
by William. J. O'Hern
In the Adirondacks, 2014

*Adirondack Wilds: Exploring the
Haunts of Noah John Rondeau,* 2014

*The Hermit and Us:
Our Adirondack Adventures
with Noah John Rondeau*
In the Adirondacks, 2014

*Adirondack Kaleidoscope
and North Country Characters*
Edited and with Biographical
and Historical Commentary
by William. J. O'Hern
In the Adirondacks, 2013

Thomas C. O'Donnell's
Life in a North Woods Lumber Camp
Edited and with Biographical
and Historical Commentary
by William J. O'Hern
The Forager Press, LLC, 2012

*Adirondack Adventures:
Bob Gillespie and Harvey Dunham
on French Louie's Trail*
By Roy E. Reehil and William J. O'Hern
The Forager Press, LLC, 2012

*Noah John Rondeau's Adirondack
Wilderness Days: A Year with the hermit
of Cold River Flow*
The Forager Press, LLC, 2009

*Under An Adirondack Influence:
The Life of A. L. Byron-Curtiss, 1871–1959*
By Roy E. Reehil and William J. O'Hern
The Forager Press, LLC, 2008

*Adirondack Characters
and Campfire Yarns:
Early Settlers and Their Traditions*
The Forager Press, LLC, 2005
*Adirondack Stories of the
Black River Country*
North Country Books, Inc. 2003

Anyplace Wild in the Adirondacks
Self-published, 2000

*Life with Noah: Stories and
Adventures of Richard Smith
with Noah J. Rondeau*
North Country Books, Inc.
Second Paperback Printing 2013

UPCOMING RELEASES
by William J. O'Hern

*At Our Adirondack Table:
Recipes and Stories from Mountain Camps*

*From Mountains to Foothills and
Campfire Tales: Gathered Memories
from New York's Adirondack-
North Country and Tug Hill Region*

*Adirondack Pastimes:
Camping and Sporting Adventures in the Cold
River Country with
Hermit Noah John Rondeau (1913–1950)*

*Remembering Adirondack Legend
Noah John Rondeau: Following a Hermit's
Footsteps Through His Final Years (1913–1967)*

Gathered Memories and Fireside Stories
A Celebration of Past Adirondack-
North Country and Upstate New York Life
Compiled, edited and with Biographical
and Historical Commentary
by William J. O'Hern

*Logging in the Adirondacks:
The Revolutionary Linn Tractor
and Lumber Camp Stories*

*The Informal History
of the Moose River Plains*

available online at www.adkwilds.com